Snowdrift

Snowdrift

by

Lisa McGonigle

OOLICHAN BOOKS
FERNIE, BRITISH COLUMBIA, CANADA
2011

Library and Archives Canada Cataloguing in Publication

McGonigle, Lisa, 1982-

Snowdrift / Lisa McGonigle.

ISBN 978-0-88982-271-9

1. McGonigle, Lisa, 1982- --Travel--British Columbia.

2. Skis and skiing--British Columbia. 3. Snowboarding--British

Columbia. I. Title.

GV854.2.M34A3 2010   796.93092   C2010-907965-5

We gratefully acknowledge the financial support of the Canada Council for the Arts, the British Columbia Arts Council through the BC Ministry of Tourism, Culture, and the Arts, and the Government of Canada through the Canada Book Fund, for our publishing activities.

Published by
Oolichan Books
P.O. Box 2278
Fernie, British Columbia
Canada V0B 1M0

www.oolichan.com

Printed in Canada on 100% post consumer recycled FSC-certified paper.

Cover Photo by Chad Chilico
Author Photo by Joe Harrison

For all the friends who feature in these pages, but in particular Lindsay and Steven "Chucky" Tallott, Ellie Maxfield and Kristen Thams, and my parents, for always letting me do my own thing.

Contents

Retrospective:
How I Ended Up in Canada
in the First Place

North County Dublin is not, you will understand, a place of towering peaks or snowy drifts. We have fields, sandy beaches, green and woody public parks. There are Martello towers, some now museums, others filled with nesting birds. There are pubs, lots of pubs, the occasional thatched cottage, golf courses, annual motorbike races around the Man O'War. There's a Round Tower into which the monks would scurry with their valuables, pulling the ladder up behind them, when Vikings came to shore. There are islands along the coast, like Lambay where those Viking pillagers first landed in Ireland, so they say.

The commuter belt stretches out this way, the trainline links towns up and down the coast and the 33 bus trundles its way out from the city. There are townlands like Baldungan with its ruined monastery and Balrothery (pronounced "Baluderry" if your family has been local for generations) which translates as "townland of the knights". Signs for "Polski Sklep" betoken a new influx of immigrants, driven to Ireland by economic necessity and who miss the comforts of home. Boy racers cruise the winding back-roads in souped-up Honda Civics, occasionally screeching on the brakes behind a chugging tractor. Teenagers text each other and on a Friday night hang around in gaggles on the beach getting "really, really drunk" off a naggin of vodka – you can't smell vodka on your breath, see, so your parents won't be able to tell. Women head out for bracing power walks after the dinner is on the table – the "walking mums", we used to term them, sitting idly on a wall as they'd stride by. In the summer, people sit out for hours "sinking" pints along the harbour road, watching the sun's slow descent, now and then tossing a chip to the gulls circling in the air.

But there's no snow.

I first saw the mountains when I was nineteen and in my second year of college. College had not proven the adventure I thought would follow once I left school. Still living at home, I was getting the train in and out to the city, glumly munching sandwiches at lunchtime, day after day. Sure why on earth would you move out, "wasting" money on rent, if you could live at home, my parents would ask? Isn't it grand and handy, they'd continue, that Trinity is right beside the train station. What could be easier! Indeed, compared to the unfortunate sods trekking out to Belfield every day, it was an easy commute (in theory). But surely starting college was the time to be striking out, fostering independence, finding yourself and that sort of thing? That was difficult to do if you were planning everything around the notoriously unreliable CIE, mindful of having to leave now because there wasn't another train for hour and a half. These may have been the boom-town years in Dublin but the infrastructure was yet to catch up. Trains would regularly break down, stopping, say, between stations for half an hour with no explanation whatsoever forthcoming from the surly station staff and so overcrowded that you'd have your face pressed against the carriage wall, arms pinned to your side.

Against this backdrop of late teen woe and overcrowded trains, two friends from school and I were talking about going on holidays together. I had a suggestion. Why didn't we try this hip new sport called snowboarding? Thinking back, I have no idea where that initial impetus came from. Throughout my youth I'd shown no inclination towards sportiness whatsoever. I'd started going swimming regularly throughout college, it's true, but that was more for fitness and headspace than borne of any natural athleticism. I'd hated P.E. in school, team sports were for me a cruel and unusual punishment, and my hand-eye coordination left much to be desired. If anyone tossed a ball in my direction I'd let it sail through the air and watch with equanimous disinterest as it landed and bounced along the ground. Nonetheless, we chose snowboarding over skiing because we thought it had more of a rebel edge. Well, that's why two of us wanted to snowboard anyway, still being very much disaffected youths. The third took the opposite approach and steadfastly refused to do anything that might be perceived as trying to be "cool". But as it was a "one-in, all-in" endeavour she was talked around, grudgingly, into giving snowboarding a go. We booked a cheapo holiday to Andorra, a duty-free principality in the Pyrenees, for the following January.

January came around, we borrowed ski-gear from whomsoever we could and off we went. I wondered if I'd turn out to be completely terrible at snowboarding, perhaps simply unable to do it at all. Beyond vague stereotypes of dudes in baggy clothes, I had no idea about its finer points. Did you just stand on the board like a skateboard? Or were you attached to it? Could you wear your normal shoes? Or did you need a pair of gumboots or something?

When we went to pick up our rental package it became slightly clearer. No, you had to wear special snowboard boots. Yes, you were attached to the board by contraptions called bindings which fastened over your boots. Snowboards slung faux-nonchalantly under our arms, we walked down to the resort base to start a week of lessons. How cool is this! I thought. I remember big, big mountains, blue, blue sky and white, white snow, many falls and crashes, the three of us having a collective crush on our instructor, a great sense of achievement when I was able to do it, sort of, and it all being a lot of fun.

Later on you forget just what a mission it is to learn to snowboard, how much you must persevere to make it through those first few constant body-slamming days. Unlike on skis, where after an initial bewilderment you just sort of point and go (the difficult bit with skiing is progressing beyond the rudiments), with snowboarding the novice stage is the most heartbreaking. You catch an edge and bang! Over you go onto the snow, your whole body jarring with the impact. Getting to grips with basic mobility, manoeuvring this thing attached to your feet without scudding wildly out of control seemed a near impossible feat. I'd gaze misty-eyed in admiration at others carving effortlessly down the mountain at high speed. How on earth did they make it look so easy?

I persevered, coming to appreciate that with snow-boarding it doesn't matter whether it comes as naturally as the leaves on the tree or whether you're the slowest of the slow. You're not on the mountain for anyone but yourself. If you try benchmarking yourself against anybody while learning it will just end up driving you mad. Whatever about a bit of healthy competition, you don't snowboard to beat other people down. You snowboard to Have a Good Time.

And this, indeed, was the best thing I'd ever done in my life! Heading home, it was clear that snowboarding for a week's holiday once a year simply wasn't going to do. Now instead of a vague, unspecified dissatisfaction about the prospect of finishing my degree and then spending hours everyday stuck in the commuter crush whilst paying off an exorbitant mortgage, I knew what I wanted to do: I wanted to be a ski-bum.

In light of this epiphany, for the next few years all my spare money went on snowboarding trips and gear. There was nothing I wanted to do other than move to the mountains. That said, I wasn't just freewheeling around. I wanted to go the mountains but I wasn't sure how viable a lifestyle move that was. Loathe as I was to start working for "the man", staying in academia for as long as possible seemed to offer an alternative. Intellectual freedom and all that. I was never one hundred percent convinced though. Anxiously I quizzed doctoral students, "how do you KNOW though?" about committing to the tenure track. (When you know, you just know.) Despite having been thoroughly underwhelmed in college so far, I just wasn't sure what else I'd do if following the snow proved untenable.

When I was in my final year of college I had an infamous showdown with our Careers Advisor. I spelt out my objections to what I saw as the road ahead. The whole "career" thing seemed like a bit of a swizz – surely it should be work-to-live rather than the other way around? "I don't want a job where I have to work in an office or wear office clothes," I said with the high-handedness of twenty-one, shifting in my chair for emphasis. "Most jobs," she said bridling slightly, "bring with them some measure of office work." Certainly those considered suitable avenues for Arts graduates. Slumping sullenly, I shrugged, refusing to budge on the issue. "Well do you want a career then?" she asked me frostily. I thought for a second, then said, "No, not really."

So with a Manichaean divide between wanting to become a ski-bum and wanting to become a top literary theorist, I worked heartbreakingly hard for my finals, focusing on twentieth century Irish literature and doing well enough to get a scholarship to do a Masters. Redoubling my efforts, I churned out a theoretically dense dissertation on the light-hearted topic of institutional abuse within the Catholic Church. Fun times indeed! By the time I was Lisa McGonigle, BA, M Litt, I was burnt out, tense, and in need of Time Off.

I hadn't forgotten about snowboarding but, focused as I'd been on such burning topics as whether Ireland could truly be considered postcolonial or whether it could more properly be viewed through a post-Catholic lens, it had been pushed to the back of my mind. That said, it was a given I was going to do a snowboard-season during this year out. Between any number of snowboard trips, I'd seen quite a bit of the Alps so for this, my Big Adventure, I wanted to strike out further afield. I applied for a one year Working Holiday Visa for Canada and was sent glossy pamphlets with pictures of the Toronto skyline, aquamarine lakes and the prairie expanse of golden wheat, all of which I intended bypassing to head straight for the hills.

Choosing a specific ski-hill to spend the winter at was like throwing a dart at a map. I wanted to live in a real town as opposed to a purpose-built resort which ruled out any-where like Whistler or Banff. After that, it was a question of thumbing through guidebooks, asking around and trawling through resort reviews. Two places in particular appealed: Fernie Alpine Resort and Rossland's Red Mountain, both in the Kootenay Mountains in British Columbia, both remote and low-key. Perfect!

Whereas Rossland remained somewhat of a mystery entity, with scant information about it available online, Fernie had several comprehensive websites. There was a "Rooms for Rent" section on the message-board of one and, still vacillating between the two towns, I posted the usual sort of thing: Irish girl, twenty-three, non-smoker, seeks room for winter. A couple called Wendy and Pete emailed me back describing their house. Since one leap into the unknown had as good a chance of success as the next, the decision was made: Fernie it was to be.

However, having spent years churning out essays for college, I'd grown accustomed to tapping away on my laptop for hours on end. Old habits die hard so, like Forrest Gump, "for no particular reason I just kept on going." I just kept on writing after I got to Fernie, mass emails to friends back home trying to capture this wondrous new world in prose.

Fernie

November 2005: Straight Outta Dublin

A chairde

Here I am in Fernie! Fernie is a town of about 5,000 people situated, and here I am shamelessly cribbing from the local tourist information, "in the Southeast corner of British Columbia, fully encircled by the Kootenay Mountains, within close proximity of Calgary, AB…and Cranbrook, BC." Close proximity by Canadian standards maybe. Calgary is 300km to the east and Cranbrook 100km to the west. I can't believe how spread out everything is here and the casualness with which people cover long distances. I landed in Vancouver last week but rather than facing a thirteen-hour, 1000km trek inland on the Greyhound – BC is so big it skirts two time-zones – I instead flew on a tiny Indiana-Jones style, twelve-seater, open cockpit propeller plane to Cranbrook. Wendy, my-landlady-to-be, met me at the airport. I'd have trouble getting my own parents to drive that far to pick me up. Petrol is cheaper here and the roads are less crowded, admittedly, but I suspect there's a fundamentally different conception of scale at play as well.

I'm renting a room in a house from Wendy and her partner Pete. There are two other ski-bums in the basement suite as well, one British and one Australian, so we're quite the international mix, representative of the seasonal population at large. This guy called Gerry from Stillorgan should also be moving into the house any day now, thereby bringing the number of Irish people in Fernie up to a grand total of three. The third is a guy from Belfast who somehow knows my brother from back home. You know how people cringe if asked something like "oh you're from Australia? Do you know my friend John?" If you're from Ireland there's a good chance that you in fact do, or that your cousins went to school together or you were in the *Gaeltacht* with their best friend.

Looking out my bedroom window, I can see the neighbours snow-blowing their drive – stop that sniggering, there'll be none of that smutty innuendo here. The annual snow-fall here is twenty nine feet and counting, something I still can't quite get my head around given that if it snows more than twenty-nine *millimetres* in Ireland it makes the front page of *The Irish Times*. So anyway, a snow-blower is a device which you push up and down like a lawnmower: it somehow funnels in and spits out the snow, saving you the heavy labour of shovelling. It's all terribly exciting in my eyes. For the locals, it's everyday life and they'd be amused and alarmed by turns if they knew of the interest with which I'm watching.

Yet despite the bounteous snow we've already received, the ski-hill doesn't open for another month. Let me explain a bit about ski-hill set up here. Unlike in Europe, where the ski-lifts are dotted in between the centuries-old hamlets and *alpages* and it's all ski-in-ski-out, in North America ski-towns and ski-resorts are not as one. The ski-hill here is 5km away from Fernie town itself, pegged out along the ridge line of the Lizard Range. And whereas in the Alps you can ski from village to village, in some instances even crossing borders, if you were to drop over the ridge line here you'd find yourself away from ski-hill land and human hand, deep in the backcountry, and certainly not likely to come across a mid-mountain chalet serving hot chocolate and *vin chaud*.

Set up during the 1960s as Snow Valley Resort, the Fernie ski-hill was bought a few years ago by a group called Resorts of The Canadian Rockies (RCR) and became Fernie Alpine Resort. Attitudes towards the big-business RCR are mixed, with a strong resistance to increased lift prices and wariness towards any future overdevelopment. But we're not there yet, Fernie is still very much in the transition stage from a local hill to the next big thing. The terrain, for example, is extensive and several new lifts have been installed of late but the other facilities remain ramshackle – the Daylodge resembles a grotty school canteen and is permeated by the lingering smell of old ski-boots.

You might wonder, by the way, why I arrived in town so far ahead of time if things don't kick off for another month. You need to give yourself this run-in to find a job for the winter, so I've been traipsing from place to place with a CV – sorry, I mean a résumé – and a winning smile. It'll happen in the end. In any case, having arrived in Fernie on my own it hasn't been hard to meet kindred spirits. Early winter in a ski-town sees an influx of like-minded people of similar age with a common purpose; i.e., to spend the next four months skiing or snowboarding to the max. Arriving here with skis or board at this time of year is like moving house as a child and taking your football out to the green to find new friends to play with.

So with all of us in much the same situation until the season starts, short of cash and idling away time, we've been hiking up the hill both to get our pre-season fix of the snow and simply for something to do. "Hiking" carries rather different connotations back home, conjuring up as it does images of cheerfully bearded middle-aged men equipped with flasks of lukewarm tea and khaki shorts as they clamber though the Lake District in their socks and sandals combo. "Hiking" here, however, simply means any sort of energetic walk beyond the parameters of a normal day's activity; e.g., one would not hike to the shops for some milk, one would, on the other hand, quite feasibly go for a hike in the woods with one's dog. Or, in our case, a vertical slog, breaking tread through knee-deep snow, kitted out in full snowboard regalia, damp and clammy with sweat. I'm not trying to bestow messianic qualities on myself, blame it on the Catholic cultural consciousness if you must, but when I imagine how we must appear, trudging onwards and upwards, stumbling in the snow, heads bowed, arms outstretched to support the horizontal beam of the snowboards across our back, I am reminded of nothing so much as the image of Jesus carrying his cross. Lisa falls for the third time.

After the hour's lung-poppin', thigh-burnin' hike up the mountain, the return was a five minute run down. But oh! was it worth the effort as we were blessed with the sort of deep powdery snow that would be considered A Very Good Show in the Alps, and, if it occurred in the Grampians, would have grown Scotsmen sinking to their knees and weeping in thanks. Being so far inland, the air in Fernie is extremely dry which in turn means that the snow is deliriously fluffy and light. Long may it last.

Going to the supermarket also becomes the focal point and structuring principle of a day during these quiet weeks. Which is fine with me, able as I am to spend hours pouring over the strange new products in this strange new land: Miracle Whip, Marshmallow Creme, Betty Crocker Brownie

Mix. But what really excites me beyond all reasonable degree is the bulk-bins. Whereas at home if you need, say, 50g of raisins or a tablespoon of cornstarch, you have to buy the whole packet, the remainder of which then languishes at the back of the press for years to come, here in North America, where the customer reigns supreme, you can simply scoop out as little or as much as you need. Amazing. I've been similarly converted to measuring ingredients by "cups" and "half-cups", having initially felt that this lacked the rigour and precision of ounces or grams. Maybe I'm being fanciful, but perhaps it's a remnant of how the country was settled, it being a lot more practical, bouncing along the pioneer trail or living in your rough-hewn cabin, to scoop your sugar and flour out of gunny sacks by the cup rather than dragging out the weighing scales everytime you go to make bread.

The dairy products, on the other hand, are severely lacking in both quality and quantity. Coming to live in the mountains, I assumed there'd be the same bountiful array of creamy yogurts, *crème fraîche* and whatnot as there is in the Alps. Alas, no. The cheese in particular is a major letdown. I've been blowing the budget buying imported Gruyère rather than the horrible, plasticky, artificially oranged stuff they try peddling here. I've already had more than one rueful discussion with other ex-pats about how much we miss proper cheese.

Right well, that's about the long and the short of it for now.

Lisa

December 2005: Work and Play

Hi

My, I'm tired. Doing a ski-season, I'm quickly coming to

discover, is like being in a human-sized hamster ball, scrabbling and scrabbling around continuously without stop. I'm now working two jobs (sort of – I'll get to that in a while) and of course going snowboarding every day.

The ski-lifts finally opened on Saturday. For whatever reason, I had a horrendous opening day, riding absolutely terribly. By the end of the day I would have been perfectly happy never again to have strapped a snowboard to my feet and was seriously questioning the wisdom behind deciding to spend a season in the snow. "Four more months of this everyday!" others were exclaiming jubilantly. "Christ no", I thought to myself. Luckily the next day I got back my snowlegs – and more importantly, confidence – and launched myself into the season and down the pistes with gusto.

I don't know how much detail I have to go into with ski-hill terminology because I know that while some of you are avid skiers and snowboarders, others, well, are not. I shall assume ignorance and proceed accordingly, trying not to get too technical but giving a overview of the basics.

The "pistes" are the marked runs on any given mountain, the interlinked green and blue and black squiggles on a trail map, and what most of you have probably stuck to if your skiing experience has been restricted to a week's holiday in the Alps. This isn't meant to sound condescending; I was in much the same situation until arriving here. Big machines with rake-like attachments – snowcats – go up and down the pistes every night, smoothing out any chopped up or bumpy bits. Hence the pistes are also known as "groomers". The off piste, on the other hand, encompasses the great swatches of the mountain which isn't manicured by ski-hill management; the trees, the powder, the chutes.

In Europe, resort management is liable for you only when you're on the groomers, their responsibility ending the second you skirt beyond the orange markers. If you get injured off-piste, ski-patrols are perfectly justified in shrugging you off with Gallic insouciance and won't necessarily come in and drag you out. I've heard horror stories of people accruing horrendous search and rescue costs after getting themselves into a spot of bother off-piste. In Canada, by way of contrast, the ski-hill boundary stretches from one side of the mountain to the other and everything in between is owned by the resort. As long as you're within bounds and as long as you don't duck into a permanently closed area, their liability and duty to you remains. So the important division here is whether you're in or out of bounds rather than on or off-piste. Just FYI.

But life is not all fun and games! After a round of résumé writing and interviews, I'm now working as a receptionist in the town physiotherapy clinic three evenings a week. The job strikes just the right balance of responsibility – neither mind-numbingly dumb nor overly taxing – and also gives me an insight into Fernie life beyond the ski-bum bubble. Fernie was founded in 1898 with the discovery of coal in the valley and the nearby mines continue to provide a great deal of the employment for long-standing locals who ski-doo in the winter and hunt in the season. In recent years, however, many socially conscious and active young types have relocated here for its enviable natural location, bringing with them their Labrador puppies and telemark gear. So Fernie is now split between these two diverse groups of people, with a seasonal influx of ski-bums added into the mix for good measure. I was expecting the physio clinic to see nothing but a parade of injured skiers but in fact it's about one-third sports injuries, one-third work-related claims (people are forever falling off ladders at the mines, it seems) and one-third miscellaneous or lifestyle complaints.

I'm also ostensibly working as a cashier in the Daylodge on the ski-hill but haven't had any shifts rostered yet, which suits me down to the ground because I still get a free staff season-pass. Haha! Beating the system and thwarting "the man"! For all the rumblings of discontent about how the corporate greed of RCR is sucking the soul out of the hill, it's not the tightest of operations and staffing arrangements are lax; far too many food and beverage staff have been taken on this winter. Whilst others are understandably annoyed about being offered a job and then getting only a few hours work a week, I'm perfectly content to work the least amount possible. In fact, so selfless am I that I'll gladly off-load the hours I do get given to anyone who wants them and go snowboarding instead.

Well better go, no rest for the wicked.

Lisa

December 2005: The Frozen Hitchhiker

Hey everyone

Question: what do you wear walking home from the bar when it's minus twenty and you live half an hour away?

Answer:
A toque (that's a woolly hat)
A fleecy face-muffler/scarf thing
A thermal vest
A long-sleeved thermal top
A cotton t-shirt
A woolly jumper (aka sweater)
A snowboard jacket
Thermal glove liners
Woolly mittens over the gloves
Thermal long-johns
Jeans
Ski-socks
Snowboots

Brr! Overkill, perhaps but, unaccustomed as I am to such cold, I'm still learning how to dress accordingly. Even though it makes me feel uncomfortably like a member of a paramilitary organisation who divests people of their knee-caps, I may start wearing a balaclava.

Strange things start to happen when the mercury drops this low. Water pipes into your house freeze solid overnight, so you have to get industrious with a hairdryer to get things moving again in the morning (making sure, that is, not to rush proceedings or the pipes may well explode and flood the house in the process), batteries die in cars, exposed flesh develops frostbite in a matter of minutes and if you breath too deeply icicles form in your nose. Similarly, hitching isn't so great at these temperatures, and thus starteth the chilling tale of the frozen hitchhiker.

Something I have neglected to mention on the phone to my mum is that while sometimes I get a lift to the ski-hill with my housemates, on other days I hitch. Not only do I not own a vehicle, I can't in fact drive. Canadians can't quite fathom how somebody who appears to be of reasonable intelligence has reached the age of twenty-three without acquiring this skill, and indeed I struggle to explain it without going into a full socioeconomic analysis of Irish society, a geographical spread-map of North County Dublin and a personal history to boot. But in brief, my synopsis runs: never a priority, exorbitant insurance rates, got the train to college, spent my money on other things. I try to explain that whereas in the Kootenays being able to drive is a basic life skill, I've hitherto always looked upon it as a bit of a luxury.

In any case, there's a designated hitching spot in town, like a goodwill taxi-rank meets social occasion; i.e., a car will pull up and the driver will say, "I can take two with skis, or three without" and queuing etiquette is strictly observed.

However, on Sunday morning it just wasn't going off. Saturday night had been the annual Mogul Smoker, a huge party centred around burning old skis in the hope that these sacrificial offerings will appease the snow-gods and ensure a good snowfall for the forthcoming winter.

What with Sunday thus being the morning-after-the-night-before for anyone who is anyone in Fernie snowlife, not to mention most people having more sense than to head to the ski-hill when it's this cold, hitching was just not happening. The people driving past were largely out-of-towners who would slow down, peer at us like some sort of local curiosity and continue on in their lovely, cosy, roomy, empty jeeps. After half an hour standing around at minus twenty-four, sensation in my fingers and toes was but a dim memory and even my eyelashes had frozen over, leaving me looking like a grizzled Arctic explorer. Luckily, along came Wes from Ontario and Scotty from Australia to the rescue in their truck! Everyone here has SUVs and pick-ups – so much more practical than dinky little cars for carrying snowboards and ski-doos in winter, bikes and hiking gear in summer and – if you're so inclined – somewhere to sling your guns and hopefully a moose or an elk if you get lucky out hunting.

Chairlift conversation that day centred mainly upon the weather. Wes described how elementary schools in Ontario close if the temperature dips below minus forty and Scotty contributed memories of Australian schools similarly shutting when it hits plus forty. I sat in the middle, unable to regale with any stories from my own piddly climes. When I tentatively offered a description of how we didn't have to go outside at break-time if it rained, they both practically fell off the lift laughing.

Regardless, I'll wait till it warms up a bit before going snowboarding again. With frostbite warnings posted prominently on all the chairlifts, it really becomes a matter of life and death that you're adequately covered up. No matter how many layers you're swaddled up in, and despite the fact that you'd be showing more skin in a burqa with your bulbous helmet-head, your face is turned to raw burgermeat by the wind-chill as you fly down the piste. The day has to be punctuated by hot drinks after every run or two and it's more about stoicism than fun.

Right, going to go fiddle with a whitening kit for my teeth, having become deeply envious of North American dental standards. You daub your teeth with this stuff from a Tippex-size bottle before going to bed and, as you snuggle down for the night, the hydrogen peroxide in the solution works its dazzling magic. Of my own devices I would have been slightly dubious about dousing my mouth with peroxide – surely that's what they use to clean toilets? But one of the skiers in the basement was a dentist in his former life and he assures me that DIY bleaching is a perfectly safe procedure even if such kits are currently banned in the Eurozone.

Yours dazzlingly
Lisa

December 2005: Haven't a leg to stand on

Hi there

I never thought in all sincerity and entirely devoid of any bravura, I'd breath a sigh of relief that it was warming up to minus ten. But it is, and I am. So festive greetings one and all!

However, I'm covered in bruises and have shooting pains down my left leg if I try to stand on it. Let me explain. It was Stephen's Day yesterday (or Boxing Day, I suppose I should call it, since no one except Gerry from Stillorgan knows what I mean when I refer to it as the former) and I went to a party last night. I haven't been drinking much since I've got to Fernie, which marks me out as an oddity against the crazy partying, non-stop boozing and mounds of MDMA of ski-town life. I am a poorly specimen, tiring easily and not functioning when impaired – if physical prowess was as key to our survival as it was for our ancestors, I'd have been long since mauled to death by a sabre-toothed beast. I can only marvel at those seemingly indestructible others who are still out shredding the gnar at the end of a three day bender. I just can't do it. Out of the ski-town triad of work-ride-party I can ever only sustain two. So partying has had to slide as I innocently romp around in the snow. I'm high on life! (I sometimes see people wearing t-shirts with slogans like "I'm special and drug-free" or "Jesus is your friend". I never know if they're trying to be ironic or not, and it doesn't do to make assumptions.)

But, anyway, last night was an exception to the norm and today, mildly groggy and a little hungover, I went up the hill. Not only that, I went to the terrain park. If the back-country is for the true mountain men, the park is where you go if you want to be down-with-the-kids. It's where skate-boarding's influence on snowboarding can be most clearly felt in terms of the tricks that go down and the features like jumps and rails. Rails are exactly what they sound like: handrails dug into the snow which bring with them myriad injury potential but also a lot of fun. Today I was trying to do frontside boardslides, a manoeuvre whereby you slide down a rail with your board remaining perpendicular, but alas I stacked it. Whilst the precise details of the incident are too painful to describe, let's just say it involved friction-burns and a red-hot gouge. Falling from height onto a metal bar whilst in motion is like being whacked with a crowbar and then some. Luckily there were few people around to witness my fall from gracefulness or to hear the sobs of agony which ensued. Thank the heavens for small mercies.

I limped home and I'm currently sitting on the sofa in pyjamas, my leg cushioned in an impromptu icepack – viz: tea-towel, ice-cubes, hair bobbin – listening to the Beatles and working my way through a tub of chocolate almonds. It is Christmas after all. I'll probably be out of action for the next few days so enough about snowsports, onto my incipient quarter-life crisis! Not only am I learning to ride park and pow this winter but also how to interact with people again. You think I'm joking? Having spent the past few years studying in solitary pursuit, sometimes after a day of dissertation writing I was barely able to string a sentence together. So now I need to decide if I really want to start a PhD come next September as planned or whether I was just falling into it in the absence of any other course of action.

I think it's the latter. When I look back over the past few years of college, what I remember is the arid monotony of scholastic life, endless essays to be written and rewritten, obscure references to be tracked down, hours tweaking paragraphs to perfect their cadence and flow. It's been a grim and thankless slog requiring an iron will of discipline but ultimately bringing only a draining sense of exhaustion. Everything in life is a trade-off: if you're going to be a ski-bum, chances are you'll be skint and it's almost inevitable that you'll accrue some injuries (I'm living testament to this). If you're going to go into the competitive arena of academe, you're going to have to make a Herculean investment of energy and time. I'm not sure it's worth it. From my current perspective, doctoral study seems unnaturally dry, insipid and tedious, and a very dull way to spend the next few years. When it comes down to it I couldn't give a fuck about the current state and critical parameters of Irish Studies, the purported topic of my PhD. The subject leaves me cold. (And certainly not in a good, snowy way.)

I don't want this to sound too bring-out-the-violins

because I'm well aware of what a privileged dilemma it is to have, but, dear friends, I'm hoping that you're fond enough of me to tolerate some navel-gazing now and then. Indeed, such soul-searching is common in Fernie where every second person has left behind a hyper-education and high-powered career to shred the gnar and earn $8/hour. In our house alone, we have an accountant, a dentist and a solicitor. There are pharmaceutical engineers and investment bankers now working in ski-school, microbiologists on reception desks and environmental consultants serving drinks. Some of them are here for a year's career break, admittedly, but others have made the move for good. So, I wonder, if they can do it why can't I?

I'd quite happily sit around here for another few years. Not, that is, plonked right on this couch with my gammy leg, but leading the good life in a ski-town at large. I might sound like some sort of hippy evangelist – let me get my tambourine – but snowboarding is more than a sport; it's a lifestyle, it's a set of values and I haven't had my fill of it yet. On the other hand, I don't want to arrive at thirty with my knees shot, a lengthy history of employment in the service industry and not much else to my name.

So what and where next? Watch this space…

All advice gratefully received

Lisa

January 2006: As I Lay Dying of Embarrassment

Hear my tale of woe part the second,

Existential crises being easily assuaged by fresh snow, my leg had healed up nicely – or so I thought – and apart from some impressive and status-earning bruising seemed to be good as new. Tuesday was a particularly super-duper day on the hill. I had the day off from both of my jobs (a rare occurrence), the Christmas crowds had gone home, there were lashings and lashings of fresh snow, and I was riding with my friend, Ali. Ali is English, flaxen-haired and, if I had to tag her in a ready-made phrase, a "free spirit". We met before the hill opened when she was volunteering at an eco-wellness fair in town, not my normal sort of thing. Anything so overtly New Age-y usually makes me cringe but in the pre-season you take your amusements where you can. Ali is at the tail end of her year in Canada, having spent the summer camping, biking around BC with her boyfriend and working at a grizzly bear enclosure. She laughs a lot and rides on "the Plank", a battered hand-me-down of such unenviable dimensions and heft that it's a wonder she can snowboard at all, much less with joyousness, which she does. If there's anyone who'll be eagerly waiting for the first lift and still be sneaking in line at the end of the day, it's Ali.

But then disaster struck! Well, that's fudging the blame a little, as what happened was no such random occurrence of fate. Ali went to work and I had one of those "hmmm, will I go home now or take one more run?" moments and chose the latter. More fool me, as in my snowy elation I had forgotten the cardinal rules of snowsports; never call last run, and accidents happen when you're tired. I went to the park, tried and landed a new rail, punched the air in triumph and then quickly scanned around me to double-check that no one had seen this cheesiness. Then I went in for the rail which had been my previous downfall. When will I learn. Down I went and whatever way I fell provoked the same burning shin-scraping agony as before. Bruise on bruise is never a good combo and was it painful.

Being a bit of a worrier, I always panic whenever I get mildly injured/fucked up on soft drugs etc. Worst case scenarios aplenty immediately rush to mind. So this time I tried to give myself a stern speaking to and carry on regardless by boarding down the rest of the mountain. However, in a weird self-inflicted inversion of the boy who cried wolf, it was not going to happen. Every time I went over any kind of bump, the minor jolt had me yowling with shooting pain. I kept having to stop to sit down and hug my leg like an injured European soccer player, packing my shin in ice for a few minutes, then boarding another couple of hundred metres before starting the routine again. About half-way down the mountain a concerned family of skiers took pity on me and flagged down a passing ski-instructor – namely Wendy who owns our house. Wendy teaches on an instructor training course for British gap year brats, and her tutees swished to a stop behind her, evidently having a hard time trying to work out how exactly this strange Irish kid writhing in agony on the snow fitted into their expensive tuition. "No, no, don't mind me, I'm grand," I shouted cheerily if wanly to Wendy and tried to shoo her and her class off on down the hill. Wendy, however, was having none of my protestations though and skied off to inform dispatch that there was an injured snowboarder, female, twenty-three, on the hill, leaving me to ponder the mantra of Rest-Ice-Compression-Elevation, leg splayed out in front of me in the snow and patiently awaiting the arrival of ski-patrol.

But for the fact that I was immobilised and my leg was rapidly swelling and turning purple, I was absolutely grand. As long as the leg was encased in ice it wasn't particularly painful, though I knew all about it whenever it thawed out or if I tried to move. As the minutes ticked by, I contemplated taking out my new iPod Shuffle – a Christmas present to myself – and start listening to it to while away the time, but I thought that that was just one step too close to feigning blithe insouciance or "I'm hard, me"-ness.

A little about ski-hill hierarchy. Back in my salad days,

I thought ski and snowboard instructors ranked highest on the ski-hill food-chain. How wrong I was! Ski-patrol are the real heroes on the hill. These are the guys – and occasionally women, though in fairness the profession is overwhelmingly male – who set out the piste boundaries, attend to first-aid crises, probe for avalanche victims, after a heavy snowfalls rig unstable cornices with explosives to trigger avalanches and perform other such tasks of manliness. I'm reminded at this point of the tale of Crazy Luke, a wild-eyed, bearded, French-Canadian loon and local living legend who, the tale goes, skied hell for leather down a particularly notorious cliff wall whilst patrol were lobbing dynamite at it. This year Dean, the ski-school director, was showing new inductees around the hill when they came across Luke in the locker room. "This is Crazy Luke," Dean announced clapping a hand on his shoulder, "don't ski with this guy." A chuckle went up from the group, assuming this was some jocular in-house banter. *"Luke you old goat!"* *"Dean you old dog!"* "No really," Dean went on, his face remaining grave, "don't ski with this guy." I suppose patrol are the ski-town equivalent of the hunky doctor, muscular and compassionately tender in appropriate measures. And with egos to match.

Anyway, Tomi, a Japanese ski-patroller, came along and we quickly determined that since I could wiggle my toes with relatively little discomfort, my leg wasn't broken, only a bit battered. He then radioed volly patrol to come and do the roughwork and haul my hefty hams down the mountain. There's also a subtle yet important difference between volunteer "volly" ski-patrol and the pro-patrol. Whilst pro-patrol get paid for their work, if you volunteer ski-patrol sixteen days a year then you get a free season pass. So the volly patrollers are the ski-bums par excellence. So this scruffy haired, twin-tipped dude arrives to tow me down the hill, bundled up in a stretcher resembling nothing so much as a horizontal straight-jacket. Normally if you get stretchered off the hill, you're in too much pain to care what it looks like. I, however, was in that boarderline [sic] zone where I was too injured to ski, but not injured enough to be beyond realising that I was the star attraction of the afternoon. Everyone was gawking at the procession from the chairlift, hoisting themselves around in their morbid curiosity for a better view of the orange bodybag of shame in which I was encased. You know that dream where you go to school with no clothes on? That was this, incarnate. There I lay dying with embarrassment, bounding and lurching prostrate down the slope, getting sprayed by snow and silently praying that nobody I knew would whizz on by. Mortification indeed.

Once back at base, Tomi wouldn't let me walk around or hitch down to Fernie town. So I spent the afternoon in dispatch, hobbling to and from the toilets on crutches and waiting for Wendy and Pete, my surrogate mummy and daddy, to come and pick me up. Tomi also gave me his new skiing magazine to read. What with it being entirely in Japanese, I didn't really understand what it was all about, but the pictures were very nice and colourful. Which added to my feeling of being about seven.

Four days later, I'm still on the couch and my leg is a strange colour and consistency, sort of tight and shiny if that makes sense. I can't do up the zip on my knee-high boots because of the swelling. However, I've been plying myself with packs of ice and one of the perks of working at the physio centre is that I get free consultations and ultrasounds and the like. The irony is not lost on me that I'm in worse nick than many of the patients.

But minor injuries notwithstanding, life remains good. Thanks to those of you who offered advice about the whole PhD thing. I'm definitely tempted to put academia on hold for a while and stay in the snow, hopefully managing to snag a visa from somewhere. Whilst the Canadians are happy for you to come for a year to staff the service industry (a cynical part of me suspects the working holiday visa scheme has been established not so much to foster cross-cultural under-standing but out of a shrewd recognition on the Canadian government's part that who else is going to run the ski-lifts, change sheets and clean rooms for $8/hour) they're less happy for you to remain.

Oh well, I'll think about that tomorrow.

Lisa

February 2006: Back on Board

I'm back on board!

Given that Fernie conversation centres almost entirely upon matters snowy, and that everyone here lives, talks and dreams snowsports, it was very trying when I was laid up out of action. I tried to be as magnanimous as I could, listening attentively to tales from the hill, exclaiming enthusiastically at appropriate moments. These efforts were offset, however, by an underlying jealousy and seething resentment.

Anyway, after ten days of comfort eating and mooching around feeling sorry for myself, I got the go-ahead from the physio to return to the slopes and test out my gammy leg last Saturday. I finished work at two, flagged down a ride and changed into my boarding gear as quickly as I could. It was late afternoon, the hill had long been tracked out, the melting snow was dripping dejectedly off the trees, the sky was a dull dismal gunmetal grey, my gloves were soggy, I was on my own; but coming down the beginners' blue runs in the drizzle had me whooping with exhilaration simply being able to ride again.

I haven't been back in the park yet because (a) I don't particularly want to continue playing Russian Roulette with my tibia and (b) aside from Saturday's unseasonable rain, it's been snowing so hard recently that all the rails and jumps have been buried in the downfall. And with conditions like we've been having it's more logical to enjoy the off-piste and the trees rather than hiking the park again and again.

However, with heavy snowfall comes not merely fresh powder but also avalanches, and avalanche danger has meant that whole bowls of the hill have been closed for days. Fernie is not an easy mountain by any standards. Beset by numerous icy cat-tracks of death, tree runs and moguls, it attracts a hardy crowd and the combination of the overhanging ridge-line, the steep gradient and the heavy snow means that it's particularly susceptible to avalanches even well within resort boundaries. Nine people were caught in an avalanche the other week, including a family with young children and the ski-patroller who had come to my aid only a few days beforehand. Luckily, however, none of them were killed. Avalanches are scary things. When sliding snow gathers momentum and rumbles down the slope, it compacts and sets like concrete. If you get trapped in the slough you have about fifteen minutes before you suffocate to death, so if you're buried in this fashion you may pray to God that someone will rapidly dig you out. It's quite the *memento mori* from the mountains.

But without being too dramatically Blakean about the whole thing, and certainly not advocating dicing with death simply for the sake of heightened sensation, the flipside of such occurrences is that life here possesses a stellar clarity and intensity. Riding with three of my friends the other day, the snow was so good we were alternately emitting spontaneous shouts of delighted surprise and shuddering low groans of pleasure. As we took a chairlift together, I put the question to our merry little band as to how snowboarding makes them feel. (I love chairlift conversation.)

"Happy", "free", "like nothing else in the world matters" came the responses, but the adjective which repeated itself more than any other was "ALIVE". Loathe as I am to use the phrase "at one with nature" and running the danger of lapsing into cheesy cliché notwithstanding, when you're out in the mountains, you're in a state of heightened awareness, every reflex poised, mind and body focused entirely upon the present moment. Colours seem more flushed, every sound from the panting of your breath to the snow turning under your board is amplified. It makes you realise that "I am LIVING!" and snowboarding trips into the quasi-spiritual. The stereotype of BC being full of granola-eating, Birkenstock-clad flakes may start to ring true at this point.

These fleeting, ephemeral moments are as addictive as any drug and indeed similarly hijack your life: you'd do anything to get your fix, such as living hand to mouth and moving halfway round the world to work for minimum wage. But oh! the effects on the soul. Being out in the fresh air doing what we love everyday has rendered my friends and I disgustingly healthy, all dewy-eyed, fresh-faced and light of heart.

Now despite my left-wing leanings, I don't wish to promulgate the great agrarian revolution by purging the cities and forcibly resettling all urban professionals to the mountains. Pol Pot tried that one and it didn't work out too well. It's not a bad idea though. Give snowsports a chance!

Yours transcendentally

Lisa

March 2006: One-armed warrior

Hi everyone

Apologies for having been so shoddy a correspondent of late but it was rather difficult trying to painstakingly tap out emails with my left arm in a cast...

Yes, I know, I know, I seem to have been beset by a horrible spate of injuries this season, every email consisting of increasingly gory descriptions of me in pain. But really, that's a misrepresentation of the winter. Most days are entirely uneventful: I sleep, work, snowboard, indulge in an inordinate amount of home-baking (despite all the exercise I'm in danger of turning into the most dreadful butterball) and that's about the sum of it. My various slams are simply the most dramatic events which is why I like to keep you informed of them all.

Anyway, I was in the park a few weeks ago with my friends Ali and Ellie. If Ali and I are matched in our unselfconscious enthusiasm for the snow, then the friendship between me and Ellie is founded on us both being driven to the point of self-destruction. Ellie is English, blonde, a geographer turned downhill mountain biker and a force to be reckoned with. She's extremely driven and ballsy and we're extremely, extremely competitive with each other when it comes to snowsports. If I go off a jump Ellie feels compelled to go off it as well. Preferably bigger and with more air. Or if Ellie takes a line down a steep face, by God I go down as well. Even faster.

So anyway, I was hiking this teensy weensy jump trying to do a backside 180 which is where you leap, spin a half-rotation in the air then land and stylishly ride it out. At least, such is when all goes according to plan. I instead stalled mid-air, landed on an edge and took the impact completely on the wrist. Although my first thought was "Phew! At least

I didn't hit my head!" – my hand swiftly made its presence felt. Unable to speak with the pain, I was reduced to a low bestial groaning, looking dead-eyed and helpless towards Ali and Ellie for aid. The remnant of rational thought of which I was still capable meant I was vaguely aware I was lying prostrate on the landing of a jump – never the best position to find yourself in, lest you should be mowed down by the next over-eager skier to fly through the air – but I didn't really care.

My friends had to unstrap me from my board and scoot me to the side of the park where I managed to croak, "I think I'd like to go home now…" in a small voice. I was going to try to snowboard down to the base of the hill, but when I stood up my legs buckled and I promptly had to sit back down again. But after the leg-hitting-rail-stretcher-of-shame-incident I was grittily determined that, so help me God, I wasn't going to be ferried down the hill by ski-patrol twice in one season. This time I was getting off that fucking mountain on my own two legs and nothing could sway me otherwise. So hardy trio that we are, together down the hill we tottered, with wandering steps and slow, Ali and Ellie taking turns to carry my board and I limply clasping my swollen arm to my chest.

Once we got to the base area, having been plied with the sugary caffeiney goodness that is Coke, I was ferried from dispatch to the doctor to Fernie General Hospital where they took x-rays to determine if my wrist was broken or not. However, the x-rays were a little unclear, yielding quite literally a grey area, an "abnormality" which could have been equally a small break or merely a conglomeration of blood-vessels. To be on the safe side, the doctor stuck a cast on the offending arm and sent me on my merry way with instructions to return a week later for the definitive diagnosis.

A broken limb is far from exceptional in a ski-town.

Walk into any given party or bar and the odds are that at least one person present will be on crutches or have their arm in a sling. Nonetheless, everyone in Fernie was so good to me during that week, supplying me with extra-strength Ibuprofen in the interests of pain relief, ready-rolled joints for the same purpose, and Matt-the-Aussie-park-rat – beneath that surly snowboarding exterior beats a heart of gold – even came over and made me a banana milkshake to ensure I was getting enough calcium for me aul' battered bones.

Luckily, a week on, the second set of x-rays revealed that, glory be, the bone wasn't broken but simply "soft tissue damage", medical speak for a horribly sprained wrist. My first day back on the hill, however, I only managed two runs and then had to give up. Whilst the actual riding posed no major problems – though I was so cautious and hesitant that I wasn't exactly having the time of my life – anything requiring torque or grip, such as doing up my boots, cranking my bindings, or pushing off a chair-lift, posed a challenge to my weak-wristed self.

However, four weeks later, though my wrist is still occasionally sore and achy and I certainly wouldn't want to launch into a set of vigourous one-armed press-ups, I'm back riding like normal, yesterday being goaded by Ellie into doing a bona fide cliff-drop. Not that I landed it but that doesn't matter. Neither did she.

I suspect I'm so addicted to the adrenalin rush of such stunts that I simply overlook all the breaks and bumps which are perhaps nature's way of telling me to stick to the groomers. There's this Fernie local who comes three times a week to the physio clinic where I work. Despite being a hard-core skier, thirty-five now and the proud owner of a Fernie season pass every year since he was three, not to mention countless adventures in the backcountry, he's not being treated for a ski injury. Instead, he was out hunting elk last autumn when he fell off a cliff and smashed his leg – "pretty spectacular really" (his own words) – leaving him to hop for four hours back to civilisation. Having been witness to the litany of injuries I've been accruing all winter long, when I arrived at the clinic sporting the cast on my wrist, he took only the merest survey of the situation before exclaiming "the park bites back!"...

Lisa

March 2006: Junket to Duke

And now to something completely different...

So to retrace our steps a few emails, you may remember my middle-class angst about whether I should do a PhD or instead continue my halcyon existence as a ski-bum. Otherwise occupied as I was, with throwing myself off crazy stuff on my board and amassing all sorts of injuries, the issue got deferred. But then the Real World intruded with a vengeance, and the decision was transformed from the abstract to the applied. You see, more fool me, before coming out to Canada I had applied to a few PhD programmes to start this coming autumn (I can't bring myself to refer to it as "fall"). One of the institutions I applied to was Duke University in North Carolina, the United States of Americkey, and I heard back from them at the start of March saying I'd been accepted into the English department with some scholarship yoke and would I like to go down for a little visit to have a look. The travel costs would be on them. Be jaysus, sez I, so I would.

What with Fernie being in the BC backcountry and North Carolina on the eastern seaboard of the States, this was no pleasure jaunt but a cross-continental trek. Over 4000km door-to-door, it took sixteen hours travelling each way – ten hours in the air, the rest sitting around various airports – leaving on a Wednesday evening, returning on the Sunday. Furthermore, the Duke travel office, in their infinite wisdom, put me on a strangely circuitous route; Cranbrook to Vancouver to Toronto to North Carolina and back again, so I was yo-yoing all over North America like a mofo.

So what came of this trip for your intrepid narrator, I hear you ask?

Not to put too fine a point on it, I was culture-shocked the fuck out of things, the sudden hike in temperature from minus to plus fifteen being the least of it. Whilst we get oodles of powder and amazing terrain to ride on in Fernie, we're in the middle of absolutely nowhere – Canada just doesn't have enough people to go around. There are no ski companies or major board stores based here, so there's scant chance of cracking "the scene" or getting sponsored: go to Whistler if you want to make it big, come to Fernie if you want to shred the gnar. Function thus ranks firmly over form here and I have never seen such ingenious use of duct-tape as in this town. "Duct-tape," one of my friends announced, "is Fernie bling." And my new Number One favourite product; years instantly added to the life of a garment through a bit of strategically applied duct-tape. I've seen it over holes in jackets, gashes in trousers and one of the lifties even has his work shoes bound together with the stuff. Likewise, having spent the previous four months in either snowboard boots or gumboots – the poor man's Sorels – I had no footwear for my trip to Duke, and had to buy myself a pair of shoes the evening before I left.

I then landed right in college town USA, straight out of the movies, featuring a mock-Gothic cathedral, frat houses with Greek letters hanging over the door, leafy quadrangles, and a cast of preppy, privileged clean-living undergrads strolling around in Gap khakis and crew-cuts, hyped up about the impending big basketball game. Compared to poor cash-starved universities in Ireland or the UK, Duke seemed to have plenty of money to go around and they wined and dined us prospective PhD folk amazingly. Earning minimum wage, I'd been living on a pauper's budget in Fernie, so in Duke I gorged myself on canapés, chicken stuffed with goat's cheese, individual raspberry tortes, and the finest wines available to humanity. Even the coffee machine in the graduate student's lounge was decked out with individual sachets of "French Vanilla" and "Java Blend".

Nonetheless, I yearned to get back to Fernie during those short few days. I'd been looking forward to getting out of town for a change of scenery – nothing like a freebie after all – so it was surprising to discover how attached I had become to the Kootenays, to the people and to the lifestyle at large. I missed not only the actual snowboarding but I missed the wilderness, I missed my friends, I missed the laid-back pace of life. I missed moments like loading groceries into my housemates' van outside the supermarket, looking up at the sunset over the Lizard Range, then grinning at each other, momentarily reminded of the glory by which we are surrounded. The snowy peaks – oh, but it's too difficult to describe the mountains without lapsing into purple prose. One of Duke's selling points is its immaculate campus, and compared to the standard squat North American towns of gas stations and malls it has its charms, but "beautiful architectural spaces" just weren't doing it for me that weekend; not a patch on God's great outdoors, I'm afraid.

But what I missed most of all was the unabashed enthusiasm and embrace of life which you get out here. What I love most about snowboarding, I discovered, is the freshness and joy it brings, the reminders that wow, life can be a lot of fun. This doesn't gel well with the cultivated cynicism of academic clabber. As every good postmodernist should, I know about truth being provisional, identity being transitory, and that I should scoff derogatorily at the idea of "certainties". Such abstruse contortions fade clear out of mind when you're psyching yourself up out at the top of a cliff, thinking, shit, it's going to be bad if this goes wrong. Standing up, your heart thumping, you hoist your pants, look around and then block out everything else and hold your nerve to straight line the fucker and not speedcheck or bail at the last instant. And if you land it, you dance on the inside, shimmering and elated, then wait to cheer your friends with a triumphant "fuck yeah!" if they do the same. Or alternately if you don't and instead bounce along the snow before scudding to a stop, you unstrap from your board, check to see if your limbs are in vaguely working order, and hike the offending obstacle again and again until it's been nailed.

With others making decisions about Duke vs. Yale vs. Columbia vs. Berkeley, they looked at me slightly askance when I admitted that I was torn not between any of the Ivy League schools, but between Duke and the lure of the snow, the call of the wild. People kept asking me what my research interests were and what school I was at – "Oh…I did a Masters in Irish literature before, but now I live in the BC Interior…." I'd trail off miserably in response.

I'm sure I must have had some sort of good reason for applying to grad school, but for the life of me I couldn't remember what it was. I had a physical ache in my stomach to get back to the snow, pining for Fernie for the four days. Arriving back in BC, I was more fired up than ever for the remaining six weeks of the season.

These are precious days, my friends, in a special, special place.

Lisa

PS: Back in Fernie, I mulled over what to do about Duke, having until the middle of April to decide. To turn down a place in a top university, which comes with a $20,000 annual stipend, for no particular reason other than "it's just not where my head is at right now, dude" seemed to be criminally insane, but the thought of relocating to North Carolina instilled in me panicky dread, heart beating faster and butterflies in my stomach, a Pavlovian reflex over which I had no control.

Though I was the only person who could make the call, I nonetheless sought advice from all and sundry, friends, housemates, patients at physio, strangers in the hitching queue – and, funnily enough, the reactions were not perhaps what one might anticipate. My university-educated friends, knowing the heartbreak and hardships a PhD would entail, counselled me to think very carefully before committing to Duke whilst the hardcore ski-bums who went straight from high school to ski-town urged me to do it in a heartbeat.

Some pointed out that I could always drop out if I really didn't like it. But it was a fantastic opportunity about which I was barely lukewarm, and I didn't want to go into it already prepared to leave. It would have been a bit churlish, I felt, when so many others would make so much more of the place. Turning it down, I realised, would be either the most exhilarating or most foolhardy thing I'd ever done. Trouble was, I couldn't decide which.

I then got offered a full scholarship to Oxford. And whilst I was willing to blow off Duke for the snow, I faltered when it came to that other illustrious institution. I'll be starting there in October. And that's that.

April 2006: Spring Skiing

The saga continues…

My return from Duke was the turning point in the season both literally and figuratively. I was so glad to be back that I positively beamed at everyone I met, high-fiving my friends, hailing them "yo dude what's happening?" and addressing them as "man" irrespective of gender. (All greetings I may have to tone down when I'm surrounded by Oxford dons.) Back on the hill it was the onset of spring. Farewell to minus twenty, you could now inhale freely without inducing lung-burn from the cold and people were starting to cultivate the first faint etchings of goggle tans. Overnight freeze-thaw action meant that while the pistes were rock-hard first thing in the morning, it sounding like the roar of a jet-engine when you turned, later in the day the sunshine softened them up into glorious slush. With an end to the "epic pow" for which Fernie is famed, everyone flocked to the park to film their spins and tricks, or as in my case simply trying to clear the knuckle without injuring myself yet again.

But the universe, it seems, looks kindly on snowboarders. During the last week of the season temperatures obligingly dropped below zero and we unexpectedly got a load of new snow, allowing us to slay the pow and scoot through the trees one final time. Which is also how my encounter off the Cheesegrater came about, this being a permanently exposed cliff-band so called on account of its ability to shred both snowboarder and equipment to pieces. It was Easter Saturday and we'd had one more bonus, late-season dump. Ali and I were ripping along, and so enthused was I about these bonanza conditions that the piste markings went unobserved. Ali was waving and shouting at me to stop but before I had time to heed her warnings I was on top of the rock face, then slipping down, then falling through the air, then ragdolling through the snow and then it was all over. Ali, meanwhile, had skirted around the chute and traversed across the bottom of the cliff, asking "Lis?" in a quavering voice, expecting to find my mangled, serrated limbs stretched across the slopes. Instead I was just sitting very, very quietly with a scratch on neither myself nor my board. By complete chance I'd somehow managed to straight-line the one almost implausibly thin section with no rocks. It was an Easter miracle I made it through that one completely unscathed.

I went home more than slightly shaken. I'd given up chocolate for Lent and even though Lent didn't end until the following day, my housemate Mike (who describes himself as Jewish-ish) explained that as Jesus was a Jew and as Jewish feasts begin at sundown on the day before, it would therefore be perfectly justified for me to start in on the chocolate again. I didn't need too much persuasion to be honest, but it was nice to have some sort of theological back-up as well. So we made chocolate-chip pancakes and smoked a joint. Then I lay on the living-room floor and watched *The Goonies*.

The ski-lifts shut for the season last Tuesday, though continuing to run for staff for the following day. Along I went, "working" in the Daylodge as I had been – I deploy the term very loosely as I never did more than twelve hours a week. Furthermore, towards the tail-end of the season there were no tourists whatsoever on the hill, only ski-bums and locals, and I was able to freely grant staff discount to anybody I knew and, um, appropriate as much free food as I desired. Add in the free ski-pass and getting to ride on Staff Day and it works out not a bad deal after all. I'm glad to have snuck under the radar on that one.

Staff-Day brought with it both sitting in the sun and boozing as well as a specifically constructed jump. It was a regatta of Fernie's finest and some of the guys were pulling backflips and rodeos (a type of inverted, spinny trick thing) like no-one's business. And then there was Ellie and me, cut-throat to the end, hiking it over and over. For my last hit of the season, I wanted to go big, all things being relative of course, and what I consider "big" being disgracefully puny by other standards. I went into the jump with way more speed than my usual measure, and despite a bit of arm-flapping action and absolutely no style whatsoever, I stomped the landing. All in all, it was enough that I could ride down to the base one final time feeling I'd had A Very Good Innings this season; bumps, bruises, breaks and sprains notwithstanding.

So what with the singing of the birds and the smell of the earth, the seasons here are a-changing. Skis have been stacked away until next year, and people are out skateboarding, running and cycling, knowing that, as the Good Book holds it, to everything there is a season. Oh, and unselfconsciously wearing shorts, an item of clothing about which people from my part of the world have a collective neuroses.

I suppose I should leave Fernie soon, a move about which I am mildly terrified. Having been here for six months, I shirk away from the idea of living, well, anywhere else. It's so comforting living in the Fernie bubble, knowing that if – as happened yesterday – a stranger pulls over in his pick-up to offer me a ride home it is overwhelmingly likely he is devoid of nefarious motives, merely motivated at the piteous sight of me plodding along without a jacket, grocery bags straining in the rain. In short, I am afraid!

However, it seems a little ridiculous to have come all the way to Canada and to have seen only one tiny town, to know all the skiing and hiking trails within a 5km radius intimately but having seen nothing else whatsoever.

Ah sure we'll see how it goes.

Lisa

May 2006: A Town for all Seasons

Me again

So here we are, the end of May, and I'm still in Fernie...

I continued to dread leaving town but told myself it would be best thing to do in terms of personal development, making the most of this chance to see Canada and so forth. However, I then got offered a summer internship in City Hall (miniscule as Fernie is, it gets classified as a city) which, though the type of bureaucratic job I'd baulk at doing back home, gave me an excuse to stay in town. Thank you Fernie city council!

Substituting a big move with a small one, I've been living in a different house since the start of May. I never went into much detail about the heating situation, or lack thereof, in our house this winter, our landlords liking to keep the thermostatat ten degrees. Ten! That's a few scant degrees above the inside of a fridge and, equally, the level to which the air-con was set down in North Carolina. Not, you understand, what one needs in the biting Canadian mid-winter. Occasionally they'd crank the thermostat up to fifteen but this did little to offset the insufferable cold. If I wanted to go hang around the living room I had to put on a fleece and toque and huddle under a bundle of blankets. I'm all for cutting down on fossil fuels but this stinginess masked as environmental concern was ridiculous, especially when they had four tenants paying more than adequate rent. The World Health Organization, by the way, recommends a minimum indoor temperature of eighteen.

I'm sure it sounds unbearably Dickensian and grim, and you probably can't understand why I didn't just baulk and move out straight away. Well, when you're in the middle of a situation like that you simply put up with it, it only being retrospectively that you think "what the fuck?". Also, I would have lost my security deposit had I left before the end of April. But by the hokey I wasn't staying put a day longer than necessary! I'm now living with a group of my friends in a rambling old turn-of-the-century house with high wood-panelled ceilings, a big basement, an overgrown garden and a roomy kitchen in which I can bake to my heart's content.

It's not all domesticated bliss though. Last weekend was the May bank holiday, local tradition being to head to nearby Lake Koocanusa for a camp out. I arrived home from work Friday afternoon to find the house asunder, the hall full of bottled water, crates of beer and coolers crammed with food and the boys industriously engaged in pulling all the camping gear out of the basement. "Come on! It'll be so warm you can just sleep under a blanket!" I was assured. I headed away hideously ill-prepared; no sleeping-bag, no tent, no waterproof clothes, it having been gloriously sunny and thirty degrees for the previous two weeks. Anyway, as we were driving down to the lake it started raining and raining and raining. Yes, yes, I know, hindsight is a great thing and of course I should have seen this coming. I was reduced to wearing a binbag over my hoodie to keep myself dry, meaning I had to be careful not to stand too near the campfire in case my beautiful new ensemble melted and shrunk.

And as for the camp itself? It's worth mentioning that the guys we were with are no namby-pamby-city-boys-let-loose-in-nature. They're all climbers, back-country skiers, mountain-bikers, and what not and indeed their gung-ho-ness was their downfall. That, and the fact they were pumped full of amphetamines and MDMA. They had brought this big tarpaulin to sleep under and whatever got into them – personally I blame stubborn masculine pride – they launched headstrong into putting it up without any forethought, shimmying up trees, tying ropes and clipping carabineers here and there without any coherent plan.

Whatever angle they installed it at, rather than providing shelter from the storm it acted as a quasi-wind tunnel, flapping uncontrollably in the breeze. Not only that, but with the boggy piece of ground they'd chosen for camp, the water collected and pooled in the bottom rather than running off as desired. It ended up with two of the most resolutely masculine Antipodeans you could meet, all wife-beater tops, muscular brawn, and construction-worker tans, spooning in a shared sleeping bag, huddling for warmth and dear life. It doesn't take much to overcome homophobic prejudice and rekindle base survival instincts when faced with wet and cold.

It was like a scene out of 'Nam. By Saturday afternoon four of us were so exhausted and drenched that we gave up and came home, long weekend bedamned.

Better luck next time, eh.

Lisa

July 2006: Exit, pursued by a bear

Hello again

After the snowboarding season had finished, I developed a touch of post-season blues, an anticlimactic flatness which was perhaps only inevitable after such a fast-paced and adrenalin-charged four months. I was jittery with excess energy and didn't know what to do with my time. But since then, as well as going for a few joyless jogs, I've bought a second-hand mountain-bike and have been scaring the bejaysus out of myself. *Plus ça change.*

Mountain-biking is a scary pastime and the stakes are high: Ellie arrived at the front door the other day, arm in a sling, shoulder scraped raw and face crumpled in tears. She smashed her wrist downhilling and now has a metal plate and seven pins holding together her arm and is only just starting to emerge from a Percocet haze. So, with a measure of self-preservation lacking all winter long, I take things very slowly on my bike, sticking to the cross-country trails and with no intention of venturing into the full-face helmet and body-armoured world of the hardcore. I shift into "granny gear" going uphill – which, by the way, is Tough Work indeed, leaving me panting, mottled purple and drenched in sweat – and on the downhill I clutch at my breaks for dear life, negotiating tree-stumps, drops and twisted roots with the temerity of "a wee sleekit timorous beastie".

While biking may be an acceptable substitute for those months of the year when there's no snow, I'm loathe buying any more equipment for it than is absolutely necessary. Over the past few months, I have amassed the most staggering inventory of sporting goods for any foreseeable climate, conditions or pursuits and I don't know how I'm going to transport it all once I try leaving Canada: e.g., wicking layers, thermal tops, fleeces, snowboarding goggles, swimsuits, running shoes, sports-bras, snowboard boots, a mountain-bike, two snowboards, more Gore-Tex than you can shake a stick at. So rather than purchasing a specific bike helmet I just wore my snowboarding one for a few weeks, which is the extreme sports equivalent of wearing your school uniform on a Saturday; i.e., desperately uncool, before procuring one on extended loan from my housemate.

However, if I continue biking alone, my Canadian adventure could end prematurely; "exit, pursued by a bear". This here is bear territory and if you go down in the woods today you'd better be prepared for a big, lumbering ursine surprise. About a month ago I heard a suspicious grunt from the undergrowth when I was in particularly dense alpine forest. Perhaps it was only a badger or something – do they have badgers in the Kootenays? – but I wasn't hanging around to find out and pedalled out of there like a maniac. However, Goonies never say die so, undeterred, I continued to bike by myself. A few days later the inevitable happened and I finally saw a bear padding across the trail in front of me. Luckily it was a black bear rather than a grizzly – black bears are less likely to attack – but still and all, it was simultaneously the most terrifying yet exhilarating bike ride of my life. Nothing like a solitary encounter with a bear for motivation to ride fast.

Fernie is idyllic in summer. (Well, my idea of an idyll anyway, the city sophisticates among you might find it unbearably slow-paced and dull. You need to make your own fun around these parts.) I've mentioned before there's been a wave of active newcomers into town over the past decade, and this is even more apparent at this time of year. I saw one woman cycling along towing not one but two children, and another out jogging with a three-wheeled baby chariot, golden retriever panting alongside. No excuses accepted here. Hiking, biking, fishing, golfing, tubing down the river; I swear I'm not being subcontracted out by the Fernie tourist board but it truly is an outdoor paradise.

Yet even paradise sometimes palls and if I had to pinpoint something which I miss about Dublin – though certainly not being one to peddle romantic illusions about the Irish or waxing lyrical about the gift of the gab – it would be the quickness of wit. Perhaps it's only the people I've had the misfortune to get stuck on chairlifts with, but in my experience Canadians lack a conversational verve and sway.

It's much more of a "doing" culture than a talking one here and whilst the Canadians I know could comfortably trap and shoot an elk from five hundred paces, white-water raft through the rapids, out-ski an avalanche and knock off a first ascent all before breakfast, it is not a culture given to the cultivation of rapier wit. My theory, entirely uncorroborated, is the pro-active resourceful family members emigrated here, becoming fur-trappers, woodsmen and starting good pioneering stock, leaving the grumblers and gainsayers behind back home where centuries of sitting around avoiding the rain has elevated the art of conversation to the highest degree.

Another change from home is that this is not a nation plagued by self-doubt. People talk frankly and matter-of-factly about their abilities and strengths rather than shirking under the excessive modesty of the Irish. When I hear people start sentences with "I'm really good at maths/computer stuff/balancing a ball on my nose...." I'm taken aback, as it's a major cultural taboo for us to openly admit to being good at something. In Ireland it's about downplaying your achievements all the way. Even overhearing statements like "pink really suits me" have left me aghast as the Irish way would be to say, "This old thing? Ah it's nothing. Sure I look like a sack of potatoes no matter what I wear."

Something which similarly threw me at first in Canada was the response "good for you!", after you've said that you're buying a new snowboard or heading on a back-country camping trip or something. In Ireland you see, a "good for you" would either carry the connotations of a snide dig, "isn't it well for some", or be accompanied by a defensive edge – the subtext being are-you-implying-I'm-inferior-for-not-following-suit? But, no, this encouragement and approbation is entirely genuine. I wonder if our slagging off of loud North Americans is in part envy of their easy self-confidence.

The flip-side of this healthy self-regard and unselfcon-sciousness is, to loop around to my original point, that Canadians just aren't very funny, at least by Irish standards. Irish humour is predicated upon self-effacement – an ability to laugh at yourself and a readiness to cut others down to size – something precluded by the unassailable self-belief of

North America. There are of course Canadian comedians: Jim Carrey, Mike Myers, Tom Green. But notice how these peddle a "zany" action-based brand of humour rather than any ludic skill.

In any case, no matter my amateur dissection of the Canadian psyche, I'm leaving here at the start of September to spend a few weeks in Ireland where I can get in all the quick-fire responses and slagging people off I want before going to Oxford to get this PhD thing out of the way. The stars, however, are inauspicious. I know Oxford is a great opportunity etc. etc. but do I really want to go back to the academic grind when there's still so much gnar to be shredded out here? Last Friday I received a bundle of official information having to RSVP for various functions where the dress code is specified as "lounge suits or equivalent with gowns". I should explain what I've been wearing for the past few months: I have never been anywhere where everyone, myself included, is so appallingly dressed. People regularly come into City Hall for meetings wearing "Calgary Marathon 1992" t-shirts. My one pair of jeans are patched, faded to a fraction of their former selves and ripped at the bottom after catching on my bike chain. I've gone straight from berry-picking to the bar, wearing my oldest shapeless cotton t-shirt, clutching a plastic bag of huckleberries, hands and mouth stained purple, and wandered around all afternoon with bike oil and chain-marks down the back of my legs.

Thinking about Oxford threw me so much that that evening I got very, very drunk in our basement on an ill-advised combination of red wine and Fireball, this bottom brand of cinnamon flavoured whiskey, before slumping in a heap against the washing machine.

Let's see what happens eh,
Lisa

August 2006: Lisa versus the Bear, Part 2

Yo

Subsequent to that first encounter with a bear at the start of summer, I vowed not do any more mountain-biking by myself: I'd only hit trails with friends in tow because I didn't want to face off against any more large scary animals on my own, thank you very much. And I stuck to this all season long. But last Sunday two guy friends and I headed out on an epic bike-ride following the power lines from Fernie into the backcountry. It's almost redundant to try to describe how gruelling and punishing a ride it was that day, but envisage mile after mile of scorched dirt-tracks up and down undulating hills in the baking, blistering heat. After maybe ten or fifteen kilometres of this, the guys decided to start hacking through the forest to discover/invent a new trail. We had neither a map nor the faintest idea of where we were, and I was hot and cranky and tired. Ah here now, I thought, deciding to bale on this particular adventure, I'm going home. So back off to Fernie along the dirt-track I set. After the whole "so you'll be alright getting home then?" routine, I'm beginning to suspect that the purpose of this particular exchange, by the way, is more to salve the conscience of the asker rather than genuine concern. "She said she was grand getting home!" one could later protest in indignation should anything go wrong.

Now, no more than ten minutes after leaving the boys I rounded a corner and came to an abrupt halt. There, rubbing their backs against a telephone pole were a black bear and cub. Who immediately froze and looked straight at me. As I at them. Black bears are highly unlikely to attack humans… unless they are protecting their cubs.

Picture the scene. In the summer stillness of the forest green, not a soul for miles around, nor a sound to be heard.

A lone girl clutches her bike, legs shaking uncontrollably, as a defensive mama bear paces towards her slowly, slowly. What happens next?

Biker-bear encounters are so common in Fernie that they have a Bear Aware programme, the basic tenets of which are drummed into all. If you meet a bear, don't try and run away – bears can outrun a horse when needs be. Stand your ground, calmly and firmly, even if the bear charges, make plenty of noise, use your bike to protect yourself. So I started talking loudly to the bear, my voice wavering, my legs still wobbling – "Please go away bear, I just want to cycle by, don't want to harm you or your cub, just want to go home" – and luckily mama abruptly changed her mind and bolted into the bush, cub scampering behind her. Terrified as I was, I nonetheless registered "how cute!" I stood frozen to the spot for a few more minutes more shouting and whooping and making as much noise as I could, singing the first things that came into my head – "Dirty Old Town" and the Irish national anthem. Incidentally, both tunes can be belted out at full volume without a great deal of vocal dexterity. Then I rode like a dervish back to Fernie, continuing to yelp and yell the whole way to warn any other wildlife of my approach.

It gladdens my heart to know that places like Fernie still exist, where your personal safety is more likely to be compromised by local wildlife than local lowlife and if rustling in the bushes makes you swivel your head sharply it's far more likely to be a bear than a would-be assailant. I've said before that, for me, what made Fernie so special in the winter was the overwhelming sense of innocence and vitality, a lack of cynicism or worldliness, and this sense was even more pronounced in the summer. My friend and I never felt we were too cool, too sophisticated, too "mature" for anything this summer, be that riding around town together on our bikes, messing about on skateboards, jumping off a rope-swing, searching for wild huckleberries, or getting a puncture rafting down the Elk River without any paddles in our cheapo twenty-dollar dinghies from Walmart.

The undoubted highlight of the summer, however, was climbing the 2100 metre peak of Mount Fernie, a phenomenally ill-prepared mission, every grunt and step and clamber more difficult than the one before. Four of us set off. I'd borrowed an ill-fitting pair of hiking-boots from a housemate and every step felt like someone was slashing at my heels with red-hot razor blades. Ellie, meanwhile, insisted on coming along despite her mountain-biking mishap. We had voiced our concerns – "dude, you had major surgery on your wrist three weeks ago and you can't even hold a bottle of beer. Do you really think it's the best idea to climb a mountain?" – but trying to dissuade Ellie when she's decided on something is like trying to hold back the tide. So she had to negotiate scrambling up near-vertical shale literally single-handedly with a battered old ski-pole for support. But well, you know the way it goes, death before dishonour, and neither of us was going to be the one to suggest turning back.

It hasn't all been clean-living and hearty wholesomeness though. At the end of the ski-season there was a mass exodus from town of the transient population and those of us who stayed behind didn't necessarily know each other that well. As summer went on, however, we huddled and coalesced into a close-knit group. They were predominantly proper ocker Australian with a few whinging poms thrown in for good measure: rude, brash, foul-mouthed, uncouth but generous and warm-hearted to a fault, and resolutely and incorrigibly upbeat and smiling. "How's your vagina this morning, Rezzie?" has been hollered across the house to let us know that Renee had hooked up the night before. On another occasion, everyone traipsed to the chemist together to obtain medication for Pado's haemorrhoids. "It's not very often," the pharmacist said carefully, "that people come in with their friends to discuss, eh, this condition...."

Falling in with this "bad set" knolled the end to my wintertime sobriety. I woke up more than once in their house wondering "how on fuck did I get here?" After the Mt Fernie debacle, for example, I drank a bottle of wine on an empty stomach, socked one of the Australians, all six feet of him, in the jaw, and had to be put to bed. I haven't been that pyrically drunk for a long time but to make use of that celebrated phrase – "It seemed like a good idea at the time."

But now it's over. If Oxford is to have my mind, the mountains keep my soul.

Lisa

Retrospective:
Brief Interlude in Oxford

It was with great reluctance and heavy heart that I left Fernie. I really wasn't sure about this PhD thing. As forefronted by the whole going-to-Duke interlude, the niggling doubt that I wasn't entirely committed to academia loomed large, but I didn't want to turn down Oxford and then spend the rest of my life wondering what it would have been like to have gone there when I'd had the chance. *Carpe diem* and all that.

That said, as it grew closer my doubts grew more severe.

The main problem was that I couldn't have cared less about what I was meant to be researching; the cheery and heart-warming topic of anti-Catholic sentiment in twentieth-century Ireland. I just didn't believe in it. No, no, I mean I do believe that anti-Catholic sentiment existed. But it certainly didn't fire me up enough to devote three years of my life to examining the issue in excruciating detail. Did I want to reach a new insight into our contemporary cultural condition? Did I want to re-invigorate scholarly debate, change the critical prism through which the country was currently viewed?

Quite frankly I'd rather keep snowboarding. Irish Catholics could drown in their own misery for all I cared. I warned my friends and family that I was half-hearted at best about this new venture; I might leave if I didn't like it. I don't think any of them took this seriously. Bracing myself for the just-in-case, I packed only the bare minimum to take with me in case I had to make a quick escape. Likewise, I took out an interest-free loan of €2000, to be repaid in one lump sum the following June, just in case I needed emergency back-up funds for any potential bolt.

Everyone kept trying to jolly me along, probably thinking that it was simply post-travelling restlessness. You'll love it once you've settled down, they said coaxingly and encouragingly. Also there was a sense that I'd had my allotted year of fun and to want any more was simply greedy. There's only so much wilderness to go around after all. Let other people have their turn. They'd soothingly say "the mountains will always be there" and I'd seethe with frustration, thinking this was an incredibly unhelpful observation. Yes the mountains will always be there but in the meantime I have to put in three years! THREE YEARS! of intellectual grief and immeasurable slog over something that I'm not even remotely enthused about. The thought of not being able to do another ski-season for that long was unbearable. Given that my long-term goal was to live in a backwoods ski-town enjoying the good life – what exactly I was going to do for money or work never really factored into this vision – I wasn't entirely sure how a PhD fitted into the plan.

I think people often find the Working Holiday Abroad experience so stimulating simply by dint of everyday items being interesting and new; e.g. the eating habits, the brands in the supermarket, the beers on tap, those sorts of little things. The Irish go to Australia, the Australians go to London, the Londoners go to Canada, and presumably the

Canadians go somewhere as well, even if I'm not exactly sure where. It doesn't really seem to matter what your actual destination is once it's different from home. Compare and contrast. Being out of your natural habitat, being exposed to other ways of living means expanding your horizons and adjusting your preconceptions accordingly. Afterwards, rather than going back to things exactly as they were and simply picking up where you left off, I suppose you're meant to take the new perspectives and insights you've achieved and inject them back into your situation to become the Better Person. Personal growth and all that.

If I'd learned any life lesson – beyond don't go mountain-biking by yourself unless you're going to start doing Grizzly Adams impersonations and befriending the bears – it was I needed to ease the self-imposed pressure and not have such a narrow-gauge focus on work. Graduate study at Oxford is perhaps not the ideal undertaking if you're trying to develop a new life-balance. Had I gone there straight from my Masters I'm sure I would have been fine, if that's the right word. Still intent on becoming the keenest cultural theorist the world had ever known, I would have become high-strung, short-tempered and shrill beyond any reasonable degree. I would have worked hard on my thesis though.

After a year in Fernie, I just didn't see the point. At the English Department induction for new D Phil students – as PhDs are known in Oxford – the "pep talk" from the Dean of Studies warned us that this would probably be the loneliest undertaking of our lives and to make sure we had at least one conversation with someone a day. Sage advice, actually, for anyone engaged in research but I just thought Jesus, I'm twenty-four. This seems like a very odd use of my mid-twenties. Shouldn't I be out there taking advantage of the irrepressible buoyancy of youth instead?

Maybe doing a PhD is like training for a marathon. You

can only do something as demanding and time-consuming and painful if you really, really want to. To get through the inevitable low days and set-backs and injuries, to drag yourself out the door when it's raining or whatnot, the motivation absolutely has to come from within, not because you think you *should*. Just as a sense of obligation isn't going to get you through four hundred plus miles of training and then 26.2 more on the day, neither is it going to get you through three years in a research library and a 100,000 word thesis. You need drive and fire to go the distance.

I straightaway made an appointment with my college tutor saying I'm terribly sorry but there appears to have been some sort of terrible misunderstanding, I have no interest whatsoever in doctoral study. She pointed out that Thursday of Week One was quite early for such disillusionment to have set in for a three-year project. She asked me if there was anything I'd prefer to be doing instead. I said I wanted to go and have adventures and snowboard. She winced.

So I must emphasise that the problem wasn't with Oxford itself. Yes, I know it's very generous of me to concede the point. On the one hand we have a centuries-old seat of learning. On the other we have a firebrand young ski-bum. Oxford is a world apart from anywhere else, a cross between a boarding school and a monastic order, everything the clichés would have it and then more: cobbled streets and bicycles and high table at formal hall. Rhodes scholars and college bops and grace in Latin and evensong in Christ-church Cathedral. Gowns and drinking port in wood-panelled common rooms. Sumptuous banquets and wine receptions and music rooms. Stone-walled quadrangles, rowing regattas and a cleaner to change the bin in my room every day.

Nonetheless, it simply wasn't for me. Fascinating as it was to see this arcane self-contained world at first-hand, it didn't set well with a hunch that whatever my destiny was,

I wasn't going to find it sitting in the Bodleian Library day after day, staring up glumly at portraits of scholars past. Under the terms of my scholarship my fees were covered and I received a stipend to live off as well. Knowing that so many people would have loved not only to be studying at Oxford but actually getting paid to do so, I felt guilty about my lack of interest. I didn't want this hesitancy to be misconstrued as ingratitude, for it to appear as if I was throwing it all back with an impetuous shrug, "nah dude I couldn't be assed". It just wasn't what *I* wanted from life.

However, rather than bolting straightaway, I was going to give it until at least Christmas time to make sure my woes just weren't dressed-up adjustment issues after all. I spent Michaelmas Term smiling weakly and forcedly, trying to Make the Best of Things by joining clubs, pedalling my mountain-bike around Oxfordshire and going to talks on various topics, usually about expeditions to far-away arctic climes. I went to a lecture by a sharp-eyed eighty-year old who'd gone on the 1952 Oxford University expedition to the North Pole. I was enthralled. I also listened to a woman who'd gone to the Antarctic for six months as an in-house writer. I sat, fascinated, as she described her trip. What struck her most in Antarctica, she said, was the sense of conviction, the sense that everyone there absolutely believed in what they were doing. This led me to thinking: surely I too should have the courage of my convictions and head back to the hills? You know those mantras that get bandied about? "Do what you love. Follow your heart. Live your dream." Well, talk is cheap – maybe I should put them to the test and see how they work out when applied.

That in mind, I left Oxford with a backpack at the end of December to go to Fernie, ostensibly for a two-week trip. My housemates waved me away joking, "You'd better come back hahaha!" I made no promises.

As soon as I got back to BC, that was it. I can never decide when I go snowboarding whether it's that the scales fall from my eyes and I achieve clarity of vision, or it's more that the blinkers go on, logic goes out the window and all I can think about is shredding the gnar. But either way, once I was "home" in Fernie, there was no way I was returning to the PhD after the Christmas break. I didn't want to become another miserable doctoral student who bitterly rued they'd ever seen Oxford, ever read a book, but felt compelled to carry on regardless because of how much time they'd already devoted to the dratted thing. I figured I should quit while I was ahead rather than two years down the line by which point I'd probably be half insane.

"Was it hard to walk away from something so prestigious, like?" someone asked me recently. Well, there was no real decision-making process as such; every fibre and instinct told me to leave. More difficult though was propelling this decision into action. It was like psyching myself up to go off a big jump: extremely nervous beforehand, the God-am-I-really-going-to-do-this adrenaline rush and then relief and exhilaration afterwards when you've gone through with it. As I'd learned from snowboarding, if you know you're capable of doing something, if it's only self-doubt standing in your way, you can't back down. You need that self-belief to push the comfort zone. If there's even a second's hesitation then it's all over.

I went to the Fernie library and sent off a string of emails to college tutors, supervisors, scholarship boards etc. saying thank you very much for the opportunity but I'm afraid I wouldn't be continuing with my studies after Christmas. None of them seemed to care very much. I imagine their attitude was that anyone who was reckless enough to drop out of Oxford to go snowboarding was evidently mentally unstable and beyond redemption. I got a short reply from my tutor saying she'd seen this coming and good luck with, well, whatever it was that I was going to do and that was about it.

I was required for "statistical purposes" to supply the reason for the cessation of my studies to my funding body, the Arts and Humanities Research Council. Rather than going for a neutral catch-all – e.g. personal issues, career opportunity etc – I instead wrote "to snowboard". I can't imagine it's one they hear too often. At that stage I was past the point of caring. Was I burning my bridges? Torching them with a manic cackle, more like. I was going down in a blaze of glory!

My parents, in an echo of the more wayward moments of my teenage years, stuck with the "we're not angry, we're disappointed" line. Essentially a dutiful daughter and not-withstanding this scorched earth policy with Oxford, I kept having dreams in which I'd been implicated in a murder and would wake up feeling horribly overburdened with guilt. Talk about transferred emotions. Evidently I wasn't fully resolved either.

After that it was along the lines of oh well, I'm here in Fernie now, may as well stay for the rest of the ski-season. It's not like I have to attend to anything pressing elsewhere. Running on the bare minimum of funds and falling back on what was left of my emergency loan I just about managed to buy a ski-pass, extend my travel insurance and change my return flight to April.

Common wisdom dictates if you've had an amazing time somewhere it's a mistake to go back as it will always pale in comparison. In fact, it felt like I'd never left Fernie at all, as if the interlude in Oxford had simply been some sort of surreal dream. A lot of people just assumed I'd been laying low for a while and that was why they hadn't seen me around. "Have you been away or something?" the girl in the supermarket asked. Something like that.

I sent few emails that winter. My first flush of Fernie love had settled into deep affection, no less heart-felt but less intensely expressed. Also, more prosaically, having abandoned my laptop with the rest of my worldly goods in my break for freedom, I had limited computer access.

Fortune Favours the Brave?

February 2007: Living on a knife edge

Yo

Deciding to do a snowboard season on the spur of the moment brings with it certain logistical and monetary hardships. Ski-gear aside, I'd brought only enough clothes for a short holiday so I'm chronically short of socks and underwear and that sort of thing. Any of the photos from this winter show me wearing the same two tops on a night-on/night-off basis. I left the remainder of my clothes in Oxford – along with my laptop and mountain-bike – and one of the guys I lived with there has very kindly bundled them all up in black bin-bags to be picked up at a later date.

I'm also horrifically poor. I'm down to my last pair of ski-socks, my thermals are threadbare and my outerwear is so unwaterproof by this stage that I might as well start riding in jeans for all the difference it makes. I've become quite the charity case, seeking refuge as I am here. One of my friends is letting me live in her spare room for free, something for which I am grovellingly and inexpressibly grateful. Another gave me first dibs on a bundle of stuff she was taking to the Salvation Army so I managed to secure for myself a second pair of pyjamas and a fleece. A third posted me a Red Cross-style care package containing teabags and toothpaste and conditioner. Were it not for such gestures I'd genuinely have trouble feeding and clothing myself.

A good quotient of my friends from last year have lingered on in town. Notable by their absence, alas, are Ali and Ellie, both of whom are now volunteering in the Scottish Highlands, radio-tracking pine martens by night. (You can't make this stuff up.) Others have come into focus though. There's Kris, a curly-haired and easy-going Australian who qualified as an Occupational Therapist last year but is in no rush to start her career. There's also Lindsay and Chucky. Lindsay grew up in Calgary and last winter she was living in Fernie full-time. This winter she's back in college in Cowtown but comes down every weekend. Chuck's this freckled kid from New Zealand with an unruly mop of red hair. He tried introducing himself to everyone as "Steve", when it emerged that he'd been known in high school as Chucky on account of his resemblance to the Rugrats character. So Chucky he has been forever more. He and Lindsay are in L.O.V.E.

[Disclaimer: at this point I need to employ some OJ Simpson-style semantic footwork. I was in Canada on a six month tourist visa, so I'm not saying that I actually *did* work under-the-table. Let's just imagine, *if* I was going to work under the table I'd go about it in a manner very similar to the description below. The following two paragraphs are therefore pure conjecture, made up purely for my own amusement.]

Discretion being the better part of candour, and what with my visa situation being somewhat irregular, if anyone ever asks me if I have a job here I'm very evasive and vague. The other day this guy in a beat-up old truck picked me up when I was hitching home from the hill. He looked like your quintessential Fernie redneck, if you'll allow the stereotyping, and when we got talking I was all prepared for him to say that he worked in the mines. Turned out he does Immigration Control down on the border. "Wonderful! Fantastic!" I exclaimed, and sat quietly for the rest of the trip. Serves me right for judging a book by its cover.

However, not needing to be similarly circumspect in the company of friends, let me reveal that I'm working in a ski-lodge in town. Shhh! Don't tell anyone. I go in for an hour in the morning to perform general cleaning duties. (When I'm scrubbing down the toilet bowls, it occurs to me that I'm not going to end up pride of place in the where-are-they-now profiles of former Oxford students anytime soon.) I then go back in the evening and help serve dinner and that sort of thing. I get to eat dinner with the guests every night which means I'm guaranteed at least one proper meal a day and, even better, it's usually healthy organic fare. This is BC after all.

It's been a good snow season, some minor dry spells notwithstanding. Today is an Albertan public holiday so I'm not going up the hill because, really, I don't feel like dealing with hoards of Calgarians, or Vulgarians as they're "affectionately" known. Calgary is 300km down the road (a mere stone's throw by Canadian standards) so there's lots of oil money being pumped into Fernie via Albertan second home-owners. Indeed, Calgarians have a particularly bad rap here for roaring around in enormous SUVs and generally flashing around their masses of cash like they own the place (as they sort of do).

They'll be back in Calgary tomorrow though and we'll still be slaying the pow.

Lisa

March 2007: In Which I Try to Ski

Whaddup.

The other day I went skiing – as opposed to snowboarding – with Kris, Chucky and other friends who claimed not to have been on skis before. Ha! This, I bitterly report, was not in fact the case. Bypassing the ignominy of the magic carpet, the conveyer belt serving the toddlers and timorous beginners, straight up the chairlift we went. Once off the lift, I clung petrified to my ski-poles, without the slightest idea how to control the skis trapped to my feet and terrified by the death-defying angle of the green run. I also wondered how on earth everyone else, ostensibly on skis for the first time too – I was yet to discover their treachery at this stage – was moving about reasonably competently when I was flailing and falling all over the place. I decided I must have even less kinaesthetic ability than the scant measure for which I'd previously given myself credit.

My friends were giving me a variety of pitying and despairing looks. Perhaps knowing how sharp-tongued I can be under stress, Chucky and Kris maintained a tactful silence whereas Eve, who's from Berlin, with the best will in the world was rapping out technical instructions in a brisk German accent, "Place your weight on your downhill leg." But her instructions weren't helping and I just didn't get it. Less than graciously I asked them to go away – "will yiz all just fuck off" was my exact phrasing, I think – and leave me to figure the process out for myself. Which they hastily did, no doubt recognising I was mere minutes away from becoming the hysterical, sobbing woman who takes off her skis and walks down the piste in humiliation and defeat.

Off they snow-ploughed. Tentatively, through trial and error I figured out the rudiments of this skiing though it took me a full hour to get from the top of the chair to the base, a distance down which I usually zip in three or four minutes. Apologising for my earlier behaviour, I got a cigarette from Eve – imagine me if you will, grim-faced and in ski-boots, puffing away – before going back up and giving it another shot. Things greatly improved from thereon in and it started to come together by the end of the day. Yes, my friends, for one brief afternoon I took my place among those beginner skiers zigzagging uncontrollably from one side of the piste to the other so no-one else can get past.

Apart from my brief excursion on skis, there's no real news from Fernie – is there ever? – just more of the same, in other words, working six days a week and snowboarding and drinking too much rum and a bit of sleep every now and then. I'm quite literally working my ass off: Clothes which at the start of the season were snug and figure-hugging are now saggy and loose, and jeans which were baggy to begin with now hang MC Hammer style. Minimum wage doesn't go far though so I'm still on the breadline.

Lisa

April 2007: Picking Up the Pieces

Hi again

The snow just keeps coming, the past couple of weeks consisting of gloriously sunny spring-skiing interspersed with unexpected temperature plummets and concomitant late season powder dumps. Easter weekend for example, was t-shirt weather and then we got 20cms of the beautiful white stuff overnight. And because there's been NO ONE around this week – not only is Fernie now completely devoid of tourists but lots of the seasonaires have already left town as well, suckers! – the hill didn't get tracked out at all and even late into the afternoon there were face-shots to be had.

All in all, however, I've found this season quite the emotional roller-coaster, if you'll allow the cliché, which I think under the circumstances you should. That's the last time I come half-way round the world for a holiday and subsequently drop out of college and unexpectedly stay working under the table for the following four months.

I reckon I'm going to go for the hat-trick of Canadian winters, maybe here in Fernie, maybe over at Red Mountain, who knows really, but I won't do it so precariously next time around. Lindsay and Chucky are also talking about doing a season in New Zealand and having met so many Kiwis here in Fernie I'm keen to check out the Southern Hemisphere. However, I don't know what I'm going to do between now and then to get myself out of debt and to get the money together for these future adventures. The options are:

- Stay in Canada, do some border-hopping down to the States to renew my tourist visa and proceed from there (Is this Canadian caper going to end with your intrepid narrator being deported? Should I just quit while I'm ahead?)

- Go back to Ireland for a penitential spell of living in my parents' house and commuting to some awful office job in the city

The more viable option is to move back home, either an appalling or appealing prospect depending on my mood. On the one hand, grateful as I am to my parents for taking back their prodigal daughter, once you've moved out of home it's hard to move back in. On the other, I've been very, very poor this season, and even though austerity and frugality are good puritan virtues, character building and so forth, it's all a bit exhausting as well. Having spent three days agonising as to whether I could afford a block of cheese to perk up my tuna sandwiches, not having to worry about paying rent or buying food for a while is extremely tempting.

Why an office job, you might wonder? Well, now that I have a brilliant future behind me and won't be taking the academic world by storm anytime soon I'm not qualified for much else. Going back to Ireland is a stop-gap to replenish funds rather than part of any long-term strategy and there's money to be made in administration, apparently. Who knew that my typing certificate would turn out to be much more useful than my Masters?

Oh well, only two more days of snowboarding left, so I'll enjoy that and decide about everything else next week. This whole following-your-heart business brings with it a measure of uncertainty. It's not to be entered into lightly.

Farewell from the nadir.

Lisa

Retrospective: Learning to Drive

When I left Canada after those strained and terse emails, I knew I'd be going back. I know a lot of people come back from travelling with the intention of taking off again but then things just happen. They get waylaid by Real Life and that's that. But I'd be going back. I'd give myself a year in Dublin to atone then I'd be going back. Next time things would be different though: I'd be financially solvent. I'd have a work visa. And, just for good measure, I'd know how to drive. So back I arrived in Ireland and if I hadn't been so intent on striking out once more for the land of wilderness and no public transport, I can't imagine that I'd have launched into learning to drive with such vigour and vim.

But there were other matters to be attended to first. I moved back in with my parents. I found an admin job in the health-care service, having talked winningly and convincingly at interview about how glad I was to be back in Dublin for good. Hmm. Having specifically said to the Careers Advisor at college that I wanted to avoid working in an office, here I was. Equally, just as I'd turned to snowsports as an escape from the humdrumness of the daily commute, here I was back getting the train back and forth every day. At least CIE appeared to have improved their customer relations if not their actual cavalcade of trains. Now they'd apologise for the delays and break-downs, even if I was fairly sure the explanations proffered were completely fictitious. Leaves on the line in June, that sort of thing.

I was also dealing with the emotional fall-out of having abandoned any sort of academic career to be a ski-bum. Brave decision? Rash decision? Away from the snow it wasn't so clear. What a miserable "summer" that was. Not only was I permanently in a black mood, but in some sort of horrible pathetic fallacy, it rained for over forty days continuously in Dublin throughout June and July. Even by Irish meteorological standards that was grim. In a touch of comic relief I kept getting sent alumni magazines from Oxford, where evidently the databases had not been set up to cope with the concept of drop-outs.

At least the "awful office job" I'd so dreaded getting was nowhere as bad as I'd feared. Aside from the commuting and having to wear horrible ill-fitting cheap suit jackets for meetings and a million and one levels of bureaucracy, the work was rewarding in its own way, the pay-cheques were more than ample and we had autonomy, responsibility, free sandwiches at meetings and other such boons.

I'm sure my colleagues thought I was an awful weirdo though. I seemed to exist in a perpetual present, with a caged wariness when talking about either the past or the future. Now, when I say I couldn't talk about the past it's not as if I were in a witness-protection programme or anything. Let's not get over-dramatic. But on my CV and at interview I'd entirely omitted the whole stint at Oxford because I figured it brought up more questions than were worth going into. It was like some sort of inverse Jeffrey Archer situation. Surely people pretend to have been to Oxford rather than pretending *not* to have been there? Plus, I figured, would you really give a job to someone who dropped out of a PhD after three months to go snowboarding? Where's the guarantee that they're not going to jack it all and do the same again? (Bingo! That's exactly what I was planning on doing.) Likewise, not knowing that I was saving away for my next Great Escape, they must have wondered why on earth I was so stingy. I wore the same two or three outfits in rotation and brought my lunch in with me everyday. Plus I was living at home and very rarely went out. "What on earth does she DO with her wages?" I'm sure they wondered.

Well I was spending a fair whack of them on driving lessons. But whatever the cost of driving instructors, by turns pricey and dicey, my dad was the real key player in my learning to drive. Just as twenty years beforehand he'd patiently pushed me up and down the pavement until I figured out how to ride a bike, he now took me on endless spins in the car, more than one of which ended up with us both storming back into the house, fuming. "How did the driving go?" my mum would innocently ask. "Fine," we'd simultaneously fume in a tone indicating let-no-more-be-said.

One of the theories about people suffering from autism is that their brains pick up on every stimulus in the environment – not having learnt to filter out what's irrelevant or unimportant – so they become overwhelmed. I felt the same when learning to drive. I wasn't able to focus in on the few salient details – e.g. car turning out of a drive ahead, intersection coming up, but instead my attention was all over the place. Car approaching on other side of road! Seagull flying over-head! Tractor turning into field! Man eating Cornetto on pavement! It took a while to learn to isolate the important points, similarly not to scream in terror every time a vehicle passed me by.

The first time I went out in the car by myself my dad

was absolutely terrified – when I got back he said it had been the worst two hours of his life – but I think it was as much out of concern for the car as for me. Every two years he trades in our current navy-blue Ford Focus estate for a new one, not because he has to have the snazziest model, he couldn't care less what he drives. Rather his logic is that not only will he never have to shell out for repairs, new Fords coming with a two-year warranty, but the longer you leave it to trade your vehicle in, the greater loss you'll incur at the end. "We can't afford not to buy a new car!" my brother and I would chorus in parody.

These trade-ins (which always occur, by the way, in spring of even-numbered years, e.g., 2004, 2006, 2008, so military is the routine) depend on the car being in near-perfect condition, as my dad never failed to remind me. So not only was I nervously learning how to operate the clutch, deal with other traffic and perfect my vehicle handling skills, I was equally jumpy about making sure the car remained absolutely immaculate and pristine. There was no added pressure when learning to, say, parallel park – watch that curb! – or reverse out of the Supervalu Car Park – God, there was a close call with a wall! The ideal situation would have been for me to have bought a 1987 white Ford Fiesta or something. I could have driven it hell for leather, taken it into stock-car rallies had I so desired, and my dad would have cheerily waved me off wishing me Godspeed rather than crankily and testily hanging around the driveway, reminding me that any scratch or dent I put in the car would decrease its value by hundreds of euros and cast our family into a downward spiral of financial precariousness towards bankruptcy. Given how skint I was though, that wasn't an option. In any case, whatever my dad's lack of faith in my driving ability, my mum was even worse. "Do you always clasp the passenger door handle in a white-knuckle grip?" I asked her when we were driving to the supermarket one day.

As for snowsports, I couldn't bear to hear, read or watch anything about them and nearly vomited with envy when I thought of anybody doing a season. Though I suppose I could have afforded it, I didn't go skiing for a week or anything that winter. I found it preferable not to have gone snowboarding at all than to have had only a few days on the slopes, hissing with jealousy at anyone who I knew was there all winter long.

Instead, I got into running. The summer before in Fernie I'd gone for a few runs in the post-season lull. The ski-lifts had stopped, the aquatic centre was on its annual six-week shutdown and, as I wrote in an email at the time, I was "jittery with excess energy". This being Fernie, it wasn't a question of *whether* I'd take up another activity, but rather *what* I'd take up instead. Being sedentary simply wasn't an option. So, yet to discover biking, I went into a local sports shop, bought a pair of runners (a size too small, as I discovered several blisters later) and decided to go for a run. Off I set, paced by my iPod. The plan, to ease me into things, was to run for one song, walk for one song. I'd pray that for the "walk" song my iPod would yield "Stairway to Heaven", the extended version of "Free Bird" or something equally lengthy. Even after a few weeks of this, when I'd worked up to continuous running and no longer needed such regularly punctuated walk breaks, I didn't exactly enjoy it much. My runners were too tight; it was hot; I was having issues with my knees; mountain-biking and tubing down the river were more fun. So that was that knocked on the head. Instant love it was not.

Back in Ireland, I still went for the occasional sporadic run, a jog really, in a very odd assortment of gear – a pair of hand-me-down runners, some shiny navy blue football shorts I'd acquired somewhere along the way as well. I kept meaning to buy new runners that actually fitted but this was low down on the priority list, something that I begrudged spending the money on, like work clothes or dental bills. Then somehow, God only knows how, I decided to enter a five mile race, having no idea if I was even capable of running for that distance. A full five miles seemed a feat of unparalleled endurance. Nonetheless, with the dauntless optimism of youth, I gave it a go. Not only was I not the last person to finish, as I'd feared might be the case, but I discovered I thrived on pre-race nervous anticipation. Equally, though not built for speed, I had a certain doggedness and unanticipated ability to dig deep for the last few miles – a cross-over perhaps from how the tenacity with which I'd keep hiking a jump until I landed it on my board. This would tide me over nicely until I could get back to the snow for the more instant adrenalin hit of cliff-drops or straight-lining into a big jump. A ten kilometre race then seemed like the natural progression, then a half-marathon. You know how it goes.

After six months, although still dodging questions at work – "So have you got any holidays planned?" "Oh yes, a really fucking big one" – I got promoted (evidently they could sense my commitment) and with the concomitant salary raise moved out of home and into a house with one of my friends a few kilometres outside the city centre. I could now cycle to and from work and not have to deal with public transport which was a major lifestyle improvement in itself. I was out of debt and future plans were falling into place. Ali came to Dublin for New Year's Eve before disappearing off to work in a permaculture settlement in Spain. Lindsay and Chucky were still planning to do a ski-season in New Zealand and I was game. Ellie and Kris were also planning to do another winter in BC, this time at Red Mountain, for which I was equally game. Things were looking up.

I went home at the weekends, having no particular reason or desire to stay in the city, and still practiced driving in my parents' car. I'd get the train after work on a Friday, go for a long run on Saturday, make dinner for my parents on Saturday night (I think my mum particularly liked that part of the routine) then on Sunday afternoon drive back through the city with my ever-dedicated dad. Every time I'd approach a roundabout or take a corner he'd shout "stay in your lane! STAY IN YOUR LANE!' – at no point, by the way, did I ever demonstrate any tendency to re-enact some sort of vehicular Dance of the Bumblebee, changing lanes back and forth at will, as he seemed to think I was wont to do. Having dropped me off he'd then drive back home by himself, week after week. Dads are great.

The driving test(s) – yes, in the plural – didn't go so well though. I kept getting slammed for Failure to Progress, which, in darker moments, I couldn't help but take as emblematic of my life situation in general, being now twenty-six and still largely direction-less. (How I hate when people ask, "What do you do?" Maybe I should pretend I've misheard them and brightly reply, "Fine thanks! How are you?")

On 28 June, fourteen months to the day after arriving back in Ireland, I left to go to New Zealand, once again finding myself in a country where not being able to drive was a major impediment. Though I might not have passed my test – a mere formality! – I nonetheless fell into the role of designated driver, rattling up and down dirt-tracks and the like.

Read on, read on!

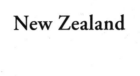

New Zealand

July 2008: Hello New Zealand

Hi everybody! Greetings from New Zealand.

Having learnt my lesson last time around, I haven't pegged out a predetermined timeframe for these – Adventures Part II. You know what they say: Want to make God laugh? Tell him your plans. It's very much a case of going with the flow and seeing what happens along the way. But to start off I'm here in a town called Wanaka on New Zealand's South Island until the start of October, that being the Southern Hemisphere spring.

On the way to New Zealand I stopped for an all-too-brief spell in Sydney to catch up with some of the wild-style Australians I met in Fernie who've since put their wild days behind them and settled down. After a year of planning and saving and thirty hours in transit, to be picked up from the airport and whisked away to Bondi Beach for breakfast was surreal. It didn't really sink in that I was finally on my way again – I half feared I was going to burst into tears from being so jetlagged and overwhelmed. As well as plenty "did you ever keep in touch with..." and "do you remember the time..." conversations, I took the requisite shots of the Opera House, the Harbour Bridge etc.

But anyway, a short hop across the Tasman Sea later, here I am now in Wanaka. Wanaka is situated on the shores of a crystalline lake with the snow-capped mountains sloping right down to the water's edge. Along the shoreline are vineyards, jetties, beaches, playgrounds, hiking trails, trees and the usual panoramic splendours. I'm sharing a house with my friends Lindsay and Chucky – Lindsay being from Calgary, Chucky from here on the South Island – and a French couple they work with.

We don't actually live in Wanaka itself though but in Albert Town – a small townland about five kilometres away – for reasons of cheaper rent. Situated as we are, not a day goes by that I don't curse the fact that I only have a Irish learner's licence and can't, legally, get behind the wheel here. Instead I've been pedaling around on a boneshaker of a bicycle which Chucky found at the dump. It has no suspension, and two working gears out of a potential twenty-one but it's good exercise, that much I concede.

Our house is heated exclusively by a wood burner which seems to be the standard on the South Island, such curiosities as central heating and double glazing being apparently unheard of. Charmingly rustic as a wood-burner may sound – and indeed it can be, blazing log fires every night, convivial communality as we sit by the hearth – the peripheral rooms (e.g.; bedrooms, bathroom) have no heating whatsoever. My first night in the house I shivered convulsively the night through under my thin blanket. Jesus, I thought, how am I going to endure an entire winter of this? Answer: by buying an enormous winter-weight double duvet the next day. I am modelling myself on some sort of Celtic chieftain – or perhaps I'm thinking of Genghis Khan or similar Mongol warlord? – swathed in layers of quilting and padding, holding forth, receiving company, conducting my daily business etc etc from my lair.

You very quickly become inured to the cold. I remember the shock of the cold and snow drifts the first winter in Canada and gaining so much respect for Canadians realising they endured this EVERY YEAR! without any particular song and dance. It was quite the realisation, particularly given the merest dusting of snow sends Ireland into mass panic. The second winter in Canada though, the cold doesn't factor into my recollections of the place at all.

I've very quickly remembered how to dress correctly for winter; i.e., by incorporating thermals and Gore-Tex into daily apparel. In the evenings, I read on the couch until I'm ready to go to sleep and then dive into bed, undressing only under the duvet and often falling asleep still clad with toque. Likewise in the morning I leap up and wriggle into my thermals and fleece, shivering en route to the kitchen, fingers numbed, to cook up some warm and nourishing porridge. As for having a shower, I have to psyche myself up to get undressed then crank the water so scalding I emerge lobster pink. As well as toughening us up, another benefit of the wood-burner is that we have a constant supply of warm water at no added cost. We're unbearably smug about how reasonable our electricity bills are compared to other house-holds in Wanaka. I should never have complained about how cold I found the house that first winter in Fernie.

Indeed, it's not particularly cold here, more European winter temperatures rather than Canadian risk-of-frostbite-minus-thirty-what-happened-to-my-fingertips cold. There's no ground snow down here on the valley floor, that being reserved for the ski-hills on the peaks around Wanaka – well, "around" is a relative term. This ain't Europe, people, where it's ski-in, ski-out villages dotted all around the pistes. It's more like the Canadian set up with the ski-hills at a remove from the town itself.

I've bought a season pass for Cardrona, a ski-hill about 30km outside Wanaka. Cardrona is definitely a hill rather than a mountain. It's small enough that you could ski its entirety in a morning if you were speedy and the annual snowfall is less than epic. If anything, it reminds me of summer-skiing on a European glacier in terms of limited area, paucity of powder, emphasis on park and pipe etc. I'm looking upon this season as my warm-up (possibly mixing my metaphors a bit here) for Northern Hemisphere Winter 08/09 – I'm going back to the Promised Land of Canada in November, HOORAY!

Lindsay and Chucky both work at Cardrona, so on their tip-off I've been leaving my ski- gear up there in the staff locker-area. This staff area is accessible through a permanently open door, the only deterrent being an A4 piece of paper stuck to it saying "Staff Only". Given that four hundred and fifty staff work on the hill, it's highly unlikely that anyone is going to cry "Halt imposter!" as I go in and out. That said, I'm as prompt and unassuming as possible. As the season goes on I'm sure some of the bona fide staff will start to wonder about the chronically shy Irish girl who scuttles around, never talking to anyone, head bowed and eyes downcast.

For the moment the set-up is working though – unlike me. Ha! I have a working holiday visa for New Zealand, but haven't been working to date. I arrived too late in the day to get a job; the season had already started; the ski-hills already had their full complement of staff and businesses in town are antipathetic – if not actively hostile – to the transient snowsports populace. Many of the job adverts specify "Locals only" and one even went so far as to unequivocally declare, "Definitely no skiers or snowboarders".

As with Canada it's advisable to get here before the winter starts if you want to work. Oh well! The cost of living is extremely low compared to Dublin so I'm not terribly concerned if I have to fall back on my euros for the next few months and become a full-time bum.

Besides, I don't know where I'd get the time to work what with my other activities: snowboarding, cycling, cooking, running, chopping kindling, tending the fire. Woman make fire. Woman happy.

So maybe I'll get a job, maybe I won't, we'll see what happens. Take care beautiful people.

Lisa

July 2008: Digitised

Hi everybody

I must have been tempting fate in my last email when I said that it wasn't too cold here, my exact words being that it wasn't Canadian-risk-of-frostbite cold; I had reckoned without my dodgy circulation, possibly the worst in Christendom. Maybe it's also that the air is damper here, a miserable soak-to-the-bones-sogginess as opposed to the crisp invigorating chill of Canada. (We'll get to the reasons as to Why I Prefer Canada to New Zealand in my next email though.) A few weeks ago it was chilly on the hilly, my digits were frozen and numb but no more than is par for the course when you're out snowboarding all day. Or so I thought. When I got home and nimbly leapt into the shower I looked down to see that three of my toes were now purply-black. Ouch. They were shiny red and engorged for a few days after that but no lasting damage thank God.

Hot on the heels (no pun intended) of this trouble with my tootsies I then hurt my finger. Now, an injured finger is hardly up there with a fractured femur in terms of grievous ski injuries but it's quite sore all the same. I was trying to learn how to spin a backside 360 (a full rotation in the air) and I jumped, spun and landed full weight down on my index finger – no I have no idea how either – which then bent backwards. Ouch again. Ah, it's fine really, just swollen and bruised enough to make me look gratifyingly gnarly. I wish, however, that the adage of "no pain no gain" didn't have to be proven with such predictable regularity in snowboarding. It's a little dispiriting but hopefully I'll get through the next twelve months with all my extremities intact.

So what with the above myriad minor injuries and occupational hazards I'm learning to ski instead! Before arriving in Wanaka, I'd only skied that one day in Fernie and I wasn't exactly a natural, to put it mildly. So last week when some friends were hiring skis for a day, I was dragged along reluctantly and sulkily. I'm happy to report however that I was just being obstinate and enjoyed myself so much that I've decided to put in the time to learn to ski properly. I love a challenge! Cardrona is the perfect bunny hill to learn on, being quite small and not too steep. In my experience, by the way, the whole skiers vs. snowboarders standoff is largely fictitious these days, certainly not borne out when you live in a ski-town when so many people can and do switch from one to the other with facility.

In any case, my choice of snowsports regardless, I'm no longer on the hill everyday because of my new job. Yes my friends I am now gainfully employed! Interesting story this. I applied for the usual slew of minimum-wage seasonal jobs – housekeeping, café staff, receptionist etc etc – with no success. So then I decided to go for broke and apply for the improbable position of part-time Office and Accounts Manager in a local property valuation firm. Reader, I got the job, although this necessitated me being...selective...in saying how long I'm in Wanaka for. I know people complain about how difficult it is to get a permanent job and how they're instead being strung along from contract to contract but I've found the opposite: I keep getting lumbered with a permanent position when all I ever want is a short-term role.

I work two and a half days a week which is perfect because I don't want to work full-time anyway. It's a small office, four property valuers and then *mise mé féin* on the admin side; filing, invoicing, typing up reports etc. etc. Even though the job title is Office Manager it's not even remotely as busy or complex as the lowliest minion position in the company I worked for in Dublin. There are some interpersonal issues, shall we say, but the biggest challenge is trying to decipher what on earth the valuers are saying on their Dictaphone tapes. And I don't mean the property terminology and jargon so much as their squawking New Zealand accents. Those mangled vowels! I suppose it's a case of you-say-tomayto-I-say-tomato but actually it's more like you say "fitted kitchen with added deck" and I hear "futted kutchen with edded dick".

So having quit my office job in Dublin and travelled half way around the world, once again I get up at seven, have porridge for breakfast, cycle the half hour to work and get changed into office garb to be at my desk by half past eight. Having replicated my routine in such perfect detail, I can only conclude that we truly are creatures of habit.

Now this cycling to Wanaka and back – five kilometres each way as you will remember from having assiduously read my last email – is fine for going to work, but less so for going out at night. That said, it's a pretty sedate season, as evinced by the fact that I polished off *War and Peace*, hefty tome that it is, in just under three weeks. With my attempts to pass my driving test in Dublin being less than successful, I've had to start from scratch again over here and now am the proud *titulaire* of a New Zealand Learner's Licence, obtained with the sole and express purpose of acting as designated driver to ferry us all home at night. One of the conditions of a learner's licence is that you must have a fully-licensed supervisor in the vehicle with you at all times. Having read the New Zealand Road Code cover to cover, however, no where does it mention that they are required to be either sober or sentient, and Lindsay and Chucky are excellent driving coaches even in their altered states.

You might ask why it falls to me to be the designated driver. Well, if I really want to hit the bottle we can always turn to the time-honoured tradition of scissors, paper, stone but I don't mind not drinking that much (or that often) because I'm training for the Auckland Half-Marathon which takes place at the end of winter. This is of course a provisional plan, everything being injury dependent. It keeps me out of trouble in any case.

More news soon to come...

Lisa

August 2008: No Second Fernie

Hey everyone
So in the last email I said that I would elucidate Why I Prefer Canada to New Zealand, or more specifically Why I Prefer Fernie to Wanaka.

In the first instance – Why Canada over New Zealand (which everyone always blathers on about being SO beautiful blah blah blah) – it comes down to the fact that I'm here for skiing and Canada has MOUNTAINS and they are BIG and COVERED WITH SNOW for months on end. Though New Zealand's Unique Selling Point is how proximate its landscaped splendours are to each other, so that you can get from the mountains to the beach year round in a few hours, I prefer the scale and sheer enormity of BC. Likewise with the brutality of the winter; how cold it can get in Canada and the amount of snowfall it receives is quite literally breath-taking (and I really do mean "literally", it being a particular bugbear of mine when people employ that term erroneously – "it was literally raining cats and dogs". No it wasn't.) The ski-fields around Wanaka are nice and I'm having fun, but it doesn't stir my soul and make it sing the way the majesty of Beautiful BC does.

But to be fair, and indisputable items such as topography and annual snowfall aside, I can't pass judgement on "New Zealand" at large, having only been in Wanaka so far. What's more, I'm very much inhabiting an international ski-town bubble, sharing a house with two French, a Canadian and a token Kiwi (Chucky). We had a party the other night and out of the forty or so people in attendance, Chucky was New Zealand's only native son. My interactions with actual real life New Zealanders are largely restricted to my job with the property valuers, which would lead me to believe that the South Island is peopled predominantly by strident financiers and ill-tempered cranks. Land of the long white cloud my ass.

Someone asked me a few weeks ago on a chairlift if I liked Wanaka. For a split second I was going to automatically squawk "I love it!" with unreflective Australasian cheer but then I thought "screw it", and gave a more measured assessment of the place. Possibly an overly in-depth answer to a throwaway question. Oh well.

There was an article in the *Wanaka Sun* with the newly appointed secondary school principal who described Wanaka as having more of a city than a small town feel. While he probably meant this in a positive fashion, I'd read it another way. Wanaka is a small town in the middle of the mountains but the atmosphere is far from congruent with its location and size. Bijou as it may be, you see, it's the hub of Antipodean snow-scene with plenty of competitions and filming and ski-movie premieres and what not going on. The result of which is that it's very much about "the scene" – i.e., the forty shades of bling, having the latest gear, the vaguely standoffish vibe – rather than skiing the hell out of it till your legs drop off, duct-taping over the holes in your worn-out clobber and so forth. Truly it is No Second Fernie.

This unfriendliness isn't just restricted to snowsporting "yoof". It seems a pretty odd sort of place in general. Training as I am for a half-marathon, I've been regularly out pounding the trails, beaming wholesomely, fresh-faced and ponytail bobbing, at anyone I meet, but this doesn't tend to elicit much of a response from any of the po-faced locals. For a place so dependent on the tourist buck they're very suspicious of outsiders and do their utmost not to make you feel welcome. I've mentioned before about the "locals only" specifications for jobs and houses, it's all a bit *League of Gentlemen* – this is a local town for local people.

You should see the spectacularly inappropriate Crimeline column, published each week by the local constabulary, aka the Keystones Cops. A weekly run down of all the traffic violations, altercations and sundry minor offences taking place in town, what its purpose is I just can't work out. Perhaps it was originally meant to be a call for information for unsolved crimes (of such magnitude as there are here in Wanaka...) but now it just serves as a general warning against visitors. My favourites – taken word for word, and if There Be Any Doubting Thomases Among Ye I can scan in the original clippings, which we've been collecting as the weeks roll by – are as follows:

"Last Tuesday a Japanese visitor working at BP Wanaka was charged with theft and is due to appear in Court. Later that evening an Australian man was charged with fighting after an incident on Dungarvon Street." (6 August 2008)

"[Concluding line of column] most of the visitors to our town are here to enjoy rather than annoy." (6 August 2008)

In a town of 4000 people you can forget about any shroud of anonymity when the local police are so fond of publishing incriminating and identifying details. In fairness though, not only are seasonal visitors to Wanaka thus named, shamed or feared, but bona fide residents can equally expect to have their personal affairs flagged for public consumption:

"Over the course of the week staff have had numerous dealings with a local couple who are battling over the custody of their son. Emotions always run high when children are involved and there have been two arrests so far in relation to these two and their associates." (13 August 2008)

[Upon the occasion of a bomb-scare in the local supermarket – don't ask]... "Wow, what a week. Grab yourself a coffee and have a seat because this week's crime line [sic] is a longer read than normal!...A local 42 year old male was arrested and has been treated by Mental Health." (3 September 2008)

Why??? Whose interest does it serve to publish this stuff?? Bear in mind, also, that any of the unfortunates featured in the column have only been charged, not actually convicted, so they still stand innocent in the eyes of the law....

Anyway, Wanaka is weird but life is good! I'm still learning to ski and having great fun altogether, the yowls of agony imparted by ski-boots aside. A friend of mine works in a rental shop in town and we have a weekly baked-goods-for-skis trade-off in place. Everybody has their price in Nanaimo bars. We also went on a road-trip to a rival resort called The

Remarkables recently (as Martin McDonagh said elsewhere, "there's an awful lot of Rs in that sentence") and I took skis rather than snowboard with me; if that isn't a sign of commitment I don't know what is. That said, I snowboarded today because you never quite forgot your first love do you.

L

September 2008: Eat-Sleep-Ski

Hi everybody

For those of you who haven't done a ski-season (yet), you might be wondering of what consists A Day in the Life of a Ski-Bum. Here in the Albert Town enclave, it's mostly constituted of eating, sleeping and skiing. Great activities all three I'm sure you will agree!

1. Eating

Do you know how I define whether I'm either badly or well-off at any given time? It's whether I can go to the supermarket and buy whatever I want without worrying about my card being declined. By that standard at the moment I am getting by just fair-to-middling. It's a case of remaining relatively restrained, of always going for the own-brand crackers and whichever type of juice is on special offer and not blowing an hour's wages on a sliver of smoked salmon or something. (I type this on my new WiFi enabled Macbook whilst sporting a goggle-tan from sunny spring skiing: is this what's known as relative poverty?)

But that said, while wild extravagance is out the window, it's hasn't exactly been Kraft Dinners and baked beans all season. Lindsay, Chucky and I do a communal shop about once a week and luckily we all like our food; this isn't a euphemistic way of saying that we're fat, I mean we all enjoy eating well and aren't loath to spend either time in the kitchen or cash in the supermarket.

We work opposite days which means there's always someone to keep the home fires burning and we take vague informal turns to cook. It's perhaps indicative of the tenor of the season that having home-cooked meals outweighs not getting to ski together that much. Likewise, when Lindsay and Chuck arrived back from a three-day road-trip one of the first things they clamoured to tell me was "we found red peppers for a dollar fifty each!!" Fruit and vegetables are extortionately expensive here in the hills, bell peppers cost $20/kg during the harsh winter months – oh how we cheered in the produce aisle, rejoicing the arrival of spring, when they dropped back down to $12/kg this week. A veritable steal! Meat, bizarrely, is far more affordable; against the rack-rent peppers and the $19/kg aubergines, venison sausages are $9/kg and minced beef is $10 for the same. The bulk of our food spending goes on fresh fruit and veg. Staving off scurvy is a costly pursuit.

But anyway, buying raw ingredients, overpriced as they may be, is still cheaper than resorting to ready-made meals or eating out, both of which are well beyond the budget of ski bums and season workers. (I've only spent $3 altogether all season long in the ski-hill cafeteria, for a hot chocolate on a particular lacklustre day.) Between our combined efforts, there's been some great eating done this winter in our house, the highlights including roasted Mediterranean vegetable lasagne ("rich man's food" as Lindsay quipped, vegetable prices being what they are), chicken and leek pot pie, curried pumpkin soup with rosemary-garlic focaccia, beer-batter monkfish, Thai red curry, butternut squash & roasted garlic quiche, chipotle-cheddar cornbread, macaroni cheese with leeks, bacon and sun-dried tomatoes. If any of these dishes sound familiar it's because the Rebar cookbook has been providing, as ever, much creative direction. Oh, and vegetable pancakes with soy-citrus glaze, otherwise known as Salt for Dinner night because each of us in turn added a surreptitious slug more soy sauce to the pan when no one else was watching. My kidneys twinge just thinking about it.

The most memorable night though – which arose by welcome accident – was a three-course meal in which each course consisted of different ingredients wrapped in phyllo pastry. (A run down: starter was special-offer brie and cranberry sauce baked in phyllo, main course was spanakopita – spinach, feta and pine nuts baked in phyllo pastry – and dessert was almond dark chocolate baked in phyllo with a side serving of chocolate ice-cream.) Oh the decadence!

What's more, these kingly feasts have been supplemented by a staggering procession of cakes, cookies, tray-bakes and muffins. People usually have a natural inclination towards being either bakers or chefs and I, my friends, am a dyed-in-the-wool baker. Even when making dinner my natural inclination is towards dishes that can be assembled and then finished off in the oven, e.g.; quiches, lasagnes, roast potatoes, pizzas. Para-baking, if you will. Usually I try to curb my sweet tooth but this season I've gone all out with sheer abandon on the baked goods; millionaire's shortbread, rugelach – cream cheese pastry filled with a chocolately-nutty-apricotty crumb – profiteroles shimmery with chocolate ganache, apricot-almond slice, peanut butter squares.

How we're not all the size of houses I don't know. Well actually I do; personally speaking, between skiing, snow-boarding, cycling to work, swimming and training for the half-marathon, my appetite has gone stratospheric this season. Nonetheless, while the onset of morbid obesity is unlikely, sometimes I can't help but worry that I'm laying the foundations for a Wanaka-wide onslaught of Type II Diabetes at which time our pancreata will collectively pack it in.

2. Sleeping

You know when you're swaying on your feet with tiredness and think you can't possibly go on? You can. You usually have another three or four days in you at that stage before total nervous collapse. This I know because being groggy and insensible with tiredness is the default condition doing a ski-season. This winter is therefore atypical in that everybody in our house is usually tucked up in bed by ten o'clock. Half ten is pushing it and in any case there's usually at least one body asleep on the couch by that point. (Possibly they're just floored by the rich dinner-time fare. Hmm.) Most of my friends here work on the ski-hill which, as I mentioned before, is about thirty kilometers out of town so this involves their getting up at a quarter past six to make their eight o'clock start. While these sorts of considerations have never impeded the constant Bacchanalian excess of ski-towns before, for some reason such is not the case here. I'm struggling to identify exactly why. But I'm (a) usually worn out in the evenings between my various exertions, and (b) a reluctant partier at the best of times, so I've been quietly gleeful about the – mostly – mellow living and all the sleep.

3. Skiing

What with all the eating and sleeping, I might make it sound like this season is merely the occasion for gluttony and sloth. Not so! Working as I am three days a week, that leaves four days a week for snowsports. In practice, conditions are such that one of these days is usually a no-go. However the weather systems work in New Zealand, when the clouds roll in over Cardrona, skiing becomes nigh-on impossible. You quickly learn to decipher the mountain propaganda, aka the daily snow report, and realise that "variable visibility" is only such in that it varies from being able to see five metres ahead of you to ten through the freezing fog. Occasionally the winds are so high they have to stop running the lifts altogether. However, patience being a virtue and whatnot, there's absolutely nothing we can do about such inclement temps but wait them out.

I'm still skiing away, with the peaks and troughs of enthusiasm that come with any protracted period on snow. Some days you feel it and some days you just don't; once again you can't do anything about this but realise that one bad day does not spell an end to your foray into snowsports. And the good days far outweigh the bad. I haven't turned my back on snowboarding altogether but I will concede that the practical benefits of skiing – i.e., traversing, skating along the flat, getting on and off lifts – are manifold. Apparently skis are a poor second to snowboards in powder but there's scant chance of putting that to the test in NZ; we've had two powder days all winter. God I can't wait for BC.

Just as I love snowboarding because it requires little mental effort at this stage so too do I love skiing because it does. Roll your ankles, sister. I caught a glimpse of my shadow on the snow the other day; hunched over, slightly knock-kneed, oddly angled ski-poles at strange angles. Likewise when I skate ski along the flat, I feel like some sort of snow-borne daddy long legs, limbs jerking and sprawling in various directions. I'm sure there must be a more graceful way of doing it. As well as actual skiing technique there are auxiliary skills to be learned as well, such as how to carry your skis – slung over your shoulder, balanced in the crook of your elbow, appears to be the most ergonomic method – or how to avoid jabbing your chairlift companions with your poles.

When apprehensive on steeper slopes, I lean back instinctively which not only leads to quads on fire, this being the equivalent of performing a continuous wall-sit but also makes the skis scud out of control. Rather than pulling back nervously, you see, one needs to lean forward and meet the steep straight on. A good life lesson for us all, I think.

That said, I'm not scared witless on skis the way I've so often been when snowboarding. Am I staying in my comfort zone, not pushing myself as much as I should? Or have I just become accustomed to the on-snow learning process? Maybe I've learned from snowboarding how pointless and counterproductive it is to panic if you find yourself at the top of something that looks way too steep/ rocky/icy/mogulled/all-of-the-above? Because you have to get down it regardless and no amount of histrionics will improve the situation. Who knows.

Well whatever the reason, there's only a week and half left of the Eating-Sleeping-Skiing gig before a month of sundry adventures around the South Island. Watch this space.

Lisa

October 2008: Tiki Touring

Hi everybody

My last week in Wanaka was good – what a bland statement but that's exactly what it was. Good clean fun! The Thursday before we left town, though, saw the singularly worst conditions in which I have ever stepped foot on a ski-hill. It being springtime, heavy rain from the day before had simultaneously washed away large amounts of the base and frozen overnight to form a patina of sheer ice. There was more snow in the car park than on some parts of the lower mountain. Thank God I'm on rental gear. I thought as I juddered along one particularly rubbly cat-track. Higher up, meanwhile, it was so icy blue you could see your reflection in some parts of the piste, and overcast to boot so there was no chance of it warming up into anything more skiable. The horror! The horror!

After two runs the gang abandoned the mission and it was a stony-faced car of snowsporteers that drove down the valley that day. I thought it was game over as regards snowsports NZ; forget about the rest of the season and put away skis, board, boots and bindings et al until Canada.

So yes, horrific day on the hill all round, which left us seeking alternative activities. The next day dawned joyfully, bright and clear, so I went hiking with my friend Yosi, another ex-Fernie head who's been here for winter as well. On first encounter, Yosi appears terrifying: a shaven-headed, bearded Israeli given to muttering "fucking bullshit" and "motherfuckers" interspersed with harsh Hebrew but in actuality he's one of the sweetest and cuddliest people I know. We climbed Mt Roy, a local landmark, and the view from the top was as spectacular as promised. However, it being blustery springtime meant it was windy and cold – there were still pockets of snow on the peak – so we took the merest cursory glance around the panoramic splendour, devoured our sandwiches and headed straight back down. That evening Yosi was hobbling from room to room with a ski-pole like the Tin Man, propping himself up with a ski-pole. It's cruel to laugh but I couldn't help it.

On Saturday it blew in a storm; conditions were so wild the entire ski-hill closed. We ate ice-cream and watched the *Back to the Future* trilogy instead. "Mark my words," I prognosticated to no one in particular, "there'll be one more dump before the hill closes. There always is." Lo and behold! The torrential rain in town yielded 30 cm of fresh snow on the hill, the third powder day all season (not that I'm complaining, never look a gift horse from the snow gods in the mouth and all that).

I finished up my season in Cardrona on Sunday with an atypically bluebird power day. And on skis. I was by myself because you know how it goes – no friends on a powder day, certainly not if friend in question is a novice-to-intermediate skier with no idea how to handle the pow. However, I struck gold in that on three successive chair-lift rides I sat beside – in turn – an off-duty ski-instructor, a retired ski-coach and an outdoors education teacher. Between their various tips – only some of which were completely contradictory – I managed to piece it together. Sort of. Red Mountain (Destination Canada) is renowned for being steep and deep so it's going to be quite the experience on skis.

That evening we had a Last Supper in the house (roast chicken and New York-style cheesecake with raspberries, upping the culinary ante to the end), and, as per the tenancy agreement, moved out the following day. However, rather than powering out of town straight away I had to finish up at work so stayed in a hostel for the next two nights. While the other guests were hiring kayaks or planning backpacking trips down to Milford Sound, I was heading off in my office clothes for a day of Rural Residential zonings and dictaphone reports.

I finished work at lunchtime on the Wednesday, and Yosi and I loaded up the rental car and sped out of town for a ten-day road trip. We were heading north for some warmth; child of the Northern Hemisphere that I am, the notion of heading north for warmer climes still strikes me as bizarre. Likewise descriptions of houses with a "sunny northerly aspect" always trip me up. Who the fuck builds their house to face north? Persons south of the Equator, evidently.

Listening to a string of appalling local radio stations, we stopped to visit the celebrated Fox and Franz Josef Glaciers. Well, in saying that, we walked to the bottom of them, did a perfunctory survey of their glacial might and then put the gas pedal down again until we reached the sun. I think we'd both just had enough of winter by that stage – this month is my brief respite of summer before heading off to Canada after all. Back to back ski-seasons have, alas, their minor pitfalls.

We drove up along the West Coast which was wet, wet, wet, stayed in two eerily half-deserted lodge motels, and saw plenty of whitebaiters wading in their sou'westers along the estuaries. An NZ delicacy, whitebait is a small translucent minnow-like fish eaten whole in whitebait patties, omelettes and the like. It doesn't really taste of much aside from being vaguely fishy and it's disproportionately expensive for what you're getting if you ask me – $80 a kilo. What's wrong with a nice piece of cod. The whitebaiting season lasts from September till November and it's big business along the West Coast. Try whitebaiting on someone else's patch, Chucky says, and you'll find yourself with a shotgun to your head. (This here is huntin' and fishin' territory but without the tweed or refinements of inherited wealth.)

A group of Korean exchange students was staying in one of the motels, and their tour leader explained that they wanted to buy some whitebait for their homestay hosts. Did the receptionist know where they could acquire any? The receptionist thought about it, furrowed her brow and puffed out her cheeks. "There's not much of it around here at the moment," she said, after a moment's pause. "But there's a guy who works here sometimes, I'll give him a call, he might know someone who's selling some." Honestly, it's worse than trying to find drugs.

We drove all the way up to Cape Farewell, the northernmost tip of the South Island, and spent a few days in backpacker proper territory, hiking in the Abel Tasman National Park, staying in hippie beach towns, that sort of thing. We're travelling in what is known as the shoulder season, I believe, the full flight of summer yet to come, so while attractions and accommodations are denuded of tourists in the main the weather is also quite variable. The plan for today, for example, was an all-day guided hiking and kayaking tour but that was scuppered by the solid rain. I went outside for a brief reconnaissance and, despite having my anorak pulled around my face like the General, was soaked through in minutes. No way was I spending the day glumly tramping around, waterproof trousers bedamned. Does this make me less hard-core? Who cares. Some days in Cardrona you'd see people getting ski-lessons in such brutal conditions that you'd just feel sorry for both them and the instructor. Some days are just not good for being outside. Period. We drove to the nearest big town, and went to the cinema instead.

We meander down to Christchurch, the main city on the South Island, after this; Yosi flies to Thailand to frolic with a lady-friend on the beach and I have another few weeks left in NZ, waiting out the half-marathon, meeting back up with Lindsay and Chucky, going to stay on various farms. More of which anon.

Lisa

October 2008: The Tiki Tour Continues

Hi everybody

Yosi and I wound down the road trip by heading south to Christchurch for Yosi to catch his flight. After a very casual and unemotional parting – ski-bums invariably pop up again somewhere around the globe, no use getting unduly upset when saying goodbye – off with him to Thailand. I went and stayed on a friend's dairy farm for the weekend then met back up with Lindsay and Chucky and the three of us headed to Chucky's parents' farm and then a B.Y.O.B. Chinese restaurant for dinner with Chucky's high school friends. And bring our own bottles we did. Still training away for the half-marathon, I was, as ever, designated driver and stuck to the Diet Coke – I can be so devilish sometimes! – but the others brought along several three-litre cartons of "Country Red". No further details about grape type(s) or vintage provided on the packaging, probably best not to ask. Nothing like your wine frothing when you pour it out of the cask....

Happy as I was to do the driving at the end of the night, I needed directions back to the farm, but Chucky was borderline unconscious by this point, occasionally mumbling inchoate phrases like "s'left here" or gesticulating vaguely in any given direction. As a result, we drove in ever decreasing concentric circles around downtown Christchurch for quite some time before finally making it out of this hell and onto the right road. Chucky at this point lurched to one side, leant out the window and threw up at a set of traffic lights. I had to stop a further three times en route for him to vomit, which at least gave me a chance to navigate. Whenever he'd take off his cap and keel towards the door, it was the cue to steer onto the hard shoulder/verge/ditch to make an emergency pit-stop. Talk about reaction to hazards. I definitely feel more confident about resitting my driving test at this stage.

Lisa

November 2008: Meet the Parents - The Bike Trip

Since leaving Wanaka at the start of October, I have fallen in love.

With New Zealand. Gotcha!

Ah, there's nothing like a good opener to reel your audience in. Anyway, though I still stand over my previous assessment of Wanaka as an odd, odd place, filled with suspicious squinting locals and I'm-so-fucking-cool faux-gangsta posturing, a month of travelling around NZ has reassured me that the rest of the country is far from being equally up its own ass. Canada hasn't been entirely displaced by Aotearoa in my affections – the skiing in BC remains, I would wager, the best in the world – but at least I no longer have such a uniformly negative impression of the place.

Anyway, since my last email I've been winding up my time in New Zealand with a one hundred and fifty kilometre bike ride and the Auckland Half-marathon. Fun fun fun!

Let's start with the bike trip. Lindsay's parents flew in from Calgary to visit their daughter and her intended during October, as did one of Lindsay's friends called Katie. So, me, Katie, Lindsay, Lindsay's parents, Chucky and Chucky's parents set out to cycle the one hundred and fifty kilometre Central Otago Rail Trail together over four days.

The Rail Trail is a disused stretch of rail line which was converted into a hiking and cycling track about ten years ago by removing all the sleepers, tossing down a bit of gravel etc, and it's unselfconsciously flagged as "No 16 on the 101 Things for Kiwis to Do!" Now New Zealand is pretty much one big farm – oh yeah, and then there's Auckland – but Central Otago is rural above and beyond the norm. I'm not going to malign the locals by claiming that we were accompanied by the plaintive twang of duelling banjoes as we pedalled along, but we were nonetheless definitely out in the wop-wops. One of the hostelries we stayed in along the way was running a drinks promotion – you went into a draw for a chainsaw whenever you bought a beer. A chainsaw! Just what you want to introduce into the mix when everybody's drunk and tempers rise.

As well as chuckling indulgently at the follies of the natives, I was just as gleeful about getting to watch how our merry band of cyclists would get along in the saddle together for four days. Would the menfolk vainly try to out-pedal each other to assert themselves as the alpha male? Good luck to them if they did – Lindsay's dad is an Ironman triathlete who recently took part in a Calgary to Philadelphia relay ride. Chucky's parents are good-humoured, straight-talking farmers, and Lindsay's parents are right-on city liberals – talk about *Meet the Parents: The Bike Trip*. If Hollywood ever comes a-calling to take our trip to the screen, no doubt it'll lapse into cliché about awkward encounters and cultural misunderstandings. But apart from one incident when Chucky got a full-frontal shot of his future father-in-law (probably) clambering into a bunk bed wearing just a pair of greying, sagging Y-fronts, any such set pieces were avoided in real life.

The actual cycling bit, about 30 or 40km a day, was fine, or at least I thought so, an ancillary benefit of continuing to train for the shaggin' half-marathon throughout all the road-tripping and general merriment of October. In order not to cut into Organised Fun Time, I generally ended up going running before breakfast, so by the time everyone else was awake and ready to get on with the day's activities, I was exercised, exorcised and showered. The only pitfall to this was that by mid-afternoon I was usually both cranky and famished.

By the end of the bike trip we were all still standing (just about, Lindsay burst into tears, Chucky was too nauseous to eat dinner, I was irritable and overtired: the older generation held up better though) and the next day I flew up to the North Island to take part in the Auckland Half-Marathon a few days later. Christ. Without getting too Nietzschean about it all, what doesn't kill us makes us stronger and while it was touch and go for a few days whether I was going to keel over, I survived! That said, my stomach degenerated into watery uselessness and I was too tired to even be hungry.

But in any case, the half-marathon went fine and twenty-one kilometres later I trotted home (read: belted across the line, blistered, chafed, about to puke). I'm back now in Ireland for ten days before heading off to do winter all over again in Canada. On the way home from NZ, I was meant to have a week's stopover in Asia for a faint snatch of summer but:

1. I'm completely skint having spent far too much money travelling around after Wanaka

2. I'm completely sick of packing and unpacking my backpack having spent far too much time doing this every day travelling around after Wanaka.

So with three clicks of my heels – or more prosaically, a phone-call to Qantas – home it was instead. For now.

Lisa

PS: Yes I am sending this at half four in the morning. The joys of jet-lag.

This is Rossland

January 2009: Back in Beautiful BC

Hi everybody

Sorry for not having been in touch before this, but there was an unfortunate episode with my laptop (to wit: glass of water, knock of elbow) which took about a month to be resolved. Merry Christmas, Happy New Year etc!

So let me think, last time I wrote an email I was back in Ireland for a ten day pit-stop, having just left New Zealand. It took about forty hours all in all to get back from NZ to Ireland, flying Auckland to Sydney to Bangkok to London to Dublin. New Zealand really is a very, very, very long way away – it makes travelling to Canada seem like a mere hop across the Atlantic. And God, was I jetlagged with the twelve hour time difference: the world seemed woolly and at a remove, as if I were on very strong tranquilisers.

So much happened during October travelling around NZ that I gave only a very abridged version of it in my last few emails; the Auckland Half Marathon, for example – and for which I'd been training for months – being disposed of in a mere sentence: "The half marathon went fine." As you may recall, o assiduous readers of mine (I do hope you've been paying attention!), the marathon came only a few days after we'd finished cycling the Rail Trail. I must have been running at an enormous calorie deficit between all these various exertions because once they were all over and I was on my way back to Ireland I was FAMISHED. I always find that on the actual day of any sort of distance event, I'm never actually that hungry afterwards, but it's during the proceeding days that my hunger really kicks in – and not just a hearty appetite but a more an urgent message – I. Need. Food. Now. It was an effective if unorthodox recovery to do nothing for forty hours but sit on planes snuggled up in a fleecy blanket and wolfing down whatever meals and snacks the air hostesses brought by. And then looking pleadingly at them for any other vittles they could toss my way.

Do you know what one of the most annoying parts of doing any long-haul travel in or out of Ireland is though? Having to spend hours waiting in Heathrow for a connecting flight to or from Dublin. Luckily I have my little rituals down pat by this stage to while away the hours, namely lingering in Duty Free, knocking back those mouthwash-cap sized tasters of Baileys they always seem to have for sampling regardless of the time of day or night, and smearing on scooped handfuls of Crème de la Mer and other ludicrously expensive face-creams until I'm shiny-faced and glowing.

Travelling abroad is like going to Narnia though – you know, with time proceeding at two different speeds, so that years and epochs can go by in Narnia and then you step back through the wardrobe to find out that actually you've only been away for a few moments and everything is exactly as you left it. When you eagerly ask people for news of what happened while you were away, they give a sort of baffled shrug. Nothing happened, they say, nothing ever does.

I hadn't actually been in NZ for that long – only four months – so despite it feeling like a vast expanse of time for me, concentration of new experiences etc etc, when I got home there remained the same pots of Thai Red Curry paste in the fridge, the same catalogues in the magazine rack. It's comforting for home to remain the same. A few years ago, though, my parents went through the Great Leap Forward and all of a sudden when I went back they had a laptop and broadband WiFi. Up until then their attitude towards the Internet was Luddite in the extreme – "you get on, do your business, and get off!" was my dad's view on things, and his emails were short to the point of crypticity. I think he thought they were akin to telegrams and you were charged by the word or something. Then he discovered eBay, and switched his wheeling and dealing for guitar amplifiers and wah-wah pedals and the like from tattered copies of *Buy & Sell* to online. Our house is now rammed to the walls with musical hardware and my bedroom has become, in my absence, a de facto storeroom. My mum tries to disguise the amplifiers by casually draping blankets over them in the hope I might be fooled into thinking that they're pieces of furniture or something, but it means that when I'm home I settle down to sleep in what's essentially an electronic goods warehouse with a bed in there for good measure.

Aside from catching up with friends and wandering aimlessly and contentedly around the house in a jetlagged haze, opening the fridge door and peering inside at roughly half hour intervals, what other excitements did I get up to when I was home for those ten days? I went to the dentist for a perfunctory check-up which developed into a local anaesthetic and two fillings. That night we were going out for a family dinner before I continent-hopped again. Out we went regardless, my face still numbed and drooping on one side from the anaesthetic, and looking for all the world,

God forbid me, like I was recovering from a minor stroke as I tried to sip my drink through a straw in a corner of my lop-sided mouth.

Oh and yes! In that ten day interval, I also managed to sit and pass my driving test. How? Well, nothing like forward planning and dauntless determination. As soon as I'd failed my test before leaving Ireland in June, I applied for another test, hoping that there'd be some way I could sit it when I got back for that brief window in November. Which, praise be, thanks to some persistent phone calls came to pass.

This time I had a different attitude (maybe) or maybe my confidence and driving skills had been bolstered by negotiating the rural roads of New Zealand. Really, I thought, I'm perfectly capable of being in sole charge of a vehicle on the road, not needing an accompanying driver being the main privilege bestowed by a full licence. I was no longer nervous: I'd dealt with dirt-roads, puking passengers, negotiating around downtown Christchurch with no idea where to go.

So I passed the test! Just about. And extremely grudgingly on the part of the driving tester who told me that I'd got it "by the skin of [my] teeth". Once again, the issue was failure to progress at traffic lights and junctions. But it's a difficult one isn't it? Because you don't want to come across in the test as some sort of speed-crazy demon, revving like crazy and accelerating away from the lights in a roar and splutter of fumes. Hence my erring on the side of caution. Anyway, I passed the test regardless so I can now, at the advanced age of twenty-six, cast aside the ignominy of L-plates and bask in the glory of a full driving licence.

No one was more pleased, by the way, than my dad who, after all, had taken on teaching me to drive as a personal project. "I'm even prouder of her now than when she got her Leaving Cert results!" he told my mum.

After ten days of R&R off it was to Canada, back, as long anticipated, to Beautiful BC. I landed in Vancouver where, by joyful co-incidence, Lindsay and Chucky were arriving the same afternoon as Lindsay was heading back to Calgary to finish off her degree, her undergrad years having been heavily punctuated by bouts of wanderlust. How great it was to see them again. Oh how the fun continues. Anyway, I had about four days in Vancouver with Lindsay and Chucky and staying with – yes, you've guessed it – some other friends from Fernie (can you see a theme emerging in my globetrotting?) before flying inland to make my way to Rossland to ski at Red Mountain for the winter.

I flew into a place called Trail, an unlovely industrial town of about 10,000 people, many of whom are employed in the big zinc mines whose furnaces are a-blazing non-stop. It's the ugly, Walmart-and-mall-filled sister to Rossland's picturesque charm, ten kilometres away. Rossland is a one-horse sort of town. It has a population of about 3000 people, the main street is a block and a half long, there's one bar, one supermarket and, um, that's about it (though during its gold-rush boom years it boasted an incredible forty-two brothels and saloons). It makes Fernie look like a cross between Las Vegas and Sodom and Gomorrah, no mean feat. In terms of BC ski-towns, it's like one of those verbal reasoning tests: Whistler is to Fernie as Fernie is to Rossland.

Rossland is smack bang in the middle of BC along the east-west axis or whatever the correct geographical term is, roughly equidistant from Vancouver and Calgary (about six hundred kilometres in each direction, I think), i.e., in the middle of nowhere. Just how I like it! The US border to Washington State is only about 10km away, not that I've had any reason to venture down there yet and it's all a bit of a mystery to me what exactly is down there.

I'm sharing a house with Ellie and Kris, whom (brief

recap) I met back in Fernie a few years ago and we arranged to come to here together for Snowtime Part II. I really didn't realise at the time how largely people who spent that winter in Fernie would loom in my future, thinking I was just there for a self-contained few months of fun before heading back to life-business proper. Ha! After the privations of our wood-burning stove in New Zealand – quaint and a "feature" at first, a pain in the ass later on when you were cold and damp and wanted instant heat – I am continually marvelling at how warm our house is. I arrived here ready to do battle with elements, swathed in layers of fleece, thick merino work socks, pyjamas you could wear to the Arctic. I haven't needed them yet.

The ski-season got off to a slow start in the Kootenays this year: November was dry, dry, dry and we were starting to worry that this would simply be The Winter When It Never Snowed (it can happen – skiers here are still traumatised by Winter 04/05). O we of little faith! The first big snowfall came on December 12, when it snowed 42cms overnight to the delight of skiers and boarders, and the chagrin of everybody else, who merely grumbled about having to shovel that much snow out of their drive.

The snow has kept a-coming fairly steadily since then, but the lack of pre-season snowfall means we're still playing catch-up in terms of getting a solid base. For the non-skiers and boarders among you (shame on you! Get thee to a ski-hill!) I won't get too technical, but in brief it means that twigs and stumps and rocks which would normally be safely and comfortably buried by snow by this stage remain precariously close to the surface, ready to gouge a hole out of your skis or, only slightly more alarmingly, yourself if you take a tumble. Even now the signs warn: "Early Season Hazards: Ski and Board with Caution."

Having picked up some shiny new skis and boots of

my own since arriving in Canada, I've been both skiing and snowboarding, depending on the conditions and how I feel. Sometimes people ask me if I prefer skiing or snowboarding but, as I said before in NZ, it's not an either-or trade off. I love both. It's preferable to take skis out at the moment, conditions being what they are and the groomers being unfortunately where it's at. But I'm sure the snowboard will come out again on the next big powder day. If I feel like shredding the gnar, slaying the pow and ripping the trees (translation: having a good time) then I take out my snowboard. If, on the other hand, I feel like a day of concentration on the groomers, remembering to roll my ankles, flex my knees, keep my arms out in front of me and keep my upper body facing down the hill, then skis it is.

Skiing is Hard Work. I know children seem to pick it up almost instinctively but I suppose when you reach your mid-to-late twenties – what exactly does pushing twenty seven count as? Late twenties I suppose. Time flies when you're having fun.... The synapses are no longer fusing as furiously, not to mention the Fear Factor, so I'm making slow progress indeed. Skiing is so much effort that it's almost in inverse proportion to the amount of fun I'm having at the moment. I learned to ski in New Zealand because Cardrona wasn't very challenging, this not being an issue in Rossland where Red Mountain is known for being "Steep and Deep" in the extreme. I have to be extremely careful what I say about New Zealand: it almost caused an international incident in Rossland when Ellie was slagging off the paucity of Antipodean snow around a group of Kiwis the other day.

That's all for now though: more next time about how I am working as a waitress – or a "server" as they're called in North America – and much else besides.

Slán go foill!
Lisa

January 2009: How did *you* end up *here*??

Hi everybody

Like I said in my last email, here as I am on a Working Holiday Visa, I'm working as a "server". Ski-town economies being what they are, not to mention North American tipping culture, serving is a high-status, lucrative and sought-after job among ski-bums, as opposed to the service industry minion they are elsewhere. What's more, working only in the evening leaves you with all day, every day, free to ski. Not that you actually end up skiing all day every day when you're doing a season. I suppose it's because (a) you only have a finite amount of energy to expend over the winter (b) when you own a season pass, you're not possessed by the frenzied zeal to get value for money which grips you when you're paying for lift tickets by the day.

Do you know something though, I really don't think I'm beaming and perky enough to make it as a typical North American server. Indeed, I probably have a somewhat Soviet serving style, not actually surly and unsmiling, but tending towards that end of the scale rather than any over the top chirpiness. Highly efficient however.

Something which makes me grit my teeth in patient frustration at work, though, is how much difficulty customers have with the "cute little accent" I'm frequently told I have. More fool them if they think my flat North County Dublin tones represent a soft Irish lilt! God only know what gasps of rapture they'd go into if someone from Galway or Cork were here. You know, a bona fide culchie.

Now I think I have a reasonable grasp of the English language. But here, whenever I speak, I can see people squinting in bewildered concentration, almost lip-reading as they try to work out what exactly I'm saying. As a result

I have to either over-enunciate my words like a pre-school teacher speaking LOUDLY and CLEARLY or modulate my voice into some bizarre BC twang. Awesome! As it were.

To add insult to injury, one of the (few) things that irks me about Canada is the denuded version of English that gets circulated in the North American media in the main, e.g., the conflation of "well" and "good", such as "I'm doin' good!" instead of "I'm doin' well"; similarly "done" instead of "finished", e.g., "I'm nearly done" rather than "I'm nearly finished"; and finally "got" instead of "have", e.g., "I got three beers here!". No! You got three beers out of the cooler perhaps, but now you HAVE three beers in your possession. Don't want to get too donnish. I also know that language is protean and that these expressions are just as valid. There is no one form of the Queen's English which one would/ should speak in plummy tones. This is Canadian English. But it makes me grit my teeth.

Don't even get me started on the closed captioning (don't worry, I haven't suddenly gone deaf or anything, it's the television at the gym) which is riddled with errors. Riddled! Most of the time these are just grammatical mistakes – the whole their/they're confusion – but sometimes the sentences are so garbled that the meaning is altered entirely: e.g., the subtitles on BBC World Service gravely informed me the other day that "the UN has condemned the excessive use of morse by the Israelis in the Gaza Strip". Excessive use of morse indeed.

Right, right, I need to get over this pedantry I know. But I can't help it. If I get this worked up about the misuse of the English language, maybe I should leave the mountains and go back to my PhD, The Academic Who Came in from the Cold perhaps?

Back to the being Irish thing – I'm looked upon here in the West Kootenays as some sort of exotic curiosity. "How did you ever end up in Rossland?" I'm asked daily in enthralled fascination, like I've been beamed down from outer space. Not a very original story, I'm afraid; like every other ski-bum in town I applied for and was granted a twelve month working holiday visa which is issued as standard to anyone aged eighteen to thirty. I suppose Irish ski-bums just aren't as common as their British or Antipodean brethren. I haven't met a single other Irish person since coming to Canada on this trip.

Now I don't want misty-eyed renditions of the Fields of Athenry every night nor am I going to launch into keening howls about Black 47 and how we were hungry long enough. But, all the same, it'd be nice now and then not to feel entirely isolated in your allusions. For example, there was a New Year's Eve fancy dress party in town, hosted in conjunction with the local radio station (Rossland FM or whatever it's called), whereby you had to dress up as something with the initials FM, e.g.; French maid, Freddy Mercury. My first suggestion of a Fenian martyr was met with blank looks all round. The Fenians were a nineteenth century revolutionary brotherhood for anyone who dozed off during Leaving Cert history. In fairness though, my later suggestions were pretty obscure as well, ranging as they did from Franciscan Monk to forensic microbiologist or – my personal favourites, though they would additionally have involved recruiting my reluctant housemates – Fleetwood Mac and a fascist mob.

Sometimes you need people from home to know what you're on about. In the absence of the same, however, to get my fill of Irishness I've taken to downloading episodes of the RTE Documentary on One from iTunes and listening to these on my iPod around town. And there you were thinking that snowboarders all went around listening to nothing but hip-hop or dope drum'n'bass. Not so! When we think no one's listening, we're all earnestly tuned into our respective national broadcasting services.

How *are* things back home by the way? Have rumours of Ireland's economic death been greatly exaggerated or are things really that bad?

Mise le meas

Lisa

February 2009: What happened to the snow?

Hey everybody

It's been a peculiar sort of winter so far. To surmise: it's as if the customary six months of Canadian winter have been condensed into one. To start, the snow was so slow arriving that the ski-hill opened two weeks later than planned, and even then conditions were marginal. Winter proper arrived, glory be to God, over Christmas time and we were blessed with two weeks of continuous snow. Fresh lines every day! January, alas, brought with it a worrying rise in temperatures and, to cut to the chase, No More Snow. It hasn't snowed a centimetre in about three weeks and we've been launched far too prematurely into what's basically spring skiing. Spring skiing is great – sunny, mellow, enjoyable – after a long, cold winter when it's nice to turn your face toward summer, welcome back Ra and the like. It's not so great, however, in mid-January when instead you just simply feel short-changed by the snow gods and denied your proper quota of pow. Absolutely unable to do anything about this though – King Canute and the waves, anybody? In the meantime, it's simply working on the goggle-tan and sticking to the groomers.

Bizarrely enough, even though the ski-hill has been sunny, Rossland itself has remained in perpetual fog. The

"Kootenay ocean" is a blanket of cloud which hangs mid-mountain level as far across the horizon as you can see, so that while the top of the ski-hill is gloriously sunny, like being in an airplane – watch me fly! – below in town it's gloomy and grey.

It's gloomy in more than one way at the moment around here though. I'm not sure if you've noticed, but there's a bit of an economic crisis going on at the moment across the world. Here in the West Kootenays, a depressed area to begin with, the free-fall is noticeable indeed. Jobs are scarce, scarce, scarce and the restaurant I work at is exceptionally quiet compared to previous winters. Well, actually it's impossible to gauge whether the lack of tourists in Rossland is due primarily to the economic downturn or the appalling winter we're in the throes of. A bit of both, I suppose. A thought: it's a dire snow year only from the point of view of skiers and snowboarders. I'm sure everybody else is breathing a sigh of relief at the unseasonably mild weather and gloating that they don't have to shovel their drives every day. Unless you're into snowsports I imagine that winter time would just be a pain up the jacksie.

All in all, what with the universal prognostications of doom and gloom in regards to The Economy: Whither?, it's not the ideal time to be freewheeling around the world, bouncing from ski-season to ski-season. Or is it? Maybe I'm just as well not being tied to any particular place by a mortgage on a rapidly devaluing property or anything. I vacillate between finding it more than a little disquieting not to be in stable long-term employment at the moment, without any sort of contingency plan, and thinking that oh well, if Nero fiddled while Rome burned, I may as well ski while the global economy collapses. As Janis Joplin sang, freedom's just another word for nothing left to lose – being a penniless ski-bum has its boons.

So let's bury our heads in the sand and talk about skiing for a while! And snowboarding! And cross-country skiing for good measure! To remind everybody: I'm a snowboarder who was transformed into a fledgling skier in New Zealand last year. My introduction to skiing – aside from that initial disastrous day at Fernie two years ago which saw me muttering and sulking and vowing never, ever again; oh how we live to eat our words – was thus done with the Kiwi baseless optimism and cheery confidence of "she'll be right". My friends took me up a chairlift to the top of the ski-hill and let me figure it out on the way down. No option really.

And for a while I was happy just to snow plough sedately and stem christy around the hill, squealing in delighted terror as I careered down blue runs. But now that familiar manic glint has returned to my eyes and I want to CHARGE! I've a long way to go yet.

In the meantime, as well as doggedly going to the ski-hill whilst waiting for the new snow, Ellie, Kris and I also gave cross-country skiing a go. What an odd pursuit. I don't think I quite got the hang of it straight away – initially I was overtaken by an old lady out for a stroll with her dog. Really, I thought, this is little more than impeded walking. Our landlords then saw fit to take us on a cross-country trip to a backcountry cabin. Hmm. It got a little trickier once the trail went from being pancake flat to, how shall I put it, more challenging terrain. I simply don't understand how you're meant to stop or turn on cross-country skis, floppy, spindly, edgeless things that they are. It's willfully perverse, I thought crossly to myself this time, to make skis with no edges on them. What does that Red Hot Chili Peppers go like again? Take Me to Your Backwoods Now. Well, I wouldn't try getting there on cross-country skis if you're in a hurry, that's all I'm saying.

Lisa

February 2009: The outside eye

Readers

You know "chick-lit", maligned genre that it is, the protagonists being in the main nice girls, not terribly together, not terribly capable, not too threatening, unlikely to disrupt the status quo. Actually, let's not get into that whole side of things now: rather, what I want to emphasise here is the backdrop to those texts, a nondescript English Everytown of working in an office (where they invariably end up dating their hunky boss called Nick), dropping earrings down the sink, going to the supermarket in an after-work frazzle and Saturday shopping on the high street. Presumably readers are meant to relate to this as their cultural norm. Reading these books in small-town BC, however, that way of life seems entirely at a remove and dazzlingly different rather than Just the Way Things Are. Tescos, Top Shop, Marks & Spencers – these things seem a universe away.

My point, which I'm arriving at tangentially, is that what's quotidian and mundane in one place is entirely exotic and novel in another. This being my third winter in Canada, much of Canadiana I now just take for granted. It seems obvious and self-evident to me that there exist small mountain towns where you hitch up and down to the ski-hill everyday, where you never ever bother to lock your front door (do we even HAVE a house key?) and where the default state is one of cheery helpfulness. Where instead of taking the Tube to work, clattering along in high-heels, you have to shovel the drive and be mindful of moose on the highway.

Some things are hardly worth mentioning – the toque and mitts and snow-boots, the drops in temperature to minus twenty that leave your eyelashes dew-dropped and frosty. When these things become the norm, they become no more worth mentioning than the air that I breath, though, on that note, it's Alpine pure and thinner here than at soupy sea-level, which made going for a run bloody difficult my first few days here. This is my reality now.

But, dear friends, you're not here with me so let me step back and describe what Rossland is like with an outside eye. I'm sitting on our couch, snuggly and cosy in my merino wool work socks – merino wool is yer man for keeping you warm – with a view onto the main street through the bay window. A guy just walked by in a "Canadian tuxedo" – jeans teamed with a denim jacket – wearing neither toque nor gloves. Brr! It's minus nine out there today.

Rossland/Red Mountain is…quirky and I'm not using quirky as a synonym for quaint or full of character or anything. No, no, in terms of both the locals and the transient ski-bums there's a much higher quotient of odd-balls and off-beats than normal. Not that this is necessarily a bad thing.

First off, let's talk about the hippies. The West Kootenays are a hotbed of tatty hippiness and pot-smoking in general, a town called Nelson – about an hour away – being the epicentre of this. I think historically it's where a lot of the US draft dodgers fled over the border to in order to avoid being sent to 'Nam, and that counter-culture vibe lives on. When I went over there to get my laptop fixed I was struck by the number of new-age figures roaming the streets in blanket-like ponchos, no doubt en route from the hemp shop to the organic co-op, or maybe the raw food vegan restaurant. I'm not exaggerating for dramatic purpose, by the way, all of the above establishments exist in Nelson. There's even a commune-run restaurant called The Preserved Seed, or the Perished Grain as I kept calling it by mistake, which somewhat removes the connotations of fecundity and fulfillment. Lots of people think Nelson is really cool: maybe my chakras are out of kilter or I'm just desperately unenlightened or something but it all makes me snigger a bit.

Rossland is infused with the same hippie-ish spirit, though thankfully to a more tolerable degree. I got a lift down from the ski-hill today with this local guy, probably in his mid-fifties or so, who was picking up his dog before heading to the timber cabin on the ski-hill where he sleeps three or four nights a week. Do Red Mountain management not mind people living on their property, I inquired? The cabin, he explained, was one of a group built in 1944 and thus predates ski-hill operations, the lifts having only been installed in 1948. A few years ago an allegation that the cabin run-off was tainting Rossland's water supply did put them in danger of being razed, but a compromise was reached and now this guy pays a $500 annual levy to City Hall to be allowed to live in peace in the woods. Firmly off-grid, with neither running water nor electricity, he uses a propane stove to heat the cabin and melts snow for water. It was about minus six in the cabin that morning, he explained to me, but the place would warm up nicely once the stove was lit. Well, he qualified, not warm to the level of central heating but Warm Enough. I nodded vigorously in agreement: I've just come from New Zealand, I explained, I know about chilly homes.

Then today I met an old man in the Daylodge who exhorted me to go to the Yukon for the summer. It was like some sort of biblical invective – I may ignore it at my own peril. You get to meet a variety of people and characters doing a ski-season whom you just wouldn't get to meet elsewhere. Certainly not in suburban Dublin do people urge you to strike out for the Great North.

Something else which strikes me about Rossland is the proliferation of moustaches around town. The older men tend to go for a Great War era approach – you know, the walrus-like look of a Prussian military general or Lord Kitchener – while those my age just go for well...moustaches. Beards of various coverage and density are pretty much a constant in ski-towns – the whole rugged man-of-nature thing, as well as the more practical benefit of extra face fur for warmth – but this unaccompanied moustache look is a new one for me. Possibly it's meant ironically, so-not-it's-hot but I remain convinced.

Now two kids are going by our window laden down with hockey gear. Ice-hockey that is, of course. I wonder if they're coming from the ice-rink or the outdoor pond which was used for last week's Pond Hockey tournament? Truly I am in Canada now.

In line with this quirkiness are the ski-bums who come to town for the winter. Some ski towns attract a crowd who want to ski hard and drink hard (Fernie). Others attract people who want to dress flashy and be part of The Scene (Whistler). Red Mountain seems to have drawn an extremely mellow, "alternative" crowd. Whereas Fernie had Monday night cheap pitchers or Wednesday night drum'n'bass, here there is just jam night and open mic session piled upon open mic session and jam night ad infinitum. I'm not a party person, I'm not even a people person, particularly, but sometimes Rossland is too quiet even for me.

There hasn't been the mass influx of Antipodeans which usually betokens a ski-town – oh, there's a smattering of Australians and Kiwis here alright, but not swarms and swarms of the blighters the way there are elsewhere. Actually, there hasn't been an influx of anyone. I'd say there are maybe one hundred and fifty seasonal ski-bums here. If that. Whereas Fernie had several different cohorts depending on where you were located on the skiing-to-partying spectrum, here it's so tight-weave a subculture that anything you do is fair game for wild-fire gossip. And forget about trying to keep any indiscretions to yourself.

With all the hippiness (not to mention the lack of much else to do in the evenings) comes the inevitable pot-smoking. Grow ops are a big money-maker in the Kootenays, apparently. I saw an ad up in the supermarket the other day from some guy looking to rent a room. As well as the normal information that you'd put into such a notice – clean, responsible twenty-seven year old seeks room – he also mentioned that he's a non-smoker so, and I quote, "There's no chance of your property being converted into a grow op." Reassuring to know that any potential rentees aren't going to go into narcotic production in your house! Evidently he felt that this would distinguish him from the crowd and give him a head-start in finding somewhere to live.

But where there are drugs, there are social ills! I mentioned Trail, the town ten kilometres away from Rossland, a few emails ago. Now poor benighted Trail is not the nicest of places to begin with. Apparently no vegetation would grow there for years because the soil was so polluted from all the smelting works and refineries. But anyway, at the start of the winter there was a drive-through shooting halfway between here and there – just a hop, skip and a jump from Rossland where, as I mentioned, we don't even lock our doors and as in Fernie where we blithely hitched up and down to the ski-hill with strangers. It turns out that this homicide was, surprise, surprise, tied in with a turf war. I wondered a bit about this at first; how much can the drug trade possibly be worth in such a sparsely populated area? Are they fighting over the custom one or two crackheads? Then someone pointed out that Trail's proximity to the US border raised the stakes considerably.... Not the kind of information I'd expected to glean while doing a ski-season in so remote a location, but there you have it.

So that's Rossland (and Trail). Next time around I'll talk some more about the actual ski-hill itself, Red Mountain.

How's everybody doing, by the way?

Lisa

February 2009: Red Mountain itself

Hi everybody

If asked if I were sporty, I'd quickly and vigorously shake my head in disavowal. I was invariably the last to be picked for teams in school (it still smarts, doesn't it?) and could be classified, as you so easily can back then, as Primary Identifier – Brainy, Subcategory – Bad at Sports. Yet, somehow I keep racking up the ski-seasons…

Now I haven't, along the way, discovered some hitherto dormant ability which has blossomed into great sporting prowess. Sometimes I get horribly demoralised and think I should have stayed cloistered away in the Bodleian rather than romping around the world after the snow. Book-learnin' came easier to me, that's for sure. But with distance running, tenacity is the key to success, and with snowsports, sheer balls can take you far. What I lack in natural aptitude, I try to make up for in enthusiasm and determination.

Having made the conversion from snowboarding to skiing – the snowboard instructor's course was my exit qualification, if you will – I can assure you that skiing is the far more technical discipline of the two. The gung-ho "Ah sure I'll give it a belt!" approach which stood me so well in snowboarding has to be tempered by accurately gauging your skill level and not going down terrain wildly beyond your grasp on skis. Compared to snowboarding, you see, there is no wussing out on skis. On a snowboard you can slip slide the entire way down the mountain if all else (i.e., courage, technique) fails. It wouldn't be much fun and your thighs would be on fire but at least the option is there. With skiing, there is no such fall-back. You Have. To Turn. And if the terrain is too difficult, so help you God.

Remember when I was in New Zealand and said I hadn't been absolutely petrified on skis the way I so often was on a snowboard? You know, heart-racing, unable to move, almost wanting to throw up? That's changed here at Red Mountain when learning to ski off-piste. Having started skiing at Cardrona, comparing Cardrona to Red is like comparing a Saturday morning kickaround to the World Cup.

Red is notorious for being "steep and deep" – unfortunately with the paucity of snowfall this winter it was merely "steep" for a while. I am aware that when I start whinging about this season's lack of snow it makes me sound like a Poor Little Ski-Bum. In terms of climatic misfortunes, a lack of snow hardly compares with a blight upon the land or a crippling drought. But still. *Ar aon nos*, after a dry spell of three solid weeks without snow we had 8cms of fresh one night! In a normal winter this would be entirely unremarkable, barely worth heading up for first lifts (I don't get out of bed for less than 20cms, darling). But after the drought that was, the whole town was whipped into a frenzy of excitement. So having mastered the groomers on skis – well, no, let me rephrase that, having made considerable progress skiing the trails – it was time for me to step up my game and take some tentative turns off-piste in the fresh. Ellie, Kris and assorted others were heading down a black, mogulled, tree run called Beer Belly and I decided to follow suit.

Ahem.

Now 90% of skiing is mental. As in, attitude is all important, not as in "Jaysus that was mental!" Though that too, sometimes. And as we went to drop into Beer Belly all fortitude deserted me. I froze, immobile, at the top of the chute, unable to make the first turn. But like I said there are no half way measures with skiing. You either turn or you don't. None of this side-slipping malarkey. So with tremulous legs and much coaxing from Ellie I got down the run. No option really.

It is hard-core here. Almost too hard-core at times. And this is from someone who spent two seasons at Fernie in my previous incarnation as a snowboarder so I'm no timorous beginner. I'm terribly tentative about striking out and exploring new parts of Red. "Are there cliffs?" I ask in a small and timid voice when someone suggests going down an unfamiliar part of the hill, much the same as a small child might ask, "Are there monsters?" In one part of the hill there's even a frozen waterfall. At some other resorts, ski-patrols cordon off hazards to warn errant snowsporteers of upcoming obstacles, but here at Red Mountain they take much more of a hands-off, be-it-on-your-own-head approach. Also, the terrain being what it is here, if they started marking out hazards, they'd be scratching their heads in bafflement wondering where to stop. They may as well just fence off the entire mountain.

The first chair lift was installed on Red Mountain in 1948 and later on, during the 1960s, lift access was also provided on Granite Mountain, an adjacent peak. Both mountains are known collectively – and confusingly – as Red Mountain Resort. Now Granite Mountain isn't thus called for nothing – cliff bands and rocks lurk everywhere just underneath the snow. If you don't know exactly where you're going off-piste there's a very good chance that you'll find yourself imperiled at the top of a thirty foot cliff – quite literally stuck between a rock and a hard place. The difference of a few metres to the left or right can spell the difference between a powder-filled bonanza and an oh-fuck-not-again ordeal.

Not only do such natural hazards abound at Red Mountain, but Rossland is an old mining town, founded during the gold rush of the late 1800s, and its surrounding hills still bear the scars of the same. There are mine shafts everywhere on Red, most of which patrol have been reasonably conscientious about filling in. Most of which. Apparently a feature to be mindful of is if you're skiing along a steep tree section and it suddenly flattens out. Do not stop! This could be an uncovered mine shaft and may cave in under your feet. Red is not a mountain to go exploring by yourself.

I have to point out, once again for people who don't ski or snowboard, that you're not in any particular danger of cliffs, mine-shafts, avalanches etc on the marked runs. So in a way, yes, if you go off-piste, you're taking a certain degree of risk and have to be prepared for things to go potentially awry from time to time. You have to strike a fine balance between trepidations to get the most out of Red and I imagine that, short of heading off to the Alaskan backcountry in a heli, skiing anywhere else is going to seem laughably tame in comparison.

Red's quite the mountain to serve your skiing apprenticeship at. Certainly it's not the kind of place where you'd come for a Euro-style, soak-up-the-sun, bring-on-the-après-ski trip. Indeed, the lack of tourists is remarkable. Because BC is so sparsely populated to begin with, and because Rossland is remote within this, there is never ANYBODY on the hill. The longest you'd ever wait for a chair (major powder days excluded, obviously) is about three minutes and that's only during the Christmas holidays. I don't know how the hill makes a profit, in fact I'm fairly sure that it's running at a consistent loss, buoyed only by the real estate sales of slope-side condos.

The only people on the hill on any given day are the seasonal ski-bums and the locals. I've seen the hostility which can arise when the ski-hill is run by an outside corporation and it's felt that local interests aren't paramount (I'm naming no names here) but no such division exists in Rossland: here the local community IS the hill. Red Mountain is a hill for all ages, with ski-bums here falling into two main categories: the under thirties (well, under twenty-fives really but let's gloss over the fact that I'm rapidly approaching the upper end of the acceptable age band for ski-bumming) and the over fifties. A huge group of retired locals meet daily in the Daylodge at half ten to ski; whoever's there is there, whoever's not, well, sure they'll turn up the next day or the day after. Many of them are Snow Hosts, volunteers who give free guided tours of the mountain to visitors, and they must be a minimum of sixty years old to a man. One of them is in his eighties and can barely walk up the stairs but he's still out every day, showing off Red Mountain at its finest. How's that for active retirement?

Lisa

March 2009: Go Team Volly, Go!

Hello again

As well as waitressing in town (where the tips are ludicrously large, short of selling drugs or going on the game, there can't be any other way to make so much money in an evening), I'm also an Events Volunteer up at Red, whereby you get your season pass for free if you do one hundred hours work throughout the winter. A season pass costs $800 so this works out at $8 an hour, i.e.; minimum wage. It's slightly hit-and-miss as to whether volly work is a good deal as some of the jobs are cushier than others. For example, one day me and Ellie spent three hours working on a papier mâché model of the ski-hill to be used in a parade. Another afternoon we spent collecting and whittling down alder twigs to toast marshmallows on at Family Night.

On the flip side, there's a lot of manual labour involved particularly when setting up the bloody ski-cross course. It's difficult to know how much detail I should go into in explaining what ski-cross is; if you've never even seen a ski-hill in the first place then there really isn't any frame of reference. Basically it's an emergent form of ski-racing where the competitors whoosh four at a time down the course over jumps and around turns and banks and berms. For course set-up, starting at the base, we had to carry bundles of two metre long bamboo poles to the bottom of the chairlift, hoist this bundle across our laps onto the lift, then ski off with it jauntily tossed over our shoulders. I staggered along, buckling under the weight and wondering how this was conceivably going to end well. It was no time for machismo but nor did I want to play the gender card by squealing, "I'm a girl! I can't do this!" Luckily someone noticed me struggling under the weight, valiantly took from me my bamboo burden and instead assigned me a garbage pail full of rope and a cordless drill. Off I set with it clutched to my chest like the baby Jesus in a nativity play or something.

Eventually we all got to the top of the piste with rope, bamboo poles and drills a-plenty to stake out the course. Once again, in deference to my gender, I was assigned the least physical task, that of running the rope from pole to pole, making sure to knot it properly on each post. Even then, at five feet four inches I was a few inches too short to toss the rope over the top of the bamboo and had to keep either standing on my tippy-toes (no mean feat in ski-boots) or make these little leaping, hopping movements. Practical I am not.

Once the bamboo poles were in place, another day's work involved setting up reams and reams of B-netting, that is, orange mesh netting sprigged down the side of the course to catch any errant skiers if they should crash and hurtle off the course. Well, such is the principle but usually the skiers are going so fast that they tend to burst right through the netting, ending up in a tangled and stunned heap on the snow. I suppose the resistance in the B-netting reduces potentially fatal wipe-outs to merely grievous ones.

Once the ski-cross course is set up as above and racing is underway, Events Volunteers also have to act as gate judges. Being a gate judge is terrible. What's that famous quote about war? That it's hours of boredom punctuated by moments of sheer terror. That's an apt summation of gate judging as well. You get assigned a section of course, along the side of which you have to stand with your two-way radio and your high-vis vest, making sure the skiers pass through the race gates or radioing up if anyone crashes or the fencing needs to be fixed. It's cold and boring and you're not allowed to leave your position at all during the day, even to use the toilet. Which is probably fine if you were a keen ski-racer yourself in your youth and are riveted to the spot by the thrill of it all. It's less interesting if you're an apathetic and weak-bladdered ski-bum who, let's face it, is only there for the free pass, hopping from leg to leg desperate for the loo. (Next time I'm going to relieve myself in full view of the chairlift. That'll show them.) And there's only so many times you can say "Section Six, Stop-Start, Skier down, B-netting down" over the radio before the novelty wears off.

Something I have gained, though, from interminable days spent gate-judging is an appreciation of how enormous a time commitment ski-racing is for child and parent alike. Here in Rossland they start off aged six with the Red Mountain Racers. For the first few years, the emphasis is on fun – so they say – but even so the standard is so high that it would easily put your once-a-year recreational skier to shame. The introductory level for the club is that your little mite should be able to comfortably ski intermediate trails, while "older children" (those classified as eight and upwards) should be able to make it down black trails such as The Cliff. (The clue is in the name.) No wonder Rossland has produced so many Winter Olympians over the years.

Once the kid racers hit the double digits, they're expected to put in at least seventy-five days on snow a year at K1 level (aged eleven and twelve), while for the K2 group (aged thirteen and fourteen) that's bumped up to one hundred days a year. So you may forget about going to school Monday to Friday if such is the case; most of the serious racers do maybe two full days of school a week during the winter and then some supplementary hours here and there. No doubt it's the same in other sports – I'm thinking of tennis in particular here for some reason, all those champions whose parents shipped them off to Florida when they were seven to train with a particular coach. And specialist sports academies exist for a reason. But, traditionalist that I am, I do feel that a formal education shouldn't be let slide. Even if you have world-class racing potential? Oh I don't know.

Oh well! Only a month and a half left of the season to ponder such matters. Thank God. No, no, I don't really mean that but I'm worn out after a year of endless winter. Some people who chase the snow from hemisphere to hemisphere for years on end – one girl I know is on Continuous Winter No. 7 at this stage – but I am Wintered Out and Ready For Summer. Not only do my knees now crack like the ricochet of far-off gunshot whenever I stand up or sit down, but my quads are about to explode as well.

Old age is a terrible thing.

Lisa

March 2009: Ellie and Kris

Hi everyone

Whatsoever I write about has actually taken place. What's so great about doing a ski-season, aside from the actual snowsports themselves, are the incidents and misadventures that simply don't happen elsewhere. Though not much of lasting significance happens, every day brings with it a new adventure. It also means, though, that describing it in prose runs the risk of becoming a bit "this one time, in band camp..."; unbearably adolescent and closed-off, an endless barrage of private references and in-jokes. I hope it's interesting for others to read as well and that what to me were hilarious circumstances doesn't in fact become boringly unintelligible, raising only a polite smile. Here's hoping.

Equally, the people who feature in these emails are very much alive. Ellie and Kris are aware that I've been writing voluminously about my travels and I did obtain some measure of clearance from them to feature within. I'm mindful, however, that, as they may not necessarily want their private business immortalised in prose, some of the best stories and juiciest anecdotes have been withheld, alas, from the public realm. Maybe some day they'll feature in the Director's Cut.

"You better make me sound cool" was Ellie's only stipulation. I've mentioned before that our friendship was founded on a keen competitiveness when snowboarding together. Towards the end of that first season we did in Fernie it was probably getting dangerous, both of us were riding as if we had a death wish, neither willing to accept the other as the alpha female. Following my defection from one plank to two, Ellie also switched over to skiing in Rossland. This time round, however, whether borne of maturity or apathy I don't know, but I could hardly have cared less if she skied harder or pulled off more impressive tricks. That's not to say that we don't still get stupidly and pointlessly competitive in different ways. One night in the bar recently both of us were flexing our calf muscles, trying to impress a volly ski-patroller by demonstrating whose were more defined. (That *is* the best way to get guys, right? To wow them with your brute musculature?)

Luckily, things are saved from turning nasty because we also share the same sense of gallows humour, cracking up over matters of questionable taste. The might of British imperialism, for example, became somewhat of a running joke all winter long. I think it started because Antipodeans in ski-towns are forever bedecking themselves in their national flags on, say, Austraya or Waitagni Day. Plenty of houses also display the red and white maple leaf of Canadiana in their windows. "That's something you never get in England," Ellie pointed out. "If you see a St. George's flag back home it means someone's on their way to start a fight at a football match." "Reappropriate the symbol!" I cried, and thus started this inexplicable and mutually antagonistic fixation upon English nationalist pride. We contemplated rigging up a flagpole in the front yard, the Union Jack flapping in the breeze, and blaring out God Save the Queen at regular intervals for the benefit of the bemused Rossland locals. Good old Blighty.

We then went to a table quiz where one of the questions was, "To which country do the Falklands belong?" "Argentina!" I cried and INSISTED on the answer sheet we refer to them as Las Malvinas and explain that, while Britain may claim unlawful jurisdiction over them (they like to do that to small islands, don't they, the Brits?), really, they were the rightful property of the Argentines. But was it my imagination or was someone humming *Rule Britannia*?

The whole England-My-England thing came to head on

St Patrick's Day, the tradition apparently being for everyone to wear green out to the bar. (This is something I never, ever encountered in Ireland by the way.) "I don't know if I really feel comfortable wearing green being, you know, English," Ellie remarked, aware of 800 years of historical context. "Wear something orange so," was my flippant return. But when the seed of an idea is planted.... This gathered momentum and Ellie ended up wearing out every scrap of orange clothing she owns that night – quite a bit actually – the crowing detail being an orange sash slung across her front. If we'd had more time we would have rustled up a bowler hat and fife and drum as well to complete the marching season attire. I'm not sure if the Canadians got it or not: there was more than one brow furrowed in confusion – dude, you're supposed to wear GREEN today. But to have the tenacity, being English, to go out wearing an orange sash on St. Patrick's Day: you have to applaud the girl.

Then there is Kris/Waffle. Kris is, I shall remind you, a cheery and easy-going curly-haired Australian who, when she's not being a ski-bum, works as an Occupational Therapist. Kris can be relied upon to be calm in a crisis and to come up with a practical solution to any problem. Waffle, on the other hand, is Kris's drunken alter ego. It's a sort of Dr. Jekyll-and-Mr. Hyde situation.

How did the name came about? It's not, as you might have thought, because of any propensity of Kris's to talk nonsense when she has drink taken. Instead, another friend of ours, Jessy, somehow acquired the nickname of Pancake when he's drunk – I don't know either – and following along the line of carbo-laden North American breakfast goods, Kris became known as Waffle.

As to whether we'll be dealing with Kris or Waffle on a given night out is anyone's guess, and the transformation from one to another is scarily swift. For example, one night

Kris left the house at ten o'clock to visit some friends, and at eleven o'clock Waffle lurched into the bar. Spencer – also known as "Young Lung" for his youth and prodigious weed-smoking capabilities – was trying to stuff a breadroll into her mouth to sober her up but Waffle was making these vague pawing away movements and trying to dance instead.

Waffle is very hard to handle; she wanders and leers all over the place, to the point that miscellaneous people come up to me or Ellie murmuring discreetly, "I think you should take Kris home now." The first few times we nodded in concern and indeed tried to bundle Waffle away – oh God, that was a mission in itself – but after this we just shrugged them off, having learnt from experience that the best thing to do with Waffle is to let her roam free. "She'll be fine," we'd say with a complete lack of concern, leaving her to stagger around. Indeed, one night after we'd already taken Waffle home twice and she'd bolted back out from the house on both occasions, showdown came with Ellie standing in the snow waving her arms and shouting at Waffle, "Go away! I don't KNOW you!" The brilliant thing about Kris is that she shows absolutely no remorse or embarrassment when she's regaled with stories of Things Waffle Has Done. Instead she just beams and carries on regardless.

I really admire Kris's dauntlessness, Ellie's too. Because then you have to add me into the mix, with my propensity for introspection, doom and gloom and a quotation for all occasions. "A dark exhausted eye, a dry downturning mouth...I read that I have looked my last on youth and little more." I kept intoning all winter long whenever Ellie would complain that we were all getting old. It's unfortunate but true: being outdoors all day every day in the snowy UV glare accelerates the craggy lines of old age.

The three of us complement each other perfectly, being so different in every possible way. Aside from skiing, we differ even in terms of the sports we like: Kris is a team-player, Ellie is a balls-to-the-walls adrenaline junkie, and I like the mental fortitude demanded of, and thinking space afforded by, pursuits such as distance running. What we do have in common is a readiness to jettison our careers at any opportunity to run away back to the snow, and we're all slightly unbalanced. It's one of those situations whereby when our powers combine.... If we were to have a theme song it'd have to be "We Could Have Been Anything That We Wanted to Be" from *Bugsy Malone* and, as Kris said, if the three of us were to return to Rossland en masse for another winter there'd be a collective intake of breath. "Brace yourselves, they're back!"

I've had a great time this winter simply by dint of my housemates being around. Now there's nowhere like Rossland for people liking to get dressed up at any opportunity. Fancy dress, I mean, not dragging out your glad rags and putting on the Ritz. Though talking of drag, I wouldn't be surprised in the slightest if there were an underground Rossland transvestite scene where all the moustachioed cat-drivers and burly mountain men regularly twirled around in feather boas and slinky dresses. And Retro Day is when everybody digs out their retro ski-gear from ski-seasons past, the tighter and brighter the better. To attire appropriately, me, Ellie and Kris queued up the day before for the thrift store. Oh yes, queued up, no less. The thrift store opens twice as week in Rossland and it's a big event on the weekly calendar. There's keen competition for the best bargains to be had as a large percentage of the ski-bum community here buy most of their clothes from the thrift store: the vogue here is for big, horrible, scratchy woolly jumpers with patterns of antelope or snowflakes and the greatest concentration of flannel shirts as I have seen. Rossland "fashion" definitely straddles the good taste/bad taste divide.

Eager and waiting as we were for opening hour at the op shop, we pounced on some beauties. Headbands, fluorescent one-pieces, shiny dungarees, leg-warmers, high ponytails, skiing in jeans: all the bases were covered for Retro Day. I skied all day, doing spread-eagled jumps at any opportunity, and then came home, reluctantly changed out of my spandex and leg-warmers and went to work. The surreality of the day's skiing was only a precursor of what was to come that evening though.

I got home from work at about 10pm and nobody was there. What a novelty! Much as I love my housemates dearly, oh how I revelled in time alone. All night long I'd been wincing whenever I had to squat down to get anything from the fridges because my quads were still so tightly knotted. I slathered myself in Tiger Balm. I sat on the couch, in a miasmic menthol haze reading *The Baker's Handbook* – I've become obsessed with bread making to an entirely new level this season – and watching trashy reality shows spliced with the French language channels. Guilty pleasures and all that.

Anyway, I went to bed but couldn't sleep. Only later did I realise Tiger Balm functions as a kind of menthol stimulant. My legs were tingling, my mind was racing. At about one o'clock in the morning I heard Ellie and Jaimie (a Kiwi girl who slept in the living room for a few weeks to subsidise the rent) come in, talking worriedly about Kris, who hadn't been seen since hitching home from the ski-hill that day. Most of the time this isn't remotely dangerous, it's usually one of the retired locals in their second ski-bumming glory who picks you up. But that didn't change the fact that, eight hours beforehand, Kris had gone to hitch by herself but never made it back to the house. Wherever she was, she was still wearing snowboard boots. Not only that, but she was MIA in her Retro Day outfit: high waisted shiny blue salopettes (ski dungarees), a hideous woolly jumper, a bright orange jacket and matching bobbly purple hat, a la the Seven Dwarves.

While trying to decide if it would be overly alarmist to contact the local police at this point – can you imagine the Last Seen Wearing description we'd have to give? – we also realised that our landlords (who live downstairs in the basement suite) had turned off the water supply trying to fix a leak and had forgotten to turn it back on.

This barely raised an eyebrow from Ellie who, at this point wearing a skin-tight cyan one-piece with matching head band, headed out into the front garden in the pitch black, grabbed the snow-shovel we use for clearing the drive, and proceeded to scoop snow into all our saucepans to be melted on the stove.

While Ellie was thus engaged, I wondered if Kris could maybe be with this guy she'd been intermittently hooking up with over the past few weeks. Why on earth she would have gone on a booty call at four o'clock in the afternoon, sober as a judge and in full retro day regalia made no sense, but I rang him at 2am just in case. Of course, Kris was safe and sound and amused by our concern. Well she could have phoned to let us know she was staying out for the night. Worried sick we were! Honestly, it's worse than having children.

Mystery solved (sort of), I went back to bed, able to sleep easily now I knew my housemate hadn't been abducted by malevolent fiends. The next morning when we woke up we found that the vessels and receptacles scattered around the kitchen, far from being filled with the pristine alpine melt waters we had imagined, were instead muddy grey with grit, gravel and earth. But Kris came home, the water went back on, we went to the ski-hill, God was in his heaven and all was well.

Just another Saturday in a ski-town.

Lisa

March 2009: This is Rossland

Mise arís

Has anyone else seen *Blood Diamond*, featuring as it does Leonardo DiCaprio as a self-declared "Rhodesian" mercenary-cum-diamond-smuggler? And did it rekindle anyone else's crush on DiCaprio to a level not equalled since his 1997 pretty-boy heyday in *Romeo & Juliet* and *Titanic*? Looks like he's a pretty boy no more though! After seeing *Blood Diamond*, me and Ellie became completely obsessed with his character in it, all rugged and manly and emotionally unavailable. It even developed into a fixation with the South African accent, which is probably ridiculous because if you're actually *from* Zimbabwe or SA your toes may well have been curling with embarrassment watching the film. For all I know, it's like saying "Oh I love how Irish people talk, just like Nicole Kidman and Tom Cruise in *Far & Away*" or "I could listen to Dick van Dyke in *Mary Poppins* all day long, I adore the Cockney accent so much."

But anyway, as well as second generation crushes on Leonardo – not to mention peppering our speech with "yar yar"s in unconscious imitation – something else we appropriated from the film was T.I.R. This is Rossland. You see, the claim made over and over again in *Blood Diamond* is "T.I.A. – This is Africa." Accompanied with a shrug, no further explanation or justification necessary, it means that things are to be taken on their own terms in Africa rather than judged by the standards and mores of the outside world.

The same sort of relativism applies in Rossland. Well no, there's no, you know, genocide and illegal diamond trading and that sort of thing going on here. That I know of anyway. But we too came to learn that the norms of elsewhere don't apply here. T.I.R - This is Rossland.

For example, it was Winter Carnival weekend. Every

year during Winter Carnival, the City of Rossland hoses down Spokane Street, the steepest hill in town. Once it's nice and icy there proceeds a bobsled race in which participants hurtle down the course at speeds reaching 80kph. Someone broke their arm last year, I'm repeatedly told. Small bloody wonder! I'm sure that was the least of it. (North American litigation culture seems to go out the window during Winter Carnival.)

I didn't get to watch the bobsledding this year because I was, as ever, doing some backbreaking volly work on the ski-hill but Ellie and Kris were around for it. We live right at the bottom of Spokane Street so it was simply a question of them stepping out the front door to watch the carnage unfold. When they came back into the house though, Kris realised that six cans of beer she'd left on the counter had disappeared. Like I've said before, we never even lock our doors so safe is Rossland, so this daylight robbery – literally – was entirely unexpected. Feckers! Kris and Ellie stood there incredulously for a bit when there's a knock on the door and in pops a smiling fireman.

Oh hello, sez he, me and the boys needed some beer earlier on so we came in and took yours. Thanks for that. Here are some bottles of Kokanee in return. That's how it works in this town.

And with that that he was gone. T.I.R.

It really is the kind of place where anything goes. The official town motto may be "The Mountains Our Treasure" but in practice it's Live and Let Live. There's absolutely nothing that I'd be embarrassed or self-conscious about walking around Rossland in – I regularly stroll down to the supermarket in thermal running tights teamed with down jacket and suede knee-high boots. I really don't think anybody cares much what you do at all here.

Possibly this is because everyone is just too baked to give

a shit. Weed usage is so common in ski-towns, particularly in Rossland, that I don't even consider it in drug terms any more, more like a mild creature comfort. Some people like rice pudding and cups of tea after skiing all day, other people like mellowing out with BC bud. Our friend Jessy, he of "Pancake" fame, broke his ankle recently but he was reluctant to take any of the strong painkillers prescribed to him. So instead he bought a two hundred dollar bag of weed to see him through his pain, feeling this was the more holistic approach. MDMA and mushrooms abound plentifully as well. But I'd never describe Rossland as having a drug problem as such; people don't seem to turn to them in any frenzied let's-all-escape-from-the-misery-of-our-every-day-lives desperation. Keeping in line with West Kootenay hippiedom, it's more of an open-your-mind-to-the-universe trippiness.

Someone asked me recently, just out of curiosity, why I don't take MDMA, deviating from the norm as this is. Just as you might ask a vegetarian why they've made a concerted decision not to eat meat. Ethical objections? Health concerns? Sometimes I have to remind myself that most people in the world at large don't take months off every year to ski and ingest as many mind-altering substances as they can.

There's an expression out here, "Kootenay time", meaning that things happen in their own good time so no point getting too stressed about urgency. If you were trying to represent Kootenay time on a clock I can only imagine some sort of warped Daliesque disc, the hands flopping all over the place.

Possibly the pace of Kootenay living has something to do with the tendency for seasonal working out here, with winter being the go-slow period. A sizeable proportion of the ski-bum community here don't work at all during winter – or work the bare minimum, anyway – and then haul for the remaining seven months of the year in primary industry or construction. I suppose it has to do with the availability of brutal but extremely lucrative manual labour available in Canada's great outdoors: e.g., tree-planting, silviculture, carpentry, working in the oil fields etc. And these are seasonal occupations, you see, it not being terribly well thought-through to build a house or go logging in January when it's minus twenty-five and the ground is frozen solid.

So it's feasible – particularly if you're a guy – to put in thirteen hour days all summer, make more than enough money to tide you over for the winter, then kick back, ski everyday and smoke your own body-weight in weed before starting the cycle again in spring. Also – and I don't know the ins and outs of it – it seems to be extremely easy to work for several months like this and then go on E.I. (the dole) for the winter. The E.I. Ski Team rides again!

When you have months and months off at a time stretching in front of you, it's hard to maintain any kind of high-octane lifestyle. It's certainly not the case that you have to productively utilise every second of the day to maximise your leisure time, tied as you may be to an allocated twenty-one days annual leave or whatever. So for whatever reason, Rossland has to be the most laid-back, whatever, place I've ever lived in. And it's not exactly like I've been based in a series of high pressure metropoles: North County Dublin, small-town New Zealand, Fernie.

Ah yes, Fernie. When hitching up and down from the ski-hill this winter, one particular conversation would play out again and again. Usually picked up by a friendly local, upon discovering I wasn't from round these parts (i.e., as soon as I opened my mouth), they'd ask me if this was my first time in Canada. I'd explain that no, while this was my first time in Rossland, I'd previously spent eighteen months in Fernie. "Fernie, eh," they'd ruminate, "that's a pretty different sort of town." Mmm, I'd agree noncommittally, not knowing what on earth they were talking about. From the perspective of suburban Dublin, you see, Rossland and Fernie are practically identical: small remote Kootenay ski-towns where you hitch up and down to the ski-hill and everyone drives around in beat-up old trucks.

Spend a little more time in Rossland, however, and you realise that different places they indeed are. Fernie is far bigger (a whopping 5000 people as opposed to Rossland's 3500) and more prosperous; a Destination, if you will. Historically a mining town, in the past decade or so there's also been an influx of health-conscious, educated types who've relocated to Fernie for the lifestyle, and who are now almost smugly self-congratulatory about how good they've got it. The disparity between Fernie and Rossland is apparent in many things: infrastructure, house prices, cultural facilities. Fernie is far more vibrant, having, among other things; more than one bar, a swimming pool, an Arts Station, a monthly publication (the *Fernie Fix*), community activism, a packed events calendar. Rossland has the twice weekly thrift store opening.

The next question I'd inevitably get asked by my hitching companion, once it had been ascertained I wasn't a total greenhorn to BC, was whether I preferred Rossland or Fernie. Up until very recently, I'd skirt around the issue. As the question was normally coming from a Rossland local who was giving me a ride home, I didn't want to be doubly rude and entirely spurn their hospitality and goodwill by crying out "Fernie! I far prefer Fernie!" So instead I'd make some wishy-washy answer about it being hard to say, what with it not being a great snow year, Red Mountain not being showcased at its finest etc etc. "But still I prefer Fernie," I'd add *sotto voce*.

Something, however, has changed. And, well, it's a harder

one to call. Whatever about summertime in Fernie, verdant paradise that it is during those months, it now seems far too busy and bustling a place to spend another winter, infested as it is by rich Calgarians and pisshead Australians by turns. "Fernie's changed…" is the refrain we heard all winter long in Rossland, with whispered rumours of lengthened lift-lines and Too Much 'Tude. Given that these rumours were coming entirely from ex-Fernie-ites who've since decamped to Rossland, they were of course entirely partisan and I don't know if there's any truth in them or not.

Equally, I don't want to get into the whole Deliberate Obscurist thing and claim some sort of superiority with Red Mountain: the reasoning being that simply because it's off the beaten track and only REAL skiers know about it, it is therefore a better hill and I am a more authentic and hard-core person for having spent the season there. Fernie, as ski-towns go, has a well deserved reputation. If it's now firmly on the map and its star is on the ascendant – or descendent, depending on what way you look at it – such is the inevitable march of "progress".

Dissing Fernie for being over-developed is not only unfair but also involves doing a 180 on my part given how small and middle-of-nowhere I found it when I went there initially. But everything is relative, right? My first introduction to Canada was landing in Vancouver and spending a few days there before heading for the hills. Vancouver is enviably located on the Pacific Ocean with the mountains in the background, filled with greenery, cultural diversity and it invariably gets voted Best Place to Live in those international indexes of living standards. It doesn't tend to drop much below zero in winter, remarkable by the standards here, so it's relatively green year round, as opposed to the washed out shades of brown and grey of other Canadian cities. Having come straight from dear dirty Dublin, I remember thinking how cool it was as a city, how liveable and how laid back. Fast-forward to ten months later, when I arrived back in Vancouver from Fernie for my onward flight home. I couldn't cope and just thought how stand-offish and image-oriented and preoccupied with worldly goods it all seemed. And I pined for Fernie. I remember walking around downtown Vancouver in the late August afternoon sun, wishing I was back wandering barefoot through Fernie's dusty streets, wearing the one pair of shorts – grown threadbare in the seat from mountain-biking – I'd been wearing for months. Then I knew that I didn't want to go to and start that ill-fated PhD, and I was wondering "what if?" about certain things and, well, it's best really not to dwell too much on matters past isn't it.

And d'ya know somethin' else, for a ski-holiday I think I'd send people to Fernie over Rossland because there's feck all else to see and do in Rossland to be fair. Also partly because I want to keep it to myself and those in the know. So stay away from Red Mountain with its ancient creaking chairlifts, its terrible grooming, its terrifyingly steep terrain! Go to Fernie! You'll have a much better time! Shoo! Nothing for you to see here in Rossland!

T.I.R., baby.

Lisa

April 2009: Rake that shit out!

Meanwhile, back on the ski-hill...

Volly work, aka The Chaingang, continues to the last. I've hauled B-netting and bamboo fencing until my biceps ache. Will this manual labour never stop? It feels as if I'm trapped in some sort of bizarre snowsports related P.O.W. camp where we're routinely put to work on whatever gargantuan task was going. *Bridge on the River Kwai*, Rossland-style.

Even when I'm not scheduled to be hard grafting, I end up doing it all the same. One day I was rostered to man the registration desk, taking race fees from the young hopefuls. Nice, I thought, a cushy job at last after God knows how many hours putting up fences. But no. I ended up, yes you've guessed it, carrying B-netting back and forth to the race shack instead. Another day I was nabbed in the Daylodge and "asked" with a steely glint to do some shovelling because one of the other volunteers hadn't turned up. I didn't even bother trying to object about being conscripted like this, so resigned have I become to the fact that anything can and does happen here. T.I.R. after all.

The continued hell of gate-judging has been enough to send some people over the edge. One guy, Tom, broke his collarbone but that still wasn't enough to get him out of it. Broken collarbone? Pah! Your legs still work don't they? So, arm in sling, off to gate-judge with him. If swine flu had hit Rossland over the winter I'm equally sure we'd all still have been put to work in between bouts of vomiting and fits of shivering. It's debatable as to whether Tom was tired, zonked on his meds or simply stoned out of his head but while supposed to be attentively watching the course, he fell asleep in the camping chair he'd brought up with him. "Could somebody please wake up the young man in Section Three?" came the crackly radioed command from the top. "We really need the gate judges to be a bit more responsive." Duly awoken, Tom later on dropped his radio in a snow-bank, half-heartedly looked for it for a minute, then skied off, his parting comment being, "Oh well, it'll melt out in the spring," leaving twelve hundred dollars worth of lost telecommunications equipment and an incredulous Race Chief behind.

Our apathy knows no bounds. As well as gate-judging, we're also responsible, in theory, for basic course maintenance, raking out the berms and corners when things got a bit cut up. Whatever. Having just skied a practice run down the course and finding it less than optimal, one of the competitors – "the athletes" – then spent a chair-lift ride back up shouting "Rake that shit out! Rake that shit out!" at us repeatedly. I stared at him blankly, my arms hanging by my side. Hamish continued playing solitaire on his iPod. Alan stayed lying back on the snow, eyes closed. The rakes lay abandoned on the ground. We couldn't have cared less. After one event one of the organisers was heard to mutter bitterly, "They're only in it for the free ski-pass." That's about the sum of it.

Even after ski-racing wound down for the season it goes on. A particularly unlucky contingent of Team Volly crew spent one thankless day hacking at ice and shovelling snow to dig the Start Gate out. The following day another group of us were sent up with wrenches and spanners to dismantle it, then sling those large and unwieldy parts of metal over our shoulders to ski them down to the maintenance shack. I have come to loathe and despise ski-racing with a zeal I never thought possible.

Ah volly work, the work I love to hate.

Not only have I been contending with the gruelling slog of volly work but waitressing has also been proving... challenging. I know it's a given to complain that your boss is mad but really, I think mine is suffering from a mild form of psychosis. No seriously. I looked up "psychosis" on the Internet, which is of course where you should always turn for medical diagnoses, and it was defined as a condition whereby "thought and emotions are impaired so contact is lost with outside reality." That sounds like a pretty apt summation of my boss. Her patterns of thought and decisions certainly don't follow what might be defined as normal channels and her reputation precedes her around town; when people hear who I worked for they ask "How do you like working there?!" "It's fine," I say, toeing the party line, but really meaning, "It's a complete nightmare."

But it isn't always so, you see, which is the tricky bit. As well as picking on staff members in some sort of chilling cat-and-mouse game, seeing how far she can push us before we snap, at other times she can be extremely friendly and generous, free drinks all round, lending out her corporate ski-pass for my visiting friends to use. It's sort of like working for Stalin, minus the bushy moustache. Who by all accounts was extremely personable when not carrying out paranoid purges.

Our own Night of the Long Knives (sorry, I know I'm conflating my totalitarian dictators here) came one Saturday night when, in the middle of service, boss-lady took exception to the other waitress and sent her home on the spot, leaving me alone in a fully booked restaurant to deal with the fray. I placed an SOS call to my housemates saying one of you needs to come up here right now to give me a hand, any of you, even Grant, our flannel-shirt clad Australian landlord living in the basement if he's the only one available. My voice was getting so stressed and shrill that soon only dogs or dolphins were going to be able to understand me, so luckily Kris came up and saved the day.

There was absolutely nothing you could do about such situations. I explained to my housemates that one peep of complaint and you were gone, labour laws bedamned. We had quite the staff turnover rate. Why have I stayed there for the whole winter? Because of the money, because of the money. It really was too good to walk away from. And indeed, I'm not walking away from it. I'm driving away from it now at the end of season in my brand-new second hand truck, bought and insured out of my tips. I can see why people fall into serving as a long-term career in North America. The money is sort of addictive. Which is probably why career criminals stay in the game as well.

Yes! A truck! My first vehicle! Now I need to clarify; it's not actually a flat-bed ute. More of a jeep-style affair, a 1991 Isuzu Trooper. But it just gets referred to as a truck out here. My heart swells with something akin to parental pride when I look at it and, like the parent of a newborn infant, I keep staring at it in rapt wonder and besotted joy, not quite able to believe that it's there and it's mine. It's a truck! And it's mine! Look at it! A truck! Then I wander away, only to be found gazing out the window again five minutes later with a soppy smile. You know the way people get so silly over babies, enthralled by little details like their eyelashes or fingernails? I've equally been going all gooey, oohing and aahing over the truck's bull bar or its barn doors or its fold down seats.

Also, like a first-time parent, I keep wanting to take photos of it the whole time to capture each developmental milestone as we bond. Here it is parked in the drive. And here it is after our first road trip together. And here it is getting its coolant topped up.

You see, for me the truck holds quite a bit of symbolic worth. (Dear God, I haven't become one of those awful people who looks upon their vehicle as a status symbol, have I?) Of what? Of having to go back to Ireland two years ago when it was the last thing in the world I wanted to do. But I did it, putting my head down, living off a shoe-string, saving all my money, getting innumerable driving lessons, taking my test, eh, several times, keeping faith and telling myself, "Someday, someday." I was determined to get my full licence, go back to Canada (legally) and buy a truck. And now it's come to pass!

There were a few raised eyebrows around Rossland

though. You bought a truck? By yourself? The inference being that I should co-own it with a man. Humph! (Also perhaps, why on earth did I shell out for a vehicle with 4WD, just how much off-roading am I planning on doing this summer?) But that said, I have actually been relying on the various transient males in my life to guide me through things like how to check the oil or how to change over to summer tyres. When I was looking for a vehicle to buy, the consensus among my housemates was that you need your dad to go along and have a look so you don't get swizzed. My dad, however, was 6000km away and despite repeated invitations and invectives refused to get on a long-haul flight to come visit, so I was on my own for that one.

Yes, between basic car maintenance, putting up fences, minor plumbing emergencies and whatnot, practical skills have been of prime importance over the past year. And never before have I felt like such a silly and ignorant girl. Really though, being not manually inclined never seemed to place me at any specific disadvantage prior to this, be that studying English literature, rarified realm of the intellect that it was, or working in administration. I was thinking about this recently: in my job in Dublin if we even had to carry a heavy box of files to the lift we could call upon Karl, the porter, to give us a hand. Then you get out here and you're given a load which, eyes bulging, arteries in your neck straining, you have to ski down an icy race course. But you know something, inept as I may be, I still think I prefer it out here in the world of disorder and misrule and engine oil.

Lisa

April 2009: By the Rivers of Canmore

In which the ski-season comes to end but the adventures continue to segue one into another...

You know, we don't have properly defined seasons as such in Ireland, they tend to merge into each other differentiated only by the degree of sogginess. So the arrival of spring isn't exactly identifiable as a distinct event. There's no particular moment where you think "thank God!" the harsh winter is no more and you can go outside without being swaddled in toque, mitts and five layers of fleece. (Though if you've been doing a ski-season, your thoughts are more along the lines of "Shit, what now?") My mother mentioned on the phone that the first of the spring flowers came up back home at the start of February. I stared out the window at the three feet of snow in our front-yard, the mercury hovering around the minus ten mark. "I think we have a while to go yet here," I said.

The first official day of spring, if we're going to bide by the Spring Equinox, is 21 March and it arrived in Rossland right on cue. Outside started the drip, drip, dripping of snow melting off the roof. This continued in a constant stream for about two weeks so that every time you went in or out our front door you got an impromptu shower down your back.

And with the melting of the snow comes the end of skiing. Red Mountain's season finished in brilliant sunshine the first weekend in April. It was just your average ski-hill closing weekend: hitting on ski-patrollers; drinking white wine and smoking substances unknown on a dodgy stomach and Kris having to take me home so I could pass out on the bathroom floor (haven't pulled that particular stunt since I was about eighteen); Ellie dressing up as Spiderman in six-year old boy's Spiderman pyjamas; the pair of us dancing on tables in the local sushi bar; wearing a trailer-park blonde wig, flannel shirt and dungarees for the last day on the hill; my boss, erratic to the end, offering me a job for the summer one day and rescinding the offer the next; tinting the milk with red food dye just because and Jaimie (the Kiwi in the living room) getting pissed off because she said she didn't want to have to eat pink porridge. Maybe we needed to expunge any remaining eccentricities from our systems before leaving Rossland.

The end of a ski-season can be traumatic at the best of times – I've touched on post-season blues before. For four months snowsports have been your constant companion and mainstay, structured your daily routine, filled your thoughts, guided your decisions, given you focus, made you smile, made you scowl and then all of a sudden – pop! No more. It's like ending a relationship, leaving you emotionally overwrought and wobbly and lost.

Furthermore, this winter I had matters on my mind above and beyond the normal concerns such as, "Will this be an epic pow season?" or "Does he fancy me or what?" (The answer, by the way, in both cases turned out to be "no".) The season's antics and amusements were founded on an undercurrent of restlessness, wondering and pondering. I won't go into the minutiae and variances of Canadian immigration law but unless I either marry a local boy pronto or pick up a trade like pipe-fitting or welding it's unlikely I'm going to be able to stay here past November when my work visa expires. Which makes me very, very sad.

(Note: I know that I'm Living the Dream but it's not always a carefree romp.)

So distracted was I by dwelling on The Future that I sometimes found myself having such heretical thoughts as "It's only skiing" (I didn't really mean it). On occasion I became incredibly demoralised and stopped trying, even powder days failing to rouse me from the muggy fog. The irony was, after all the time spent mulling thus all winter long, I still had no plan whatsoever by the end. The vague idea had been to load up the truck and drive the four hundred kilometres over to Fernie for the summer but then for some reason, despite having spent the best part of two years pining after Fernie, I baulked at the last minute. So rather than heading to Fernie by myself – where, really, solitude could have propelled me into a spectacular meltdown, only to be found three days later dancing naked around the forest, babbling in tongues – I was instead talked into detouring up to Banff and Canmore for the weekend with Ellie. Safety in numbers and all that.

We had entirely different reasons for going there. Ellie was meeting up with some friends to keep skiing for a few last days before she headed back to Blighty, but I was skied out by that stage. But remember Lindsay and Chucky, who featured so prominently in the series of emails from New Zealand? Now living in Calgary while Lindsay finishes university, they too were heading to Canmore for the weekend. How's that for narrative continuity? Anyway, they had An Announcement. Having hooked up drunkenly in Fernie three years ago, they're now engaged and getting married in September! Romance lives on and ski-bum dreams can come true!

You may be wondering if Banff is as spectacular as its reputation would dictate. Yes, it is beautiful but early spring is a scrubby sort of time to be in the mountains. The snow has melted and the earth is still parched and brown. Also, I was too preoccupied to care. What's that biblical psalm turned Boney M song – by rivers of Babylon I sat down and wept? Well, on Easter Sunday by the river in Canmore I sat down and didn't exactly weep but, after gentle questioning from Lindsay, admitted that I just didn't know where I was going. Starting with where I was sleeping that night, for example. Was I precariously close to becoming one of those lost souls who end up living out of their car? It's better to have some sort of plan, ANY sort of plan, for after a ski-season rather than nose diving into the abyss like this.

If they ever make a film of my life, the tag-line could be "She lost the plot but found herself."

Lisa

Here, There and Everywhere

April 2009: *La Belle Province*

Me again

Rather than sitting by the stream indefinitely until I reached enlightenment (the Rockies in April are too cold for that sort of self-indulgence) I went down to Calgary with Lindsay and Chucky and spent a few days on the internet trying to come up with a Life Direction. What I'm going to do next in the short term, you see, is largely determined by in the long term. In other words, if I'm going to head back to Rossland to do another ski-season next winter I'd like to spend the next few months doing something vaguely responsible, earning a regular wage, perhaps even taking an evening course. You know, self-actualisation, personal development, that sort of thing. If, on the other hand, after this allotted year in Canada I'm turning my back on peripatetic wandering then I might as well stay with the live-for-the-moment-let-it-all-hang-out vibe for another while. Given that I don't have a clue what I'm doing come November, depending entirely as this does on whims and variances of

Citizenship and Immigration Canada, this reasoning proved somewhat of a dead end. So stay in Calgary? Head to Fernie as planned? Go back to Rossland? Even randomly put the foot down on the gas-pedal and roar away on a cross-continental road trip to Montreal (pronounced Mawh-ray-AL if we're going to get all French-Canadian about it)?

For years, you see, I've had a hankering to get to Quebec. This fascination with Quebec arose because my first few experiences abroad consisted of working in Switzerland for three summers whilst at college. And somehow travelling and snowboarding and living in the mountains became enmeshed in my mind with doing it all through French. (My first thoughts upon reaching BC were how easy it was doing this living and working abroad thing through English.) Another reason I've become so curious about the place over the years is that, although I'm not prone to generalisations, I'm yet to meet a French-Canadian who wasn't slightly unhinged. I wanted to see if this was only the case with the ones who made it out west to ski-towns or whether it was a more general population trait. (I recently found out that half a million Québécois claim Irish ancestry which may go some small part towards explaining their crazy-eyed, hard-drinking demeanour.)

However, adventure as it would be, I was reluctant to drive four thousand kilometres across Canada on a whim. So I had a thought. Why not leave the truck in Calgary and check to see if there were any last minute deals on flights? Go on a bit of a holiday. Rejuvenate. Cheap flights there indeed were so I booked a return Calgary-Montreal flight giving me a week to explore *La Belle Province*.

Off I headed with my backpack the next day. I didn't take too much with me at all: a pair of jeans, two flannel shirts – what can I say, I've spent a lot of time in the Kootenays by this stage – and my running gear in case I wanted to go for a jog while I was there. (Take note of this, it becomes significant later on.) It was a novelty to travel with a manageable amount of luggage rather than buckling under the strain of various sporting goods. Travelling with a snowboard bag, for example, is like lugging a coffin around and only slightly less conspicuous.

It was equally novel to be visiting a city in and of itself, rather than simply en route to a ski-town. You see, urban Canada has always seemed something of an anomaly to me. I could never understand when people in college would get a Work Canada visa and then spend the summer in, say, Toronto. Surely the whole point of coming to Canada is to experience the wide open spaces? The grandeur of the mountains? To head off into the wild?

Equally, until I came to North America I never really got it when people would harp on about how "cultured" Europe was, not seeing anything remarkable in having cathedrals and medieval walls and, well, old things every-where. Here, however, I've seen here the streets are laid out thwack thwack thwack on a grid system rather than developing and meandering over time and there are an awful lot of ugly, mall-ridden, highway-strip towns scattered through Canada – Trail, Creston and Cranbrook are just three examples off the top of my head.

So having decried cities and sung the virtues of the land for so long, my only thoughts on Montreal were: what a cool place! (Has the time come for me, like John the Baptist, to re-emerge from the wilderness?) Without resorting to guidebook-like clichés, it really does have the best of both worlds, North American dynamism spliced with European *joie de vivre* and good food. Bilingual, multicultural, new and old and bustling! What's more, springtime is the perfect time for a visit. I find it terribly depressing to be in the city on a summer's day when it's hot, dirty and noisy, everyone huddled onto tiny patches of grass in their office clothes. Likewise, in winter you have to deal with snow and cold and dirty slush without getting any of the benefits of the same, i.e., snowsports, but spring brings with it no such climatic constraints.

I had no particular itinerary for my time in Montreal: just wander around, see the sights, go to cafés (I always get this idea that I'll immerse myself in café-culture before remembering that not only do I not actually like coffee, I'm also too self-conscious to go linger by myself over a latte all day long), soak up *la francophonie*.

Canada is a bilingual nation, French having as much official import as English, but in BC you don't tend to see this in practice beyond the fact that food packaging is legally obliged to be in both languages. (That said, even Rossland, miniscule as it was, has both English and French-speaking primary schools because it's your right as a francophone for your progeny to receive their education in French if there are enough of your ilk around.) So I sort of assumed the situation in Canada was like it is in Ireland, where English and Irish are both official languages, but despite the small communities clinging to the western seaboard and the quasi-fascist *Gaelagoirí*, really, outside of government communications and TG4, Irish is not really in widespread use. I don't want an angry mob coming after me with their hurleys telling me how their granny spoke Irish every day of her life, Lord rest her soul, blah blah blah by the way. The exception only serves to prove the rule. I figured nobody actually went about their daily business in French over here or anything.

How wrong was I.

I then met many French-Canadians whose whole lives had been entirely in French, at home, in school, the television they watched. To whom English was a thoroughly alien tongue. One girl I know only picked it up when she went abroad to Australia for a year. These people were as franco-phone as anyone from Poitiers or Nice.

And determined to remain so. While, as I said, at the federal level Canada is bilingual, there's a great deal of autonomy at the provincial level and the only officially bilingual province is, interestingly, New Brunswick. The other provinces have English as their official tongue except Quebec where, French and French alone rules the day. Unlike the other provinces Quebec also has control over its own immigration channels. As far as I can tell, the main criterion for being accepted as an immigrant to Quebec is speaking French and committing to continuing to do so, including sending any current or future progeny to French speaking schools.

Despite coming from a country with our own particular separatist debates, I certainly can't pretend to have reached any sort of insight or understanding into the Quebec separatist situation after so brief a stay, but in I did notice that the adjective "national" when used there referred not to things Canadian but to things Québécois; e.g. *la fête nationale, la bibliothèque nationale.*

Montreal has the greatest anglophone presence in all Quebec so it was interesting to see (and hear) how French and English played off each other around the city, being greeted with *bonjour*-hello. As opposed to the dead-eyed apathy and general low-ebb I'd been sent into since the end of the season, I was enthused and invigorated by this complete change of environment, possibly in fact verging on mania. Overexcitable! Surviving on scant food and sleep! Believing myself capable of prodigious feats! Which may explain what happened next.

Lisa

April 2009: Montreal Half Marathon

Comrades.

First off, it may sound counter-instinctive but skiing doesn't necessarily get you fit. Taking the chairlift up and then simply swoosh-swoosh-swooshing down the corduroy groomers may lead to strong legs – witness my grossly over-developed quads – but aerobic exercise it is not. Skiing off-piste is a bit more of a workout though, particularly if you've had to hike for your turns. You have to work hard to make it through the moguls and chop – those hot squirts of lactic pain! Luckily the pow is worth it.

Also ski-seasons are so busy – if you're working that is, and not merrily cruising along on E.I. – that routine goes out the window and you guzzle sugar and caffeine just to keep going. Couple this with the raucous drinking that's an almost inevitable part of ski-seasons and it's not surprising how many people come out of winter huffing, puffing and ten pounds heavier than before.

When I went back to Ireland for a year I got into running, initially to maintain some vestige of base fitness for when I would return to the hills. I somehow started enjoying it on its own terms rather than it simply being a means to an end. Though I kept running in NZ, the skiing there being far from all-consuming, once back in Canada this winter running took a back seat. It's not that I'm a fair-weather runner as such, having started training for my first half marathon last January in Dublin. Which was dark, damp, windy and miserable. I'm just not equally enthused about running in subzero climes, wuss that this might make me. Apparently dealing with the snow and ice involves faffing around with plastic bags over your socks to keep your feet dry and hammering crampon-like spikes into your soles to get some grip. Frankly if there's enough snow to ski, I'd rather go shred. As I've said before, to everything its season. And winter is the season for, eh, winter sports.

But now that the winter was over it was back to business. So when I was in Montreal I wondered if there were any five kilometre or ten kilometre events on that weekend, not to go out and set a PB, just to ease myself back into training. But no, nothing of that length taking place. There, was, however the *Demi-Marathon de Montréal* the following day. A half-marathon. Hmm. Hmm again. Could I? You know, just to see? No! That would be crazy! But, well just to give it a go? Mmm...well it would be interesting to see what toll the winter had taken. Oh I don't know...Go on! Why not? Oh fuck it then the worst that can happen is I'll throw up and pass out. Right! Where do I sign up?

So I decided to run the Montreal Half Marathon with a day's notice. *Mon dieu!* I was accused of being flighty recently. Which is funny because on an everyday basis I'm not. I'm far too responsible and serious for my own good. But when it comes to major decisions like whether to drop out of college or buy a vehicle or hare off across the continent by myself or enter distance races on a whim then yes, perhaps I am given to seemingly insane moves. I like to play it safe on the small scale and gamble on the big one.

Far from following any carefully calibrated nutritional plan, I'd been eating exactly what I wanted all winter long with gay abandon; spoonfuls of peanut butter straight from the jar, loaves and loaves of homemade bread and obtaining a sizeable quotient of my calorific needs from licking the spoon when making cakes. (We got through this winter, among other things: 25 kg of white flour, 10 kg of wholemeal, a jar of yeast, a pound of baking powder and two pints of molasses. A household of hungry skiers can really pack it away.)

As for the crucial few weeks immediately before the race? Rather than avoiding alcohol altogether, as might be advisable, I'd been coping with particularly stressful nights in the restaurant by shotgunning the spirits at the end of my shift. Amaretto? Down the hatch! Van Gogh espresso-flavoured vodka? I'll give it a go! Left over coffee in the pot? Better mix it with some Bailey's so!

But anyone who brings their running tights and Asics on a week's backpacking trip isn't a total *ingénue* and it's not as if I'd been leading a sedentary lifestyle. For the previous four months I'd skied most days at a gnarly, gnarly mountain, made occasionally trips to the swimming pool, had gone for some sporadic runs and had even put in some treadmill sessions at the gym. These exertions may have come under the category "Damage Limitation" rather than comprising a concerted training regime but, I figured, it was better that nothing. Besides, getting through a ski-season alive is a good exercise in endurance in itself.

The following morning, chilly and crisp and bright, I took the Metro out to the starting line in Parc Jean-Drapeau with my sinewy, lyrca-clad brethren. I was beaming away like a loon thinking "God! This is mad, isn't it?!" and the actual bit about having to run twenty-one kilometres never really registered.

Off went the gun and off went we.

It was a great day. The course was extremely flat compared to the half-marathons I've run before – the first half-marathon I ran was in Connemara and contained a section known as "The Hell of the West", a two-mile uphill incline from Mile Nine onwards where, alas, one brave soul met his maker and returned to the great running track in the sky the year before I took part. Also helping in Montreal were the copious number of aid stations, water and Gatorade to hand every few miles. A golden rule of racing is never try anything on race-day that you haven't already tried in training. That I'd never drunk Gatorade before didn't, of course, stop me now from grabbing it at every opportunity. When you've come this far in How Not to Train for a Half Marathon 101, why stop?

I don't normally rely on my iPod in races because, if I'm going to be completely honest, I like eavesdropping in on other runners' conversations. But that day I figured I could use whatever help I could get. So what did I listen to to keep me pumped? The entirety of Handel's *Messiah*, all three choral acts (skipping over the slower and more boring solos though), followed by the "Theme from Rawhide" over and over again for the last few kilometres. *Chacun à son goût.*

Having invested neither time nor emotional energy in training, I put absolutely no pressure on myself. I wasn't trying to beat any particular time and trotted along at what seemed like a snail's pace. Everyone else was glancing at their watches and grimacing. I was having a grand old time of it, checking out the scenery, singing away to myself, and even high-fiving one of the race marshals along the way. Distance running is like taking a long-haul flight: you have to accept that you're going to be there for a very long time, and asking "is it nearly over yet?" really doesn't help. The only slight pressure came from the fact that the course would close after three hours which, as half-marathons tend to go, is a fairly slim margin. It later transpired that the Montreal Half Marathon attracts a particularly elite crowd – today, I thought, I ran with the Kenyans – and in fact also doubles up as the 2009 Canadian Half-Marathon Championship. Oops!

Many, many things can go wrong when you're in a race; stitches, cramps, dehydration, needing to poo, just a general feeling that your legs are on a go-slow and every step is an effort. I was lucky in that everything went well in Montreal, one of those Bonus Days that seems to be a gift from the gods. (Or as Del Boy used to say in *Only Fools and Horses*, "He who dares, Rodney, he who dares.")

Rallied along by the crowd with their ding-ding cow bells and their various encouraging shouts of "*Allez allez!* Let's go, let's go! Bravo! *Bouge, bouge!*" I crossed the finish line still grinning like an idiot only two minutes slower than the Auckland Half Marathon for which I'd trained for months. Hmm.

And having been immortalised in the race results as "Lisa McGarigle" (who's she?) of Rossland BC, that was that.

Lisa

April 2009: Peanut Butter and Ottawa

Dia dhaoibh aris

So at the end of the last email, I'd just belted across the finish line in the Montreal Half Marathon. A quick recap: my training for this event had fallen somewhere between the markers of "sporadic" and "non-existent". And while the run itself went absolutely fine, the post-race recovery period wasn't similarly so sprightly.

I never know how seriously to take the advice offered in running magazines and websites and the like. It seems to be aimed at serious "multi-sport athletes" – a phrase which makes me snigger in its humourless self-estimation – rather than "steady plodders" like myself. Anyway, apparently after a hard run there's a short window of opportunity during which you should refuel with a specific ratio of protein and carbohydrate. After an event like a half-marathon, my face cracks with dried salty sweat and I want to throw up. The thought of forcing down solid food is about as appetising a prospect as stuffing a hand-towel into my mouth. Having no doubt anticipated this, those in the know suggest chocolate milk as the optimal post-run snack.

Nonetheless, I've been variously a student and ski-bum

for so long at this stage that the hunter-gatherer instinct in me is particularly keen: if there's free food to be had I'll pounce and forage as much as I can. At the end of the Half Marathon, despite the thought of eating anything being absolutely anathema, I automatically queued up for the free carb-heavy foodstuffs – bagels, bananas, muesli bars – they tend to hand out after races, I suppose to reduce the chances of participants keeling over in their droves. So I grabbed two bagels, a banana and countless bottles of water and ate one of the dry bagels mechanically and without relish. Ugh.

Then I got the Metro back to the hostel I'd been staying in. Lunchtime! But what to eat?

A note here on peanut butter: peanut butter is a peculiarly North American persuasion. In Ireland you might find a token jar or two of it in the jam aisle but it's nothing to write home about. (Though hang on, that's exactly what I'm doing right now. That's the trouble with clichés – they divert meaning all over the place.) Over here in Canada, however, entire sections in the supermarket are devoted to the stuff in its many varieties. My favourite type is natural peanut butter which has neither added sugar nor salt and is satisfyingly gritty. No – "gritty" makes it sound like it's been scooped up from a driveway, embedded with bits of gravel. I mean it's slightly granular in texture compared to the curiously repulsive whipped smoothness of other types.

Since coming to Canada, peanut butter has become one of my favourite foods. It's 50% fat which, if you're a cash-strapped ski-bum – I'm time rich, money poor – is an excellent price-calorie trade off. Not to mention being filled with protein. If you have a jar of PB to hand, you're only a slice of bread away from a balanced meal. Indeed, the UN uses a fortified peanut butter paste called Plumpy'Nut to treat malnourished children in the developing world, so close is it to the complete food-group.

Where was I going with all this anyway? Oh yes! The night before the Montreal Half I'd bought a jar of peanut butter, a multi-pack of bagels and a bunch of bananas. (You've a fine bunch of bananas there missus.) Not only has peanut butter become one of my staple foods, but the night before the Connemarathon last year, my first half-marathon, I was staying in a B&B in Oughterard where dinner options were limited indeed. So I rustled up a tasty peanut butter and banana sandwich to fuel me through the day ahead. Though I don't really observe any pre-race superstitions such as always wearing the same pair of lucky socks (though come to think of it, I *do* always wear the same running socks ones by default because until very recently I only had the one pair, bought in Lidl last year) this tradition has remained. Hence in Montreal it was the classic PB and banana combo for dinner. Ditto for race-day breakfast, along with a bowl of porridge. Now at lunchtime, using the goods to hand, same again. Devoted as I am to peanut butter, if you're exhausted and dehydrated, it's not the easiest thing to digest in large quantities, dry clagging stuff that it can be. I was starting to feel a bit peculiar.

Growing progressively queasier, I rang Aongus McGreal from Co. Roscommon. He doesn't live in Roscommon anymore though, he lives in Ottawa, two hundred and fifty kilometres west of Montreal.

Aongus and I met when we were both spending the ski-season in Wanaka, New Zealand, last year. Though we're both serial expatriates at this stage, having someone around from the same cultural frame of reference was great. He's a teacher-man and one night we sat cross-legged with an atlas testing each other's primary school geography.

"Which river goes through Waterford?"

"The Suir!"

"What's the name of the island in Clew Bay in Co. Mayo?"

"Em…"

"I'll give you a hint, the Saw Doctors did a song about it. Will you meet me on…"

"Electric Avenue?"

"No. Clare Island."

"Here, give us that atlas. Name the island off the east coast of Ireland which – "

"Britain!"

Anyway, last October Aongus moved to Ottawa, saying there was always an open invitation to come stay should I find myself in that part of the country. (Don't ever tell me that I'm welcome in Sydney or Vancouver or deepest darkest Peru if I'm ever passing through because before too long I'm guaranteed to be on your doorstep with a backpack full of stinky sportsgear.)

I rang him from Montreal to see if the invitation still stood and he assured me I was more than welcome to go over to Ottawa for a few days. So, stomach heaving, I hoisted on my backpack and headed to get the Greyhound. My legs were also starting to seize up at this stage, I grimaced every time I had to go up and down stairs, clutching at the handrails like a geriatric.

A few hours, dull and woolly-headed, I hobbled up to Aongus in Ottawa Greyhound Station – "Howiya McGreal". I was welcomed with *cead mile failte* and back with us to *Tigh* Aongus. Are you hungry, I was asked. Not a biteen, said I, but that's probably only because I'm too tired to register much. (Also still queasy from OD-ing on peanut butter.) Hang on a second so, says Aongus, and disappears off into the kitchen in the spirit of Irish hospitality. Back he arrives a few minutes with, you've guessed it, peanut butter bagel Number Five since the night before.

Shortly afterwards I went to bed, very very tired and not feeling very well at all.

The next day Aongus gave me the walking tour of Ottawa. As in, he strode on ahead while I brought up the rear with a stilted, wooden gait. BC is run by hippies and foresters, while Calgary is the Dallas of the North, a city of oil-prospectors and cowboys: something you're not really aware of out west is that Canada remains part of the Commonwealth, subject to the English throne. But in Ottawa, seat of Canadian parliament, it's apparent how it's still very much bound by dominion status.

The parliament buildings are a replica of Westminster, for a start. I went on a free tour of them and the tour guide explained how the Queen is the head of state and the Governor General her representative on Canadian soil. I booed under my breath. Down with that sort of thing. Call it atavistic prejudice, call it youthful indoctrination, but I simply can't understand why a country wouldn't want to sever the ties from their former colonial master and become a republic. Simply can't understand it.

Aongus may now be a Canadian permanent resident but to become a citizen and obtain voting rights he'd have had to take an oath of allegiance to the Queen. The man from Roscommon, he says no. He'd rather be permanently disenfranchised than take any such oath. Although I'm the last person in the world to buy into myths about romantic Ireland and harp on dead martyrs dying for the cause – I'd just watched *The Wind That Shakes the Barley*, a good illustration of the trouble you can get into being too hard-line over that sort of thing – I can see his point. Something at a visceral level rankles at the idea of being in thrall to the British monarch even if it is only words, words, words.

Grappling with such weighty national issues, Aongus and I continued our tour of Ottawa. Outside parliament a throng of teenagers and assorted youths were gathered on the green smoking spliffs, one young fella even toting an enormous bong. Would you get a load of that? Even though there's a fairly liberal attitude taken towards weed in Canada, I was still surprised to see so many people toking away on Parliament Hill in full view of the police. Aongus also noted how many of the kids were waving Jamaican flags and wearing rasta hats. Considering a Canadian plane had been hijacked in Jamaica that week, it seemed an unusual way of pledging solidarity to one's countrymen.

Aha! Eventually we realised it was April 20, 4/20, a day of pot-smoking celebration and campaigning for legalisation the world over. Given that the median age of the crowd in Ottawa was about sixteen, I don't know how committed a group of social revolutionaries they were. Nor were they even a particularly hardcore cohort of smokers. An audio recording would have captured panasonic coughing and hawking from all directions, the sound of virgin lungs unaccustomed to such poisons and pollutants. I think they were getting the bigger high from how devilishly daring they thought it was to smoke weed outside parliament, defying the heavy hand of the law. The bystanding police meanwhile, were jocular and indulgent, smiling away in amused indifference, letting them puff away with not an intention in the world of intervening. Maybe on a different day they would have taken a harder line, but on 4/20 such folly is par for the course. God bless the innocence of youth.

Abhaile linn to Aongus's house, where we got our reciprocal fill of Irishness, drinking Barry's Tea, watching the DVD set of *In the Name of Fada* (about Des Bishop in the Connemara Gaeltacht), and employing ridiculous sayings that no one under the age of fifty even uses anymore. I said something about needing more time to explore Quebec properly. "Well now," said Aongus, "the man who made time made plenty of it." "Indeed and he did," I replied.

Since November I've visited Vancouver, Calgary,

Ottawa and Montreal, in addition to having spent the winter in Rossland of course. Something I've been wondering through all this is how does Canada *work*? From expensive outdoor-gear Vancouver to the hippie West Kootenays to the redneck hicksville of Alberta, not to mention Ontario and Quebec, it's just so enormous and diverse. And I haven't even made it to the Maritimes or up north yet. I spent the following day in the Museum of Canadian Civilisation pursuing an answer, only to come up with more questions still.

Thus dwelling on Canadian multiplicity, I flew back to Calgary on April 22, where it was minus four and snowing heavily. For the first time in my life I groaned at the falling snow. Once you're no longer living in a ski-town you take an entirely different approach to winter, one of when's-it-ever-going-to-end, rather than oh-goody-more-snow. Would spring ever come to Cowtown?

Lisa

May 2009: Living in Cowtown

Hi everyone

When I was in the Museum of Canadian Civilisation on my jaunt to Quebec, there was an interactive touch-screen display: "Which Canadian Historical Figure are You?", the first question being "What season were you born in?" I hesitated. Was this a trick question to weed out non-Canadians? A recap of the seasons as we learned them in school in Ireland (being the progeny of a Montessori teacher, I stand on solid ground when it comes to days of the week, seasons of the year, letters of the alphabet, that sort of thing): Autumn – August, September, October; Winter – November, December, January; Spring – February, March, April; Summer – May, June, July.

It would be ludicrous, however, to even pretend that there are four seasons of equal length in Canada. Winter drags on for a disproportionately long time – the running gag is that there are two seasons: winter and construction. A famous Québécois song starts *"Mon pays ce n'est pas un pays, c'est l'hiver"* (my country isn't a country, it's winter). Indeed, Canada *is* its winter, sort of, given how dramatically winter structures daily life, be that shovelling your drive, plugging your car in to stop the battery going dead, leaving a tap slightly running overnight so that pipes don't freeze and burst not to mention simply learning how to dress for those days and weeks when it plummets to minus thirty. There's ground snow from October to April as standard, but snow can and does fall at any time of the year. I'd been drafting an email about the arrival of warmer weather when I got caught in a snowstorm on 5 June.

Likewise, my birthday is 8 May which by Irish standards means I was born in summer, such as it is in our soggy land. Summer most definitely does not start in Canada in early May. On the May Bank Holiday weekend we went out for a bracing round of frisbee golf in the snow and hail. Frisbee golf is a North American thing – take the basic concept of golf but with frisbees instead of balls and enclosed basketball net type targets in place of holes. It's not just a novelty pursuit, by the way, but just as you have different irons or clubs or whatever they're called for regular golf to optimise your game, so too for frisbee golf are there discs of various weights and radii. (I could have just said "width" but I love obscure Latinate plurals; radius, radii; alumnus, alumni; stadium, stadia.) There are even professional frisbee golf players who make their living from it. Anyway, as we trudged around the frisbee golf course, we were Determined to Enjoy the Bank Holiday so doggedly played on in the driving wind, bundled up in down jackets and toques.

How the school year is divided in Canada is a bit of a hint as to the climate, I suppose – there's the Fall Semester from September to Christmas, the Winter Semester from January to April and the Spring Semester from May till the end of June. There is, you will note, no mention of summer; telling nomenclature indeed.

It's not that Canada is a frozen wasteland year round. Summer here is beautiful. It's just...rather short. Maybe six to eight weeks long and even by August the nights start to get cooler again. I met some people from the Yukon recently. The Yukon skirts the Arctic Circle at its northern-most extremities and gets twenty-four hours of daylight at this time of year. They were saying how glorious this can be (strange things being done in the midnight sun, whooping it up in the Malamute saloon, that sort of thing) but the flip-side of so northern a latitude is that the Yukon summer is shorter than elsewhere in Canada. Christ, I thought. It's short enough as it is.

That said, Ireland isn't exactly known for its blistering climes so I haven't really got a leg to stand on. Indeed, I'm yearning for sun because it's Been a While. Remember: my Adventures Part I in Canada came to end in April 2007. My work visa had expired, I was in debt etc etc so I went home for a hiatus to turn my personal fortunes around. (Yes children! It's true. For a brief spell in Ireland there were jobs for all.) Summer of that year in Dublin was a non-event and since then I've been chasing the snow from hemisphere to hemisphere, having gone through any number of springs without ever reaching summer. Now that summer and I have finally been reunited, I'm stricken with guilt about staying inside on a sunny day, conditioned by my Irish upbringing to rush outside the door for any brief snatches of warmth that may come my way. Patience, Lisa, Patience.

Oh! I'm living in Calgary now by the way. At an altitude

of 1000m, Calgary is one thousand kilometres from the coast so the air here is largely devoid of moisture: this means that it benefits from a wonderfully dry heat in summer rather than any smothering humidity. Less pleasing is that despite slathering on any amount of lotions and unguents my skin has dried out to a reptilian scaliness.

I suppose I'd better backtrack and explain how I've ended up here away from my natural mountain habitat. After my trip to Quebec, I flew back into Cowtown on April 22, groaning at the snow on the runway and the continued sub-zero climes. I stayed put for a few days and then tootled off in the truck to Fernie, my New Jerusalem.

As I've said before, all winter long in Rossland we'd been hearing rumours of how Fernie had become crassly overdeveloped in the meantime. Arriving back, there *was* an unprecedented number of vehicles and people around. Though the ski-season was finished, I drove up to the ski-hill for the sake of fond nostalgia, only to be similarly met with scaffolding and wooden framing everywhere. What had happened to the so-called recession and what was behind this Fernie mini-boom?

It then transpired that a Hollywood crew was in town making a film called *Hot Tub Time Machine*. Apparently it's about a group of middle-aged guys on a ski-trip who get transported back in time to their 1980s hey-day via their hot tub: I don't think it's going to be the second *Schindler's List* or anything. In any case, it explained both the influx of people into town and the new construction on the ski-hill which, on closer inspection, was in fact only a temporary set of fake building fronts.

Visiting film crews aside, not a great deal happens in Fernie in the interval between the ski-hill closing and the mountain-bike season kicking off in June. I spent two and a half weeks in a state of suspended animation, staying in my friend Darren's house, though Darren himself was back on the farm in Alberta helping out his dad for the spring. I had no phone, no internet, no television and no housemates, and did little but write and write and then write some more in a prodigious spurt of industry.

But after two and a half weeks spent thus it was time, alas, to leave Fernie, time to get a Real Job again for a while. Not that there's anything wrong with ski-bumming – that has, after all, been my *raison d'être* for the past few years. Though bigger than Rossland, Fernie is a small town still (therein lie its charms) and jobs are scant. So leaving my beloved BC behind, back it was across the Albertan border to Calgary, a city of one million people and employment opportunities galore.

As you may have gleaned from some of the emails I've sent over the past three and a half years, I quite like it here in Canada and I'd like to stay for a while longer after my work visa expires in November. The road to residency, however, is byzantine in its complexity. It would probably be easier to become the grandmaster of a Freemason lodge than to navigate through all the bureaucracy. I could hold an entire conversation in acronyms when it comes to immigration paperwork: LMOs, HRSDC, NOC, AINP, CIC. I bore even myself trying to explain what these all stand for and how they're related.

But in short: one potential route through the mire is to secure a permanent, full-time, skilled job (i.e., no more waitressing) and get your employer to lobby on your behalf. My move to Calgary to find such an employer was my last gasp to try to stay in Canada. One successful interview later and I'm now the "Accommodated Exams Co-ordinator" at one of the third-level institutions here. Any students with a registered disability who require particular supports for exams – e.g., extra time, a distraction-free environment, scribes, use of a computer – well I'm yer woman to ask. How strange is life. This is not what I'd envisaged myself doing, living in Calgary of all places, but a permanent position is a potential golden ticket to residency and so here I am.

So, after four winters and two hemispheres of ski-bumming I'm back to a regular, salaried job. The regular hours pose no problem, the salary is obviously quite welcome, but harder to adjust to is the concept of only three weeks annual leave a year. I often think that your salary isn't payment for the actual work you do – it's more like compensation for your lack of liberty. I'll "only" get to ski at weekends next winter, assuming I am in fact still here. Let's see what happens with the paperwork. It could go either way.

As to what Calgary is like? Well, if I met someone else on a year's working holiday visa living here I'd look at them askance – what on earth are you doing? Get out there, see the wilderness! Or alternatively, if the great outdoors isn't your thing and you're determined to pavement-hug, hang out in one of Canada's cooler cities. Like multi-cultural Euro-vibe Montreal. Or Vancouver, groovy right-on enclave that it is. By no means would I recommend that anybody base themselves in Calgary for their Great Canadian Experience. In a previous email I gave vignettes of it as "the Dallas of the North, a city of oil-prospectors and cowboys." Massively spread on a grid system, it's the hub of the Albertan oil industry but apart from a glut of shiny business centres doesn't have a downtown as such, just a seemingly endless parade of shopping malls, parking lots and subdivisions. Not known for its vibrant urban culture, it's stereotyped as brash and rednecky and indeed there's a lot of stone-washed denim and cowboy boots around these parts. They play both kinds of music here – country AND western. And you're nobody in Alberta if you don't own a Ford F-150.

Maybe there's no downtown in Calgary because at weekends, rather than flocking into the city centre, everyone flees for the hills. Calgary's proximity to the mountains redeems it considerably. Banff and Canmore are a mere hour away while slightly further afield, back across the BC border, is Fernie. It's only a three hour drive from Fernie so the next best thing to actually living there is going down there at weekends – as you can see, I'm thinking in Canadian terms about distance as well now, "only" a three hour drive each way. Truly I am a Calgarian now, invading small mountain towns at any opportunity. Given the stigma attached to being from Calgary in Fernie, it will be a sad day when I trade in the BC plates on the truck for Albertan ones, as I'm obliged to do within three months.

So in conclusion, though Calgary may not be the most exciting city in the world, or even in Canada, it's not a bad place to ride out the economic storm, bolstered as it is by oil money. It may not be as idyllic as small-town BC but for all the times that you should live for the moment, at others you need to keep an eye to the future. If I want to stay in Canada beyond November, this is the trade-off for now. But like I said, I will do Whatever It Takes to stay in Canada. Even becoming a Calgarian for a while.

Lisa

June 2009: Is It About a Bicycle? It Should Be.

Hello again

Newcomer as I am to Calgary, until I find somewhere to live I've been staying with Linsday and Chucky in their one-bedroom apartment. Rather than sleeping on the sofa though – how plebeian! – by fortuitous circumstance Linsday's parents (who also live in Calgary) were clearing out their old furniture just as I moved to town and there was a single bed going spare. This is now installed in the corner of the living room, where I sit propped up like some bad-tempered old granny who'll rap people on the head with her cane as they walk by.

Luckily Linsday & Chucky and I have lived at extremely close quarters for extended periods before. Recap: we shared that perishingly cold house last year in Wanaka where it was simply not an option to spend time anywhere other than the toasty and glowing circle of warmth sent out by the wood-burning stove. When the ski-season finished we then travelled around the South Island together for a few weeks, sleeping in creaky bunkhouses, hostel dormitories and campsite cabins until any need for personal space was reduced to a minimum. Hence I sleep in the living room now. It's the ski-bum way.

We don't exactly live in the most genteel of neighbourhoods. There's a dumpster outside in which homeless people forage for whatever treasures they can find, clanking their shopping trolleys along. They're primarily looking for cans and bottles to bring back to the recycling depot, driven not so much by environmental concern – though who am I to say, maybe this does indeed feed into their motives – but because you get a few cents for every receptacle you return. And every penny counts in these tough economic times.

That said, this local, eh, "colourfulness" has its boons. (I should clarify: it's a dodgy area only by Canadian standards, it's not exactly Jo'burg or Tallaght.) The other week, in the first of many automotive mishaps I'll go on to describe, I managed to lock all my keys in the truck. I'd been there about ten minutes, muttering, cursing and fruitlessly trying to pry one of the windows open with my credit card – not as easy as it looks in the films – when along comes an ill-shaven local. Quickly assessing the situation, he hummed and hawed, disappeared for a minute before returning with a chisel and a twisted piece of wire. Getting to work, he effortlessly levered a small gap through the rubber seal at the top of the window with the chisel, fed through the piece of wire, skillfully manoeuvring and looping it to pull up the lock. Bingo! A carefully honed routine evidently.

Talking of trucks, in emails past I mentioned how I'd been bonding with my truck. Alas, for all the maternal solicitude I've bestowed upon it, it has my heart scalded. Sharper than a serpent's tooth is it to have a thankless truck. Now I find driving around Calgary terrifying at the best of times. That it's on a grid system with several main criss-crossing highways doesn't stop me getting lost on an almost daily basis trying to negotiate my way around. It's a baffling spaghetti junction, one-way system ordeal. Getting on and off the highways, making sure to make your exit and changing lanes at HIGH SPEEDS leaves me simultaneously dry-mouthed and with hands slipping off the steering wheel, slick with sweat. Skiing down a black diamond mogul field. No problem. Nearly breaking my wrist in the terrain park. No problem. Coming face to face with a bear on my own in the wild. No problem. Driving along McLeod Trail in commuter traffic. Terrifying. I spend so long planning and replanning, double-checking my route and envisaging which lane I'll need to be in at various junctions that for journeys of under ten kilometres it's far quicker to cycle.

Yet I know that I need to get over this dread fear. So, like a recovering agoraphobia, I've been taking small steps and little trips to this end. One day I drove to a nearby neighbourhood to buy some new runners. (I was going to call them "running shoes" there, slipping into the North American vernacular.) And then. The clutch had always been a bit sticky and sometimes needed...encouragement...to yank from first into second gear. This time, however, when I jabbed my foot the clutch just went to the floor and stayed put. Though the engine was running fine, I couldn't change gears and thought it was going to be like some sort of *Speed* situation featuring Keanu at his wooden finest where I'd have to keep veering around the glinting chrome of Cowtown for hours on end before careering off a pier. Of course, nothing as dramatic took place. I rolled to a stop into an adjacent parking lot – notice the use of "parking lot" rather than "car park"? – and did exactly what you're supposed to do in a situation like that: I rang Chucky and wailed in despair.

Five hundred dollars, one stealth towing mission, one new clutch cylinder and one new master cylinder later, I used the truck for its express purpose – to take me back to the mountains whenever I want. Or, rather, whenever I can afford the petrol after all these recent capital outlays like vehicle repairs and residency applications. Off it was to Fernie for the weekend! I'll skip over the incident where my windscreen wipers stopped working in a rainstorm and I had to roll down the window and peer myopically through the windscreen to finish off the trip. (It turned out to be a loose connection in the wiper mechanism, easily resolved by a strategically fixed cable-tie.)

No, instead let's focus on the return trip to Cowtown after just another summer's weekend in Fernie (i.e., perfect weather, hot-tubbing, barbecue feasts and hitting the trails). I normally vaguely enjoy the drive to and from there, entirely different as it is from the multi-lane trauma and overcrowding of city roads. There is a stretch along Highway 22 at the start of which you are warned "No Gas or Services for 135km". But as I was driving along this particular section of road last weekend the steering seemed a bit, well, loose, I suppose is the best way of describing it. Then things started to get a bit rattly. Then Holy Jesus it was as if the truck was being blown in a tornado, rattling uncontrollably. So I pulled over and discovered that one of the rear tyres had exploded with metal wires poking out everywhere. I stood for a minute, flummoxed, and trying to work out what to do about this blow-out. Remember: this was in the middle of the Albertan badlands with nothing for dozens and dozens of miles in any direction and scant traffic passing by. Furthermore, I was wearing a pretty green sundress, not the optimal attire for heavy duty maintenance.

I have trouble operating the tin-opener tool on my penknife, how the fuck was I going to jack up the truck and change a tyre? Yes, yes, I know it's incredibly straightforward and you're probably chuckling at my ineptitude but when you've never even watched anyone perform the procedure before it's a little daunting. Well, I thought, there's nothing for it. Let's hope the instruction manual is comprehensive. So I found the tool kit under the front seat and, as per the instructions, got to work loosening the wheel rim with the wrench, vowing to keep some WD-40 with me in future. To add to the challenge, when I went to remove the spare tire from the back of the truck I discovered it was helpfully padlocked in place for extra security. Not that I'd ever received the key when I bought the truck. Great, I thought rattily. Should I fashion a primitive hand-tool in line with my Neolithic instincts by finding a large rock and hacking away to smash the lock? I stood there ineffectually for a few minutes when along came the most astounding *deus ex machina*. So incredible that if it hadn't happened firsthand I wouldn't have believed it.

It was a mechanic driving a tow-truck. Just like that, through the middle of nowhere, late on a Sunday afternoon. In fact, not only was he in a tow-truck and carrying a huge industrial jack but was fully clad in overalls and work-gloves. He changed the tyre almost without looking. He was SO nice and helpful – so Canadian, he even apologised for not having any air with him so he couldn't pump up the spare a bit more and I had a feeling it would have offended him greatly if I'd offered to pay him. Maybe it's a professional code that you can't very well drive a rescue vehicle around and then zoom past girls in sundresses who evidently have no idea what to do at the side of the road in rural Alberta.

I'd like to thank all the various men who've helped me deal with matters truck-related over the past few months. Talk about reinscription of gender roles. I was over at a friend's house recently and we had to specify what we were looking for in a partner, e.g., must like animals, must be financially solvent or whatever. As well as the normal provisos – must ski, preferably holds a Canadian passport – one of my major stipulations was "should know about engines and be able to fix things around the house". And who said romance was dead.

But in the interim it looks like I'll be spending the greater portion of my next pay-cheque on a new set of tyres. As a first-time vehicle owner, and having already had to deal with defective clutches, blown-out tyres etc etc, my conclusion on motorcars is that it's a lot easier and more reliable to cycle or walk whenever you can. I'm with Bob Marley on this one: My feet is my only carriage.

Lisa

July 2009: This here is Cowboy Country

Ahoy!

After the Drama on Highway 22 incident, I went into a local garage once I was safely back in Cowtown. "Change my tyres, my good man!" I cried to the Portuguese mechanic. Which he did and, while so doing, described in great detail Calgary's demise since he arrived here thirty-six years ago. It was a good place starting off, he said, but no more. It's too expensive and it's racist. There's racism everywhere, he continued, regretfully adding that even his own children have succumbed to the same. As I was nodding sympathetically, the conversation broadened out to the current financial ruin, the situation in Iraq and much more besides. My new friend lowered his voice and, with a conspiratorial hiss, explained that the Jews were to blame for the plight of the world at large. I coughed awkwardly and steered the conversation back to the more neutral topics of the Canadian climate and any vehicle repairs I may need.

Anyway! As well as imparting his...uniquely informed take on global geopolitics, the mechanic also described how, throughout the 1980s, each of the main routes into Calgary was marked by a bill-board proclaiming, "This is Cowboy Country – like it or leave it." I don't know if any such road signs really were in place or if this anecdote has been so embellished over the years that no truth remains but in either case it's a pithy summation of Alberta.

Let's start with this "like it or leave it," carrying as it does a note of challenge and confrontation. The oozy black oil which courses through Calgary's veins, its economic life blood, has rendered Alberta both nigh-on recession proof and aggressively self-assured. Oil builds the skyscrapers, keeps enormous SUVs on the roads and buys up fancy condos in outlying ski-towns, thereby earning Calgarians the jealous loathing of ski-bums eking out an existence on Kraft Dinner and minimum wage.

But even if Calgary is as brash and swaggering as it gets in Canada, the bottom-line is that this is nonetheless CANADA which means that it remains incredibly polite and courteous and safe. I have to watch my tongue here – they're easily shocked by the foul-mouthed Irish in full swing. Not only do I have to refrain from sprinkling my speech with the f-bomb as liberally as I'm accustomed to, I also have to go easy on the blasphemy. There's a lot of keenly believing earlier marriers and evangelical types here – Baptists, Mormons, Jehovah's Witnesses, you name it we got it – which means no more "I swear to God" to emphasise my sincerity, no more "Jesus, Mary and Joseph" as shorthand for "I am quite surprised and dismayed right now." I've even transmuted the bog-standard "oh my God" to "oh my Go…sh" a few times mid-speech. The things I do for cultural assimilation.

I'd be absolutely shocked if, say, a group of teenage boys shouted smart-arse comments after me in the street or some gouger tried to steal my bike while I was in the cinema, things which I simply expect as par for the course back home. Of course, crime does happen here – apparently gang-land shootings occur reasonably frequently in Calgary. (Is "reasonable" quite the right quantifier to be used when talking about the incidence of drug-related killings?) But in the main you can be quite assured of your personal safety in Calgary, if perhaps not to the unmatchable degree you could in the Kootenays. Last time I was down in Fernie I locked my truck when going into the supermarket to "do the messages" and my friend smirked to herself at such city-bred paranoia.

But while it remains to be seen how hard-line the ultimatum of "like it or leave it" is in practice, this nonetheless indeed remains "Cowboy Country". This has been particularly evinced over the past week as it's Stampede time! Yee haw! Along with the 1988 Winter Olympics which, as anyone of my generation who saw *Cool Runnings* at an impressionable age can tell you, were held in Calgary, the city's major claim to fame is its annual Stampede, an enormous ten-day rodeo and celebration of western heritage. (A side-note on the Winter

Olympics: Lindsay grew up here in Calgary and amidst the hazy fog of early childhood, the Winter Olympics stand out for her in vivid technicolour. As far as she was concerned for years, the Winter Olympics were the "real" Olympics, the summer games being a mere addendum and conciliatory sop for countries skilled in neither bobsledding or biathlon.)

At the bus-stops, in the bars, along the streets – wherever you look during Stampede are swarms of Stetsons, checked shirts, tight Wranglers and bandanas knotted loosely around necks (as opposed, that is, to the round-the-forehead-Sylvester-Stallone-in-his-Rambo-hey-day or I've-listened-to-too-much-gangsta-rap bandana styles). I saw one woman wearing a sari and a cowboy hat at the same time – cultural fusion, innit. Workplaces abandon their customary dress-codes in favour of denim skirts, tasselled shirts and oversized belt buckles. Even the police have specially commissioned cowboy hats for the Stampede with golden sheriff-type badges emblazoned on the front.

It's the norm for companies, churches and community organisations to put on a free pancake breakfast at some point during Stampede. A pancake breakfast if properly done is an incomparably hearty feed: pancakes, scrambled eggs, sausages, hash browns, baked beans, waffles, jugs of syrup to pour over the top. I suppose it's what you eat on the ranch before going out to corral those steers or buck those broncos or whatever exactly it is that cowboys do all day.

Events really kick off with the Stampede Parade, during which the city centre – sorry, the "downtown", get with the lingo Lisa – shuts down. Any Calgary business wanting to retain a modicum of respectability gives its employees parade morning off work in addition to the regular gamut of statutory holidays. People head out with their folding deck-chairs to get into prime curbside position up to three hours ahead of time and by the time the parade starts at precisely

8:55am there are 300,000 spectators along the route, dozens deep in parts. There are marching bands, there are horses, lots of horses, there are miscellaneous Wild West styled floats, and there are spangled and sequined rodeo queens.

Every time Stampede comes around Lindsay winces – I suppose it's akin to my horror of St Patrick's Day in Dublin, a sea of inflatable green shamrocks and American tourists wearing tweed flat-caps trying to blend in. However, this year she very nobly overcame her cultural cringe to take me and Chucky (her Kiwi betrothed) to the Stampede show-grounds for the self-proclaimed "greatest outdoor show on earth."

And what an array of activities and attractions there were. There were real-life cowboys competing in the rodeo. There were livestock displays. There were sheep-shearing competitions. There was live music. There were carnival rides, ferris wheels, haunted houses, merry-go-rounds. There were medals and ribbons being awarded for every assortment of craftwork: sugarcraft, quilting and blacksmithing. There were chuckwagon races, a particular nod to the pioneering days of yore. You start by shackling your horses to your covered wagon, your pot-bellied stove on the ground. When the gun goes, you have to stow the stove into your wagon before heading off with a whoop and whip-crack-away around the racetrack.

One of the main attractions at the Stampede, though, is the food. We're not talking haute cuisine here, we're talking down-home rodeo: kettle-corn, slushees, mini-donuts, fries, corndogs, deep-fried Oreos and – Alberta being cattle-ranch territory – enormous chargrilled steaks. A veritable smorgasbord of county fair snack foods, all washed down with bucket-sized vats of Coke.

When I was younger and would read books set in North America I never knew what certain of the foodstuffs mentioned so casually were. What was an Oreo? Or a Twinky? Or a Tootsie Roll? This was before the Internet, you see, you couldn't just turn to Google to find out what these wondrous items were. Oh no! You had to use your imagination. (And we had to walk eight miles to school and back every day, without shoes and uphill both ways.)

Though some of these culinary mysteries I'm still decoding, I can now speak with great authority on the subject of Oreos and, alas, they're nowhere near as exciting as I had envisaged them snuggled up in my bunk-bed in the early 1990s. An Oreo is a small round biscuit – or cookie, if you absolutely must – consisting of two cocoa-tinted rounds sandwiched together with a layer of vanilla filling. So they're no more remarkable than Bourbon biscuits or custard creams, staples of an Irish childhood such as those were. Had I but known. Anyway, at the Stampede they were deep-frying them. What is a rodeo without deep-fried Oreos? Incomplete. With them an abode of bliss…

Corndogs also merit description for the uninitiated. Are you all familiar with cornmeal? Whereas in Ireland it's a specialty item, nigh on impossible to find without paying an arm and a leg in Donnybrook Fair or whatever that other poncy food emporium on George's Street is called, here you can find enormous sacks of it in any supermarket for next to nothing. As to how to assemble a corndog: Take a wooden skewer. Spear a frankfurter on it. Cover it in thick cornmeal batter. Deep fry. Coat with ketchup and mustard as desired. Eat, eat, gloriously eat.

I ate without restraint at the showgrounds as that morning I'd run in the Stampede Road Race, a hot and hilly ten kilometre race. (I now spend more time than I'd ever thought possible in lycra running gear, but I'll get to that another time.) Alas, running in the heat plus delightfully plump thighs equals raw and chafed skin. I had a decidedly cowboy stagger as I ambled round from food-stall to food-stall, wincing with the pain. At least I fitted in, I suppose. By late afternoon I was overstimulated and all worn-out – no, not even the deep-fried Oreos could perk me up – so home it was, happy, tired and well-fed.

Hope y'all are having a stampedin' good time wherever you are.

Lisa

July 2009: Running Joke

Greetings.

My knowledge of maths and physics is scant at best, dumbly incomprehensive at worst, but something which *has* penetrated the woolly fog of my mind is that there are no fixed reference points in the universe. To reiterate; there are no absolute and immutable points from which matters can be objectively referenced and gauged. What you see depends on where you're looking from. Everything is, you will understand, relative.

Certainly, any of the descriptions I provide of places are highly subjective and partial, quantum physics having proven that I am not, alas, the centre of the universe. Take, for example, my impression of New Zealand. The dominant depiction of NZ holds how beautiful a backpacker's idyll it is, temperate and lush, and how easy-going and good-natured Kiwis are. I, by way of contrast, ended up working for a firm of hellish property valuers when I was in Wanaka last year; so over-worked and belittling and rude were they that I couldn't leave town soon enough at the end of the winter, no desire ever to return. Even now when I hear about anyone heading to NZ I give a cynical snort, thinking, good luck to them with that shower of wankers down there. I should know better but it's all a question of perspective.

My impression of Calgary and its denizens has been similarly skewed, though this time favourably rather than not. As far as I can now see, Calgary is populated predominantly by wiry distance runners, not the Albertan good ol' boys by which it gets broadstroked. Calgarians, in my eyes, are a uniquely spry and speedy breed, constantly out doing tempo runs or interval training. Surely everyone here owns wicking t-shirts and sat-nav watches that let you know your distance and pace at a mere click? Isn't everybody in this city preoccupied with achieving negative splits?

Similarly, if asked to give a description of the cityscape my first response would now be not to bemoan the miles of urban sprawl but rather to enthuse about the admirable trail system. Calgary is bisected by the Bow and Elbow rivers, with a six hundred kilometre network of running and cycling trails up and down their lengths, linking various parks, nature reserves and glittering reservoirs along the way. You can run for miles and miles and miles without having to constantly stop and start at traffic lights or dodge the ire of cranky drivers.

That I've become so acquainted with these trails and view Calgarians in such athletic terms is because I too have been out there running a lot recently. Having also run the Calgary Half-Marathon at the end of May I'm now stepping it up and training – fanfare – for the Dublin Marathon, the full whack, which takes place at the end of October. Even though there is a whole slew of marathons taking place across Canada during late summer and autumn, I figure that if you're going to put in months of training and then slog it out for 26.2 miles you might as well do it somewhere with a bit of personal significance. Not to mention somewhere with parents to take you home afterwards, feed you up and patiently listen to your glory tales over and over again.

It's funny, this one. I'm not normally reticent when it

comes to writing about where I went, what I saw and how I felt about it. Yet I'm incredibly diffident when it comes to explicating upon running. You see, I fundamentally feel like an imposter, given my complete antipathy towards any form of physical exertion when I was at school. I hadn't discovered snowsports at this stage. For me, "real" runners are the skinny kids who did athletics and went to the Community Games when they were younger and have continued suit into their adult lives. Evidently I've missed the boat on that one a bit. Despite avidly watching the Olympics whenever they came around, I would rather have clawed my own eyes out than gone on a run voluntarily. Furthermore, sporty host of friends such as I have, many of you reading have done – nay, WON – triathlons, bashed out sub-four hour marathons and clocked times over shorter distances I can only dream of. So when discussing running I feel I should preface every sentence, eyes downcast, with the disclaimer, "Not that I know much about it." On my way to the Calgary Half-Marathon I heard one man ask another on the C-train "so what's your race strategy for today?" If similarly asked I could only respond, entirely without guile, "em, start running at the gun and not stop until I reach the finish line."

That said, I won't be disingenuous and talk myself down too much. Neophyte as I may be, I'm not exactly lolling around on a sheepskin rug eating chocolates all day and assuming it will somehow miraculously come together at marathon time. I'm training four times a week; sometimes I run fast, sometimes I run long, most of the time I run an unremarkable distance at an unremarkable pace, but it's not much of a day if streaking a finger across my cheek doesn't, at some point, yield a crystallized trail of salt. I'm intimately acquainted with my lactate threshold, have grown accustomed to wincing slightly when going up and down stairs, reaching to the bannister for support, feel a slight aching in my quads at all times, and scowl in disgust whenever I hear anyone denigrating carbs.

But being in essence a recreational mid-pack runner and staying put, though my running clothes aren't quite as motley as when I started out a few years ago, I still resist getting too technical or coordinated. In Elizabethan England, sumptuary laws meant certain fabrics or colours remained the preserve of certain social classes. For example, only those at the rank of earl or above were entitled to wear purple silk, while you needed an annual income of £200 or more to sport a velvet cloak or gown. It truly was a case of th'apparel oft proclaiming the man. Though we may no longer be legally impeded when filling our wardrobes, a relationship between clothing and status is still in place. An unspoken rule of snowsports, for example, is that if you want to rock the bling, you have to bring the skills. If you're going to wear anything outrageous or flashy (eg, a bright yellow one-piece, hideous fluoro gear, big fat powder skis) then you'd better be able to ski hard or pull off some impressive tricks. There's a hierarchy on them thar hills. To paraphrase from *Spinal Tap*, big air talks, bullshits walks. I have a dread fear of becoming the running world equivalent of one of those skiers with all the high-end equipment and GoreTex gear who can then barely snow-plough down the nursery slope. I had to buy a new top recently and shied away from my first choice because it matched my shorts too perfectly. I'd feel like a right sap all decked out in matching kit and then be barely able to maintain ten minute miles. (And that's on a good day!)

These preoccupations also affect my "hydration strategies". It's so warm in Canada at the moment that it would be foolhardy in the extreme to head out on a long run without anything to drink. But how to carry it? One option is these special Velcro belts which fasten snugly around your waist with pouches for several mini water·bottles. They sort of look like grenade-holders actually. Again, a puritanical streak in me resists acquiring one, running after all being the low-tech activity par excellence. So I've simply been clasping a plastic bottle filled with diluted orange, the contents sloshing around frothily with every step. This no-tech approach, however, has its pitfalls. By the end of a slow nine-miler last weekend my hand had curled into a raptor-like claw from holding the bottle in place for so long. Maybe I do need to come up with a better solution, without falling into the consumer trap of thinking that acquiring more stuff will make me faster. The only way to get better at running is to, well, run. After all, you don't see Haile Gebrselassie burdened down with gadgetry, do you?

What's that? You don't know who he is? Haile – pronounced "Highly" – Gebrselassie – pronounced, oh, you can figure this one out on your own – is an Ethiopian distance runner, probably the greatest of all time. He grew up in a mud hut and used to run ten kilometres barefoot to school and back every day with his schoolbooks tucked into the crook of his elbow. Indeed, he still runs with a slightly stilted upper gait as a result of these book-carrying years. Having smashed world record after world record, he is now rich and famous but remains cheerful and humble, continuing to live in his homeland and funding, among other enterprises, an orphanage where the youthful charges are trained up in trades. I got a goldfish for my seventeenth birthday which I named in his honour and my friend Lena and I also came up with some catchy slogans to cheer him on in the Sydney 2000 Olympics – e.g., "We think highly of Haile", "Haile is smiley." It was definitely the world's loss when we didn't go into copywriting as careers.

Anyway, as well as plodding around Calgary by myself

several times a week, I've also surprised myself by joining the marathon training group of a local running club. As far as I was concerned until recently, club runners were those lean figures in singlets and split shorts who, in races where I'm still to reach the turnabout, are belting back in the opposite direction towards the finish line, faces contorted in a rictus of anguish and pain. (It's some consolation to see that they don't make it look effortless at least.) True, there are a cohort of such figures in any club. But they're not the only ones. I'm not going to say that there are runners of "all shapes and sizes" in the group – you'd have to really be packing it away to remain portly when you're putting in the sort of mileage some of them maintain – but they're not uniformly the gaunt skeletal types I had imagined.

We meet every Tuesday night and just as important as the agonising speed sessions we do – speed being of course a relative term in my case – is the camaraderie and encouragement. Having found people with the same obsessive interest means I don't have to bore my housemates with the details of how I ran twenty seconds a mile slower today than on Sunday, why this might possibly be and the precise degree of the tightness in my calves. Instead of asking, "How was your weekend?" the conversation opener is, "Did you get your Long Run in?" The weekly Long Run being the lodestone of marathon training. Similarly, rather than "Are you going on holidays anywhere this year?" it's "Have you got any races planned?" Age, by the way, is no determinant of fitness with this crowd. Just as how I was out-skied in Rossland by septuagenarians, so too do wiry sixty-year olds easily trot past me now when I'm jelly-legged and about to throw up. Luckily I'm not in it for the ego.

Why am I in it, I sometimes wonder? Why on earth do I want to run a marathon, illogical, arbitrary and punishing distance as it is? I can only parrot George Mallory's alleged response when asked why he wanted to scale Everest: "Because it's there." With a bit of luck, however, I won't similarly perish several hundred yards from my goal. I'm not doing it for bragging rights: I don't expect anybody to particularly care what odd compulsions I get up to in my spare time. It's just something I want to do. I've long admired the dedication and stamina of anyone who's trained for and run a marathon. And, well, imitation is the sincerest form of flattery.

It *is* a uniquely masochistic hobby though. For every one day that you head out and the air is crisp and joy it is to be alive, there are three or four where your legs appear to have mutated into sticky pillars of treacle. Or, as last Saturday, when the relentless summer sun meant that by the time I was finished I was so hot, slick-skinned with sweat, water bottle empty and in desperate need of respite that I dove into a clump of dewy bushes and rolled around like a dog trying to smear any available moisture on my face and limbs. If running is a form of lunacy, then perhaps I am a "real" runner after all. In either case, when I cross the finish line in Dublin, I may have to slough off my long-held self-description as non-sporty. It's becoming increasingly hard to justify these days.

I can't go on, I'll go on.

Lisa

October 2009: Time to Taper

Hi again

It's been a while, eh? I haven't sent an email for nearly three months, during which time my life has become increasingly dominated by continuing to train for the Dublin Marathon. It's not that I've nothing to say about this; quite the opposite in fact as it's amazing at what length I can now talk about the simple act of putting one foot ahead of the other. You've probably heard the joke, "How do you know who's the marathoner at a party? They'll tell you." Oh yes; the precise pace at which you should do a tempo run; how often you should change your runners; the best tactic for bagging a personal best; the optimal breakfast for fuelling a long run; the perils of not leaving enough time for aforementioned breakfast to settle in your stomach. I could drone on for hours. But even in my most self-absorbed moments I appreciate that distance running lacks an inherent dramatic appeal. It's perhaps not as interesting for the non-runners among you to hear about the hours I've spent trotting along in solitary contemplation as it was for the non-skiers among you to hear about cornices, chutes, cliff-drops and hot young things with goggle tans.

In any case, even if I had wanted to keep you in the loop with weekly bulletins reporting how I had to rinse the blood out of my sportsbra after a particularly bad chafing incident or how shortsighted it was to devour a platter of sweetcorn-and-jalapeno salad the night before an eighteen miler, I've had neither the time nor the energy to do so. By the time I get home from work, go for a run and then have dinner, I can barely get myself to bed, let alone compose an email.

However, I'm now tapering. When building up to a marathon, you see, you gradually increase your mileage until it's almost but not quite untenable, and you are a ragged mess; legs swollen with lactic acid, positively misanthropic with exhaustion. Having reached this point (about three weeks before the marathon itself), you then scale down your training to allow you to go at it full throttle on the day. Tapering gives you a chance to attend to the daily duties you've been neglecting of late, such as catching up on correspondence, but mostly you use these rediscovered hours to drive yourself around the bend worrying about twisting your ankle or falling victim to swine flu (or both, if the gods were feeling particularly cruel) the day before the race.

If such were to occur it would be particularly upsetting given that I've been training for what feels like an unfeasibly long time, from the last snowfall of one winter to the first snowfall of the next. (Such is life above the 49th parallel.) Not to mention through the summer in between. Adjusting to hot weather running was quite the experience. In real life I'm riddled with the usual host of body-image issues: I'm self-conscious about wearing a bikini and shy away from hot-pants on the grounds that it would scare animals and small children. When it got up to 30C though, any modicum of modesty went out the window and I had no qualms whatsoever about wearing only a sports bra and the shortest of short shorts to struggle against the relentless sun. I was also getting up ludicrously early on a Saturday to beat the heat on my long runs. One time when I was down in Fernie circumstances were such that I got up at half past five to fit in ten miles, whooping and cheering as I ran through the forest to announce my approach to any snuffling bears. "This," I thought at the time, "is the abandonment of all reason." And then – just as I'd grown used to having the clothes stuck to the back of me with sweat – fall, eh, fell and it's now back down below freezing again. O Canada. Luckily after four ski seasons I have enough winter wear to drive MEC (Mountain Equipment Co-op: outdoor goods emporium and site of all holiness here in Canada) out of business and can layer up adequately for any cold weather activity you can name. Last night it was blowing snow, minus 6, minus 14 with windchill, but there was a five miler in the training plan so out the door it was anyway. Talk about the highs and lows of life as a distance runner.

Let me backtrack a little and elaborate a little about

these long runs, fabled and feared as they are. I'm still going along to the Calgary Road Runners – "the skeletors" as Lindsay and Chucky branded them – every Tuesday night. A few weeks ago one woman exclaimed how tired she'd been after a half-marathon the previous weekend. Her legs felt so heavy and she even had to take a nap that afternoon, she said, shaking her head and rolling her eyes in good-natured disbelief. Imagine feeling like that after a mere thirteen miles! See, in the normal world if you run a half-marathon you then sit on the couch for the next week, basking in the glory. And rightly so. In the latter half of marathon training, however, every Saturday morning you're out there surpassing that distance with no fanfare, no applause, no aid tents, no volunteers arms outstretched with paper cups of Gatorade for you to slug and toss with impunity, no spectators cheering you on with those sweet little lies "nearly there!" (the encouragement is appreciated but let us not shy away from the fact that there are still four miles to go) and "looking good!" (Once again, I thank you for your kind words but I am aware I look sepulchral right now.) Nope: Instead it's just you and your feet.

At the start of the summer I kept getting given energy gels and electrolyte drink powder in race packs. I was baffled but figured they'd make more sense once I started doing the long, long runs. And indeed they do. Running requires a ready supply of glycogen. However, pausing mid-run for a snack – a nice hang sangwich and a cup of tea, say – is out of the question unless you want to vomit it all back up a few minutes later. But with energy gels it's one convulsive gulp down your gullet and ah! feel that sugar hit. None of that low-GI, slow release softly-softly nutrition; they're instead for I-need-glucose-NOW moments. I'm a convert to the point of having found myself cross-legged on my bedroom floor, frowningly comparing the various electrolyte and carbohydrate contents of different brands. Bizarrely though, the makers still base the percentage of daily nutritional needs on a typical 2000 calorie a day intake, when even the briefest of thoughts would indicate than anyone engaged in the sort of endurance activity where they're guzzling energy gels patently has a greater calorific need than the norm. Equally bizarrely, you sometimes see displays of energy gels set up in ski-hill Daylodges. It's a tad overkill if you ask me because when you're out skiing for the day you can always pause for a second to fumble in the inner recesses of your jacket for half a squished peanut butter sandwich or a zipperbag of trail mix. That's what chairlifts are made for.

Heading out for one of these gel-fuelled long runs – and long they really are, capping out at twenty miles by the end – is like some sort of meditative or yogic practice where you have to achieve emptiness of mind and learn to relax into the task at hand. With time and distance becoming elastic concepts, you can't allow yourself to think too much about how even though you've already run seven miles you still have another nine to go, nor that your calves feel like blocks at which someone is steadily chipping away with a meat-tenderising hammer. Apparently one of the quickest ways to speed up your recovery afterwards is by plunging yourself into an ice-bath immediately upon your return. Now after running for over three hours straight, I don't want any more masochism. I want to have a warm shower, eat exactly and as much of what I want and then go for a nap. Clambering into a frigid bath-tub does not factor into my idea of self-indulgence. And whereas some people swear by them and their ability to minimise muscle inflammation, the scientific evidence is inconclusive so I haven't bothered. The whole notion just reminds me of eminent Victorians clad in blue-and-white bathing suits striding vigorously and briskly into the sea, pipes gripped firmly under their bristly moustaches, harrumphing and believing the cold swirling water to be doing wonders for their constitution and virility.

Furthermore, it's not my legs or muscles which pose the problems with the long runs, it's more my gastrointestinal tract, be that during or afterwards. En route, all that churning has meant I've had to make one or two emergency pit-stops in Calgary's public "washrooms" (why do North Americans have to be so euphemistic when they're referring to toilets? I'm not really going in there for a quick scrub down.) Similarly, I'm used to feeling quite wretched and nauseous. Possibly this is because of plummeting blood sugar, as energy gels can only do so much. I've discovered an effective treatment is eating several handfuls of liquorice allsorts – how's that for evidence-based learning – even though I don't have any real actual appetite. Which is a pity because one great thing about marathon training is having absolute carte blanche to eat what you want without feeling "guilty" for so doing, that being the current orthodoxy for women in the Western world. I saw an ad up recently for some brand of the Pill. It featured an empty tub of chocolate ice-cream, spoon still balefully within: control your hormones, stymie your cravings, it urged. I instead thought what a good idea! and bought a pint carton of Ben and Jerry's Cookie Dough to devour over the weekend.

Do you know something; training for your first marathon is what I imagine being pregnant for the first time must be like. Even though it's a fairly common and far from unique experience, you're fascinated by the process, shrouded as it is in mystery and ritual. You wonder at the changing contours of your body, fret about whether you're doing the right exercises, eating the right things, getting enough rest. As the months pass, you're constantly tired, everything aches, and going from a sitting to standing position grows increasingly problematic. And throughout it all you know that ahead of you lies an ordeal of incomparable pain, but one which, everyone assures you, is absolutely worth it. Well, only seventeen days to go and then I can report back from the front line.

Lisa

October 2009: Ubi Sunt

Ahoy.

The more I discover of Calgary's interlinked park system, the more I marvel about what a great place it is for running, during the verdant splendour of summer at least. I've gone into rhapsodies over this before so there's no need to repeat myself except to reiterate how well we, the running community, are served.

It's a good thing that Calgary has such enviable running trails because it has little else going for it. How do you define a city? The definition rattling around my brain is that it has to have a cathedral, which is probably not the clincher in North America these days. However, rather than wasting time with taxonomy, let us simply take a city to be a "very big town". That there's no love lost between me and very big towns will come as no revelation to anyone. All the buildings and crime and grime and cars get in the way of the good things in life. Like skiing and mountains and fresh air! But even putting my initial antipathy aside, Calgary is particularly lacking as cities go. Consider the great cities of the world: London, New York, Paris. Why are they celebrated? Why do people visit? The history, the architecture, the museums, the shopping, the food, the culture. Calgary has none (or few) of the above. It doesn't feel like a vibrant urban centre, primarily because it's not. It feels like a clump of skyscrapers plonked down in the middle of the prairies. Oh! We appear to have a city now!

As a result, you get the worst of both worlds. You lose out on wide open spaces and the great outdoors but you don't gain any urban energy or dynamism in return. Now I write this slumped on the couch in old shirt and jeans, truck parked out front, planning which backwoods I'm going to slope away to this winter, so I'm no to-the-bone culture hound. (When I hear the word "culture" I reach for my snowboard.) It would be hypocritical of me to diss Calgary for its cultural denudity and unsophistication when part of the reason I fled Dublin so fervently was having just spent four years amidst the scarf-tossing horror of the Trinity Arts Block. But still. If you have to deal with the frustrations of city living – traffic jams, urban sprawl and aggressive drivers (quick, hurry! We need to make some more oil money!) – then surely at least the cultural backdrop should be edgy and outré rather than hockey and Hooters.

I'm not sure if "edgy" and "outré" factor into the Canadian psyche at all though. I've postulated before that Canada is more of a "doing" than a "talking" culture and adept as Canadians are at outdoor pursuits, verbally they're not the quickest off the mark. When the DJs in particular try to be risqué, it makes me want to wail in despair. The dullest provincial announcer on Mullingar FM reading out hospital requests – "this is for Mrs. Mary Moriarty from Ballynaclin. Get well soon Nanna love Jason, Sophie and Grace" – has a faster line in repartee than the prime-time DJs over here. I was driving back from Fernie to Calgary on a recent Bank Holiday Monday (never again) and got caught behind every single Alberta in their RV. Having mislaid my iPod, I was stuck with the radio for the four hours. As the cavalcade crawled along I considered the lilies and composed lengthy and colourful hate mail to the DJs in my head. "You're not funny!" I was shouting at the dashboard, "you're not funny!"

Every time I cross the border back into BC on the drive

down to Fernie I cheer; when I re-enter Alberta on the return journey I groan. It's not that Alberta isn't beautiful. On one of these trips recently the highway was closed off because of an accident and everyone had to take a detour. In a country as expansive as Canada, a detour isn't simply a matter of a quick U-turn and slipping down a side street. Circumventing the accident meant an hour of rattling down back roads through a dust storm, the sun sinking over ranch land and rolling hills. Very nice indeed.

Similarly it's not that Calgarians aren't perfectly pleasant as a collective whole, leaving me a bit shame-faced about having cursed them as "rich Vulgarians" in Fernie. But it's extremely conservative here, both socially and politically. Every single MP in the city and its environs is Conservative; in fact, there's only one federal representative in the whole province who's not. Evidently I'm going to have to single-handedly rouse the proletariat into consciousness.

Marx's line about religion being the opiate of the people probably won't go down too well though. Though the Kootenays have a sprinkling of Baptists and Jehovah's Witnesses – not to mention pockets of polygamous cults – among the weed-smoking ski-bums it's more about communing with Gaia, a decontextualised Buddhist belief in karma and a vague notion of all being one. Once you cross over to the Prairies though, this ramshackle pantheism and nature worship gives way to other forms of belief. Praise Jesus!

Now, it might seem odd for someone from Ireland, dominated and dragged into misery by the Catholic Church as that country has been for centuries, to be unnerved by the religious sentiment with which I'm met in Calgary. On paper, at least, it appears to be far more secular. I rummaged through recent censuses for the stats – this is what ski-bums get up to in the off-season – and whereas in Ireland only 4.4% claim no religion (the blaggards), in Canada it's 16.2%. In County Dublin a shameless 6.8% are doomed to burn forever in the flames of hell versus 23.1% in Alberta. And while 6.2% of Skerries remain unsaved, in Calgary this rockets to 24.6%. However, the difference is that when they believe here they *really* believe. There's going to Mass at Christmas time and maybe even the odd Sunday to set a good example for the kids then declaring it on the census and then there's the North American religious right. It's Ned Flanders and *7th Heaven* in real life. Sometimes at work when I ring people I get through to their answering machines: "Hi, you've reached the Dreislers but we're not in right now. Leave a message after the tone and we'll get back to you when we can. Blessings!" I equally get any number of emails with sign-offs about God's magnificence and munificence.

I think it's the cheerfulness which gets me. Such open enthusiasm and zeal for Our Lord would be looked upon with great suspicion in Ireland, where every parish has had a crazy lady prostrating herself at the back of the church during Mass, babbling away in tongues. Grudging adherence and quiet piety is as much as we're comfortable with. Careful now.

I'm equally fascinated by the Hutterites and Mennonites, spurning modernity and leading the simple life on the land. Well, spurning some of modernity anyway and their selection criteria remains somewhat unclear to me. In August I went up to Edmonton to do the Edmonton Half Marathon (where I finally broke the two hour marker and though this hardly ranks with Roger Bannister's sub four-minute mile as a Great Sporting Achievement of our Age, I was delighted). Afterwards, swaying and tottering on my feet, I went to the West Edmonton Mall, the largest mall in North America. Though too dazed to take much in, one thing which did register was a family of Hutterites out for the day, the women in home-sewn dresses and black kerchiefs pinned on their heads, the men likewise soberly clad. Why shun vanity and worldly things and then spend the Sabbath in Canada's greatest temple to filthy mammon?

Similarly, every time I go down to Fernie I stop in the Tim Horton's in the Crowsnest Pass. This is not for Tim Horton's coffee which, though I'm no coffee connoisseur, is particularly vile sludge, even though millions of Canadians can't get through the day without it and I'm denigrating a national icon in speaking the truth. No, no, a few years ago when I was running away from Oxford back to the hills I had a particularly fractious journey; Dublin-London transfer cancelled, diverted to a different airport, getting stuck in gridlock on the M25 or whatever the ringroad around London is called, arriving in Heathrow after check-in had closed, bursting into distraught tears at the Air Canada desk, being plopped onto one of those golf cart thingies for celebrities and old people, arriving at the boarding gate with seconds to spare. Upon landing in Calgary I decided to stay put in Canada for the winter and got on the shuttle down to Fernie. On the way we stopped in the Crowsnest Pass and my first meal "home" on frozen Canadian soil was a Tim Horton's blueberry bagel with strawberry cream cheese. So now every time I'm driving through I stop and order another to commemorate my flight into the wilderness. Consider it a personal Passover. Anyway, last time I was in Tim's there was a coach load of fourteen or fifteen year old girls and their chaperones. Again dressed in home-spun smocks and lace-up leather shoes (though my fashionasta friend Niamh assures me these are the height of fashion this season), every second one of them was clutching a digital camera. Back out they trooped onto the Manitoba-plated coach with their Timbits in hand while I watched, baffled and fascinated by it all.

As ever, I feel bad sniping at Canadiana given how very, very nice Canadians are in general. Too nice sometimes when you're Irish. (Here I go again!) As the marathon training intensified over the summer, I became progressively tireder and crankier, incessant Canadian chirpiness started to wear me down and it became apparent how irrefutably Irish I am, not that I want to be met by Dublin Bus driver surliness at every turn. As in Ireland, every conversation here starts with, "How's it going?" Back home this doesn't even require a response; a slight inclination of the head or maybe a grunt if you're feeling particularly expressive. Here, however, the only acceptable return before conversation can proceed is "good!" Do not attempt to respond with anything else even if your leg is hanging off or you've just been told your whole family has been wiped out by a freak typhoon – they simply won't get it. A few times I tried "ah you know yourself" and might as well have been speaking Ancient Aramaic for all that I was understood. I then went for a noncommittal "grand, grand" but "grand" in Canada loses its original denotation of fair-to-middling and instead mistranslates as something large and excellent in sweep, a grand piano for example. "Grand!" the Canadians exclaim, "well isn't that something." Indeed.

The amateur psychologists among you have probably discerned a seething frustration throughout this email, which might as well be sub-titled Yeah Well Your Country's Not So Great, I Don't Want To Stay Anyway. Which brings us onto the sad topic of why I'm in Calgary in the first place given that I despise nearly everything about it and how my fail-proof plan to stay in Canada has, well, failed. A reminder: I came to Calgary to get a Real Job, thereby demonstrating to Immigration Canada that as a contributing member of society I should therefore be allowed to remain indefinitely rather than getting booted out on 15 November when my current visa expires. To that end I've spent the past five months working in the Disabilities Services of a third-level institution. Yes, yes, very worthy but most of the time it's just the usual bureaucratic frustration and sludge green walls. This, I thought one day whilst doing battle with a recalcitrant photocopier under flickering fluorescent light, is not why I came to Canada.

In other words, it's just another job. It was tolerable when I thought it might be my route to residency but less so since the master plan was thwarted last month. When I was applying for residency in June I asked the HR department at work if we needed to obtain this thing called an LMO (a Labour Market Opinion), which is where your employers are obliged to prove that they had to employ you, a Farangi, only because they couldn't find a Canadian to do the job. Oh no no, Mr. HR Man assured me, smiling serenely, it should be fine. The HR man is very nice – he is Canadian after all – but a gentle soul you might say, wind chimes and water fountains tinkling in the background. You need to be a bit more cut-throat when you're going to bat for a foreign worker against Immigration Canada and indeed, a letter came back in September from the powers-that-be saying well now Ms McGonigle, as your employers haven't provided us with an LMO your residency application has been refused. Cue much consternation at work and much stony-faced I-fucking-told-you-so fulmination on my part. So then the job had to be re-advertised nationally to prove that every last Canadian cretin and moron had been trawled through before resorting to bringing in the Irish. As a result, over five hundred applications were received for the position, including my own. Oh yes, I had to reapply and re-interview for my own job:

"Why do you think you're suited to this position?"

"Primarily because I've been doing it for the past four months."

"Where do you see yourself in five years time?"

"Hopefully still in Canada, the only reason I'm going along with this ridiculous charade."

The renewed paperwork was sent off last month so now I have to wait and see (again) but of course, there was some additional drama. If I went to Dublin for the marathon would I be able to come back into the country with only two weeks left on my current work visa and an LMO pending? It would make far more sense to avoid the attentions of border officials altogether. So, my manager said, maybe the trip home would have to be abandoned. Take a day or two to think it over.

Oh.

What a horrible symbolic choice: Ireland vs Canada; to go home, get to see my friends and family, but potentially blow my chances of staying in Canada for good, or else to stay in Calgary on the outside chance this LMO would be approved and miss a marathon for which I'd been training for months.

Crestfallen, I tried to convince myself that one marathon was much the same as another. Even though I'd spent most of the summer envisaging what it was going to feel like to run down Nassau Street towards the finish line (absolutely horrific is my current guess, based on what I feel like after the long runs) I resigned myself to not going home, glumly deciding to do the Victoria Marathon in BC instead. That weekend, however, while out doing an eighteen mile run – do you like how I just slipped that in there? – I realised how pitiful a prospect it would be to run 26.2 miles with no one to cheer me on or meet me at the end. I've spun out an analogy about running a marathon being like giving birth, let's turn to Zoe Williams' riposte in *The Guardian* when it was suggested she go to hospital to deliver her second child alone while her husband stayed at home with their toddler:

"nobody goes to hospital to give birth alone...[e]ven a pregnant murderer would arrive with some kind of case worker". Similarly, nobody goes to run a marathon alone. Everyone has someone to be meet them at the end. If I went to Victoria I'd have to bribe homeless people into waving banners with my name on them, much like how they used to hire professional mourners for medieval funeral processions. And if you're thinking this is a tenuous comparison then bear in mind that much of the time marathon runners are indeed as ghastly and grim as anything out of Hieronymus Bosch.

Christ, I thought, I'd like to get Canadian residency but not at this price. Though I said I'd do Whatever It Takes to stay in Canada let me now formally retract that statement. And anyway, didn't I get into ski-bumming in the first place to avoid becoming a browbeaten admin lackey? Maybe the Greeks were right – you can't escape your destiny. So back to a slightly modified version of the original plan it was – flying out to Dublin on 21 October, running the marathon on the 26th and back to Calgary on the 28th at which point immigration officials may well ask – and rightly so – why I only went back to Ireland for a few days and why I've booked a series of transatlantic flights in quick succession. None of it makes any sense. To which I'll only be able to nod my agreement; I know, I know. Not only will I be bombed out of it with jetlag I might as well douse my savings account in kerosene, torch it and be done with any vestige of financial solvency.

Given the "current economic climate" and Alberta's Conservative government, I'm not overly hopeful about the LMO being approved but visa processing tends not to be to the speediest of affairs and it's unclear whether I can keep working after 15 November if I haven't heard back yet one way or the other. Apparently there's this amorphous entity called "implied status" whereby you can keep working if you have a visa application pending, even if your initial visa has expired. However, I can't get this verified by any source of officialdom. The LMOs come from one governmental division, the work visas from another and all their websites do is refer me from one to the other. Ringing the automated "help" lines doesn't yield any useful information much less the chance to talk to a real life person, and the HR department is as dithering and useless as usual. Relying upon the mysterious limbo-state of implied status could be as shaky and potentially disastrous as putting your faith in myths like you-can't-get-pregnant-if-you-do-it-standing-up and I don't want to have to hot foot it out of Cowtown in a hurry.

Either way, this is the penultimate chapter in my Canadian adventure. I'll either get a last minute reprieve and move back to BC, become a pillar of the community in Fernie and spend my days skiing and writing and baking into sweet oblivion and the moral of the story will be that you should never abandon your dreams. Or else I won't and I'll brush myself down and head off to do something else, somewhere else entirely and the moral will be that you can't always get what you want but the journey is as important as the end and see how I've grown as a person along the way.

Onwards!

Lisa

November 2009: Amor Omnia Vincit

And finally…

It's difficult to describe momentous events like weddings or marathons, difficult to capture the exalted emotions and sense of occasion without becoming bombastic or falling into cliché. The bride was radiant. The food was divine. The last six miles were hell. Jane Austen didn't even bother trying to be fresh and original when faced with the union of her two protagonists in *Northanger Abbey* and instead disposed of their wedding, the culminating event of the entire novel, in a few stock phrases; "Henry and Catherine were married, the bells rang and everybody smiled". (As for distance running she simply avoided the topic altogether.)

But having been privy to so much information about my friends Lindsay and Chucky over the past few years – the genesis of their relationship in Fernie, the travelling we did around New Zealand together last year, the announcement of their engagement this spring, the three months I spent sleeping in their living room this summer – I'm sure you've grown as fond of them as I am and are eager to know how their big day went. Similarly, having mentioned the Dublin Marathon, oh, once or twice over the past few months, the least I can do is furnish you with narrative closure on that one too.

So ladies and gentlemen, without further ado, let's wrap up all the loose ends and bring this thing to an end. Take it to the bridge!

Now people are imperfect beings. Call it original sin, call it a tendency towards self-preservation and self-interest, but the most we can aspire to being is partial and flawed. Outside the rigour of mathematical formulae, perfection is not an entity we should expect to observe. But sometimes universal laws are defied, or gently pushed aside and there is a meeting, a moment, a match so perfect we are privileged to look upon it. Like Lindsay and Chucky's wedding.

I made a speech at the reception – oh those Irish, such a way with words – saying how neither of them ever got so caught up in wedding preparations that they lost sight of what the day was really about, the fact that they love each other more than anything. The food and the flowers and the finery remained ancillary to this simple crux and the day was the better for it. It was a small affair – fifty guests or so – held in Lindsay's parents' back garden, though "garden" somewhat undersells the expansive lawn with the pristine Rockies as a backdrop, a river gorge in between. Chucky's family flew over from New Zealand and while there weren't official bridesmaids as such, Lindsay's friend Katie and I did the bridesmaid-y things: cake-tasting, staying with the bride the night before, getting our hair done together and other such onerous tasks.

"Here Lindsay," I said, reading from the stack of wedding etiquette books her mother had festooned around the house, "apparently the bride should try to eat something small the morning of the wedding, even if she doesn't feel like it." At this point Lindsay was at the stove making french toast for the entire bridal party and any miscellaneous relatives who happened to be in the house. Oh yes, on the morning of her own wedding.

Later on, hiding in the master suite, we changed into our frocks. Katie and I scurried to and from the kitchen, squealing in girlish anticipation, ushering Lindsay into the bathroom so Chucky wouldn't catch a glimpse of her ahead of the ceremony. Then as we sat in the garden, waiting for the bride to walk down the aisle, I sighed in starry-eyed awe at how wonderful and joyous it all was. At this point I took a tissue and dabbed discreetly at my eyes. Even hard-bitten hacks like myself have their sentimental side.

When we were in New Zealand we knew this English guy called Paul who was tragically stuck between the nicely brought up young man he was and the playa he thought he should be. He felt obliged to constantly emphasise his sexual magnetism and prowess, even crocheting a toque with the national flags of "all the girls I've *known*", his leery emphasis making clear he'd known this array of lucky ladies in the Biblical sense rather than simply having had the pleasure of their acquaintance. But every day on the staff bus up and down to the ski-hill he'd quietly bury himself in *The Count of Monte Cristo*, confessed to me once that his favourite book was *Emma* by Jane Austen, and after a night of alcohol-fuelled gyration would maudlinly turn to Lindsay and Chucky saying, "I just want what you two have!"

It's all that anyone really wants though, isn't it?

In the face of all this undiluted emotion, Katie and I were a bit wobbly the next day. Out we went for brunch and rang Lindsay to chorus our happy hellos. She told us that her residency application for New Zealand had been approved so her and Chucky would be moving to NZ for good in the next few months. Though long expected, this was wrenching to hear. Why do people have to head off half-way round the world? Poor Reg and Barb, I thought, that their only daughter will be so far away.

Poor Reg and Barb indeed, though I could do worse than to be as considerate of my own mum and dad. My tunnel-vision focus on snowsports has meant the occlusion of everything else, not least of all the feelings of my parents who I'm sure would love to see me more often than they do. I've spent only two weeks in the past eighteen months in Ireland and foregone four out of the past five Christmases at home to ski or snowboard instead. Not that I've been going without. The first winter in Fernie, Gerry from Stillorgan stepped into the role of mammy with aplomb, staying home from the ski-hill and whipping up a full Christmas Dinner, sprouts and all. Last year in Rossland we hosted a raucous pot luck which nearly propelled me into a gravy-splattered breakdown but everyone else had a great time. All in, I've given barely a thought to my family as I've shredded the gnar and slayed the pow. I know that parents are all for you spreading your wings and making your way in the world but surely only to a point?

But I'm starting to mellow in my advancing years. When I went back for the marathon there was the usual tearful reunion at Dublin Airport, the difference being that this time there were tears on my part as well. Until now I've only ever gone home because I've been skint or my visa for whichever country has run out. This was the first time I'd ventured back of own volition and appreciated being there. I'm a terrible person, I know.

Back on native soil, I took it very handy for the remaining few days before the race; sleeping for fifteen hours the first night to knock the jet-lag on the head, going for a final three mile leg-stretcher, carbo-loading and heading to the RDS with Lucie, a fellow snowboardeuse who'd flown in from London, to pick up our race numbers and swag bags. Carbo-loading, incidentally, isn't as enjoyable as any poor Atkins-starved crayturs among you might envisage. Having put on hold the high mileage to which your body has become accustomed, you just feel lumpen and bloated not to mention daunted by what lies ahead. Wholemeal toast for breakfast, sandwiches for lunch, pasta for dinner topped off by a late night snack of more pasta. Though I devour carbs with a gusto rare among girls in their twenties, even I was getting fed up by this stage.

Then the Bank Holiday Monday, the day of reckoning, arrived. Weather-wise we couldn't have asked for more; sunny, calm, a bit "close" perhaps, though only someone who'd been living in Calgary could have been so staggered by the heat and humidity of Dublin in late October. (I'd gone for a six mile run when it was minus 16 and skin-crackingly dry two weeks beforehand.)

Arriving in town with plenty of time to spare, Lucie and I sat on the Georgian steps of Merrion Square and discussed the biggest indicator of how the race would go, namely whether we'd managed to poo or not that morning.

As a distance runner you quickly lose any compunction in discussing every convulsion of your GI tract. We queued over and over again for the portaloos and, after one final piddle, moved down to the starting corral where 12,000 people were huddled together in the greatest conglomeration of lycra, knee-supports and quivering Irish flesh I've ever seen.

"Ah", I thought, "I love the smell of Deep Heat in the morning".

What is it with the bizarre stream of consciousness that race MCs tap into though? Last year at the Connemarathon Half the announcer urged us to pack back further behind the start line: "Come on now, keep moving there, move back from the front unless you're Kenyan or something and you're going to be getting around in less than an hour." At the Dublin Marathon we heard over the PA system how "I was watching the X-Factor last night with Cheryl Cole, sexy and sassy she is. But there's 12,000 people in front of me this morning and every one of you are every bit as sexy and sassy as that!"

We mumbled our way through *Amhrán na bhFiann* then bang! Off we went, shuffling slowly towards the start line then working up into a trot. There are plenty of times for heroics but the opening miles of a marathon are not one of them. Rather than going out guns blazing then collapsing in a quivering heap along the Stillorgan Dual Carriageway, I stuck to a steady pace and the first twenty miles slid by like silk, buoyed on by the crowds and their unmatchable cheer. The New York Marathon has an estimated two million spectators but I doubt they're anywhere near as spirited and giving as those lining the streets in Dublin. People were clapping until their hands hurt and handing out jelly-babies, chopped up Mars Bars, plates of Jaffa Cakes, lollipops, barley sugars, and spray-on Deep Heat. One man in the

Phoenix Park was shaking his head going "Marathon running! Fantastic! Absolutely unbelievable! Running marathons!" at everyone going past. Another guy rigged up a professional sound system in his front garden, playing cheesy hit after cheesy hit, and families dragged their kitchen tables into the street to set up extra water stations for those in need. There was a particularly savage hill turning onto Fosters Ave and for every step of it there were shouts of "Nearly there! Nearly there! Go on girls! You're nearly at the top! Last hill on the course lads!" Dubliners are great, culchies are great, the whole fucking world is great when you're on a runner's high.

I'd been warned, however, to approach the marathon as a six mile race with a twenty mile warm-up. "Now it starts," I thought when I reached the twenty mile marker. At this point the body starts to run out of glycogen, the mind games kick in and things get tough. There were plenty of casualties in the bleak no man's land of those last few miles; one runner bent double and vomiting, another clutching his leg in agony on the UCD flyover and most worryingly of all one man simply passed out face down on the course in Ballsbridge. Marathon running is an unforgiving pursuit.

As well as desperately needing to go to the toilet but being unwilling to break the pace and stop, I also wanted to throw up by this stage, so full was I of energy gel and Club Energise Sport (this isn't intended as product placement, it's more how incorrigibly Irish the on-course support was – none of that foreign aul' Gatorade muck on this day). Right, only two miles to go and then I can vomit I thought at the twenty-four mile mark. In the closing stages of a marathon you take comfort where you can.

Down Pearse Street and round the bend onto Nassau Street, eight hundred metres to go, four hundred metres to go, some runners barely tottering along, others managing to find one final explosive burst of speed. After 4 hours 19 minutes and 42 seconds of running I crossed the finish line. Fuck yeah! Then just fuck! Everything seized up in an instant, my hamstrings sung with the pain and I thought my right knee had had it, so swollen and unnatural did it feel. There was no striding it out purposefully now and I was reduced to piteous hobbling geisha steps to pick up my medal and my finisher's t-shirt, the hardest earned t-shirt of my life. A woman behind me was crying with exhausted relief and there were wan figures slumped against the railings, lying flat out on the ground or being ferried from place to place in wheelchairs. Walk it off! Walk it off!

I made it extremely slowly to the other side of Merrion Square and met up with my parents outside the Natural History Museum (has that place reopened after the staircase collapsed last year?) who were even more excitable than I was at this point. Having given me a lift into town early that morning, they'd watched the race start then, fortified by a rucksack full of sandwiches and a flask of tea, walked out along the Grand Canal – "it's absolutely gorgeous along there, Lisa, swans and everything" – to the eleven mile marker. Just in time to see the elite runners power by in pure concentration, they waited until I too went past with a bashful grin before cutting across the city to the twenty three mile point, shouting encouragement and handing out jelly-beans to those in need: "And they were so grateful Lisa! Full of the thank yous! Ah there was just, just a great buzz altogether".

Then along came my friends, two of whom had run as well, two of whom had been cheering and one of whom turned up with a box of champagne truffles. Manna from heaven! Time for a hard-earned drink but where to go, given that the city centre was now thronged with 12,000 thirsty runners and their entourages? We needed a bar where tourists or endurance athletes would be unlikely to venture. A bar untouched by the demands of consumer culture, where the Celtic Tiger and its demise had gone entirely unobserved, where the lack of atmosphere is its very charm. Only one place for it: Hartigan's.

The unassailable air of stasis in Hartigan's reminds me of that line from *Withnail and I*: "even a stopped clock tells the right time twice a day." I doubt they even knew in there a marathon was taking place outside the door. "Well," someone asked when we were propped up on wonky bar stools in the anteroom, "would you do it again?" Without a doubt, my friend Graeme and I quite cheerfully agreed. (Graeme's unorthodox taper included the half-marathon distance the Wednesday before and ceilidh dancing at his cousin's wedding all night long.) Really though, the challenge is as much the training cycle as the marathon itself. "We know 26.2 is the short part" is the slogan for one brand of running gear, it taking so much to even get to the starting line that the actual marathon is almost just a victory lap.

Only one more thing to attend to at this point. "What are you going to eat after the race?" a fellow runner had asked me during the summer. "Chicken nuggets and chips," I replied without a second thought. Evidently it's normal to spend the hollow-cheeked hours of training planning your I-don't-give-a-rat's-arse-about-my-cholestrol-I've-just-run-a-marathon meal. All summer long I'd been dreaming of chips, not skinny unsubstantial french fries but proper Irish chips from a proper Irish chipper, stuck together in a claggy mass of salt and fat. I went home, got in the shower, yowled when the water hit my raw and chafed skin, went back down the stairs sideways (if you've run a marathon you'll understand) and ate. Aah. The day was complete.

Though I really should know better, the marathon has given me a completely skewed impression of Dublin as a sunny place where everyone smiles. However right now it's no bad thing to have such a delusion, despite it being one of which I'll quickly be disabused. I flew back to Canada after the marathon only to discover yesterday that my work permit thingy hasn't been approved so back to Ireland it is after all. For now at least. Now, I'm not as devastated as you might imagine. My primary emotion is delight to be getting out of Calgary even if it means waving goodbye to the Canadian dream. I ran out of milk for my porridge the same morning and was more upset about having to eat watery gruel.

I'm finishing up work next week and leaving Calgary for one final world tour of the Kootenays. The skis are waxed, the winter tyres are back on the truck and I'm raring to go. (Anyone want to buy a 1991 Isuzu Trooper by the way?) Consider it a Greatest Hits Tour: visiting all my friends who remain behind and hopefully getting in some early season skiing if the snow is up to it. The plan is to go home for Christmas and take things from there.

I don't know though – this is a terrible time to be heading back to Ireland. I'm abreast of developments about NAMA, collapsing railway viaducts, lengthening dole queues, the economy down the jacks and, ironically, every second young professional doing a legger abroad. A misty-eyed emigrant I'm not.

So back to the auld sod? Back to tutting over the weather forecast for wind and rain. What do we expect? It's the North Atlantic. It's not an aberration when it rains: this is the climate. Back to Beckettian waits for buses which either come when they feel like it or not at all? Back to complaining to bus drivers about the discrepancies from the timetable only to be told, "Don't believe everything you read?" Back to interminable drunken arguments in the rain on Camden Street about whether giving a pint smuggled out of Whelan's to a homeless man can be considering a kindness or not? Back, thank God, to less Nickelback on the radio. (Canadian radio stations are mandated to devote a certain percentage of air time to Canadian artistes and Nickelback rule supreme.) Back to good quality dairy products, a more straightforward tax system and a laxer attitude towards drink? Yet paradoxically a more hard-line approach on drunk-driving.

We'll see.

Lisa

Back At It

November 2009: On The Road Again

Why hello there…

You know those experiments in which lab rats are offered the choice between food and cocaine and the wily rodents go for the coke every time? That's what snowsports are like. Once hooked, you abandon any foresight, security or monetary success in pursuit of that snowy high. At this time of year, just as the geese know it's time to fly south and the bears know to go into hibernation, I instinctively know it's time to go back to BC. "I want to ski. I want to ski. I want to ski" is the message of blinking insistence stemming from some part of my brain that knows nothing of reason.

So Kootenay World Tour 09 is a go! I left Calgary wearing my new ski-jacket, truck fully loaded and in the passenger seat was my best friend from Ireland who flew over last Sunday for the next weeks on the road.

Now she's very chary of developing any sort of online or print presence, still resisting Facebook etc so I'll simply refer to her by the fiendishly clever pseudonym of Maximilian.

Anyone who knows her well will realise who this is, but all others will be baffled by this impenetrable cloak of anonymity. Aha!

When she arrived last weekend, Maximilian brought with her some Irish newspapers. I fell on them immediately, starved as I've been of quality print journalism here in Canuck-land. You know Lord Macaulay's incendiary statement that a single bookshelf of Western literature contained more merit than the entire literary tradition of India and Arabia? Well I'd take a single issue of *The Irish Times* over a year's worth of Canadian rags.

"Are things really this bad at home right now?" I asked her, looking up from yet another story about negative equity and financial mismanagement. She nodded vigorously.

"Yeah, there's a pretty bad atmosphere in the country at the moment. People are –" she paused, looking for the right word, "angry. There's a lot of anger about how much of a mess it all is."

Right. Not the ideal time to be a returning émigré. Maximilian says she was shocked when she heard I intended coming back to Dublin at Christmas time rather than lingering on here to eke out one final ski-season. I shrugged. I have to leave Canada for good at some point so why postpone the inevitable? Furthermore, I only ever intended to do one winter in Canada and still can't quite fathom how I've ended up doing three.

We headed up to Banff National Park, the heart of the Rockies, to stay in a wooden hostel lodge in Lake Louise for the night before making a break for the BC border. Thank God. I've had enough of Alberta to last me a lifetime and then some more. The next day we drove to Fernie through pine forests, mountain passes and national parks. In Fernie it was the usual pre-season entertainments: hiking through the snow, helping my friend nail Christmas lights to the front of his house (my duties: holding the ladder, shouting encouragement), wandering around Canadian Tire. We tramped on the trails around town and hiked the hill for some early season turns. Snowshoes and skins on the way up, faceshots and faceplants on the way down. Pow pow pow – it's shaping up to be a good season. Nice for those who'll be here to enjoy it…

One evening we were sitting around chatting, an *Aliens* marathon idly playing in the background, when a friend rang. There was a bear about one hundred metres down the road. No way! Not that there's anything exceptional about seeing a bear in Fernie (as I've discovered the terrifying way), bounded as it is on all sides by mountain forest, but shouldn't it be hibernating by now? On with the jackets, winter boots and toques and out the door it was. No bear but we found its tracks in the fresh snow. The following night I was driving up the street when a black shape lumbered across the road in front of us. The bear! But quite a young one by the looks of it, evidently separated from its mother and at a bit of a loss what to do. Oh dear.

Fretting over the plight of ursine orphans, we left Fernie and continued to drive westwards across the Kootenays. This evening I missed a deer by milliseconds when it darted across the road. Looks like the bull bar on the truck could come in handy on this trip…. Though I'll miss the excitement of bear spotting, in some ways it'll be a relief to go back to Ireland where the most severe automobile vs animal mishap would be knocking down the neighbour's dog.

Next stop - Rossland!

Lisa

December 2009: Winter - whither?

Hey hey

This isn't the first time Maximilian and I have travelled together to snowy parts. When we were in second year of college (nearly eight years ago! Christ!) we went on that fateful snowboarding holiday to Andorra at which point I saw the light, abandoned the notion of ever pursuing a conventional career, finished up college as a mere formality and headed off to chase the snow, never to look back (only occasionally and fleetingly, anyway). Maximilian wasn't quite so easily distracted, however, and after six years of medical school launched straightaway into work as a junior doctor. She's thus spent the past three years regularly putting in seventy and eighty hour weeks, racking up innumerable sleepless nights on call and waving goodbye to ever enjoying a bank holiday weekend. Though I've been exhorting her to visit me in Canada for years she was never able to do so until now. She could only ever get one week off at a time, annual leave being contingent upon staff shortages, what other members of the team were up to etc. And while she loves the actual work – the patient interaction, the thrill of diagnosis, the emergency procedures – she's less keen about the status-seeking and extreme competitiveness of the medical world.

But after a few short weeks in BC she's seamlessly sloughed off any traces of this and has adapted to Kootenay time with alacrity. When we arrived back in Rossland she met the shower of ne'er-do-wells I happily call my friends and quickly became versed in the whole culture of tree-planting, seasonal work and claiming EI. She was talking on Skype to her mum, who wondered how exactly the ski-bum thing worked. Do they just go skiing at weekends, the people in Rossland? "No, no, they go to the ski-hill every day. I don't know, they work in the evenings or something. Or they just go on unemployment benefit for the winter. It's fine!"

The life of a ski bum is quite the contrast to the career-climbing of medicine where no gap on a CV can go unaccounted for. Indeed, Maximilian only had the time off for the road trip in the first place because she's currently on a career break for a very specific purpose. Having spent the past few months studying for a Diploma in Tropical Medicine, she's heading off to work in rural Zambia where she'll be the only doctor in the locale. However, there have been ongoing issues with the placement organisation (name withheld to protect the guilty). She was originally meant to be leaving in December, then the end of February, then back to December. She checked her email the other day and sighed.

"Now they're saying that it might not be until the middle of January again. This is…."

"Rubbish. You thought you were going to be heading off as soon as you got back home and now…."

"I'm going to have another month just sitting around Skerries…."

"And being stuck in Dublin for New Year's Eve."

"Oh God."

"Oh God."

(We've been friends for so long that we can finish each other's sentences with ease.)

I mulled over this for a second.

"Maybe we should both just stay here in Rossland for the winter," I suggested, half in jest.

"Really?" she asked eagerly.

"Yeah!" I exclaimed, then clapped my hands over my mouth. You know when you suggest something that's so joking, daring and preposterous it doesn't bear thinking about but once it's out there, there's no going back. Could we? Could we stay in Rossland for the next few months?

Well...why not? Let's examine the potential difficulties in both instances. Maximilian would have to tell the placement organisation that after all the messing around she'd just go to Zambia at the end of February, the date suggested at one point. She'd simply say that "an opportunity" had arisen which she was keen to pursue in the interim, glossing over the finer details involving powder skiing and the BC Interior.

Then there's the issue of parental opposition. Maximilian rang home again to break the "good news" that her four week trip to Canada might be turning into a semi-season as a feckless ski-bum. Her mum quizzed her about how this would be looked upon when she has to slip back into the system next year and apply for medical jobs again. Hmm.

Though I have no such career considerations – ugh, the "c-word" – if I were to stay I'd be suffused with guilt about not going back to Ireland for Christmas AGAIN. Like I said before, I've missed four of the past five Christmases at home to ski. Well, as Johnny Logan put it, what's another year....

Oh, I'm seduced by the Kootenays, addicted to snow, whatever way you want to look at it. Ski-seasons are an unmatchably wild and joyous time particularly if the alternative is going back to Ireland for 14% unemployment and sackcloth-and-ashes.

But let's not rush into things. I need to put some critical distance between Rossland and myself before reaching a final decision on Winter 09/10, so on with the road trip it is.

Westward ho!

Lisa

December 2009: Livin' the Dream

Where was I again? Ah yes! Rossland!

Maximilian and I left Rossland for the seven hundred

kilometre drive to Vancouver, with an enthusiastic estimation (on my part at least) of how much ground we could cover in a day. Note to self: even the most perfunctory survey of the BC Road Atlas should have indicated that Highway Three, rather than roaring flat across the province in the multi-lane highway I had perhaps envisaged, is a twisted, sinewy affair encompassing mountain passes and hair-pin bends. Furthermore, if you undertake such a drive in icy late November when darkness comes at 4:00pm it's only to be expected that progress will be slow.

As we neared the coast, the driving snow gave away to sheets of rain. We pulled off the highway into the optimistically named town of Hope and checked into a motel for the night. Motels are an expressly North American phenomenon, so our impressions of them had been gleaned from films and television rather than personal experience. As a result, we'd been led to believe that they're peopled exclusively by criminals, fugitives, persons conducting seedy affairs, and those awaiting placement in witness protection schemes. Maximilian was particularly taken with how the doors of the individual units opened straight onto the motor-court rather than via a central reception. All the better for dodgy dealings, you see.

"This is the sort of bathroom where people wash out bloodstains," I called out from the dated, pine-walled facilities. Well, that or they dye their hair to change their appearance and evade the intelligence agencies in hot pursuit.

The night passed without incident, a bit disappointing really when I'd been hoping for gunshots or at least a door being kicked in and someone dragged out in cuffs.

On it was the next morning, pushing west, pushing west. We reached Vancouver and went into a mall, where I was dazzled by the bright lights and consumer durables of the city. A guy from Rathmines was working behind the till in one of the shops and the whole you're-Irish-I'm-Irish-how-long-are-you-in-Canada-for exchange arose. Maximilian explained we were on a road trip and had driven over one thousand kilometres across Alberta and BC, from the prairies to the Pacific via various ski-towns.

"How were the roads?" the Rathmines boy asked.

"Oh", Maximilian said airily, "you know, it was a bit snowy, you'd need the four wheel drive." In fact the only time we'd gone into 4WD at that point was when whirring on ice in the Rossland trailer park. But why let such details get in the way of a brag?

All that remains to be said about the roadtrip is that having reached Vancouver and the coast we promptly turned around and headed back to Rossland for the winter. Because really, who was I kidding when I thought I'd be able to leave the Kootenays at the start of December when the ski-season is just kicking into action? Flights were changed, parents were informed, accommodation was sourced, season passes were purchased. Baby let's get this show on the road!

Now finding accommodation in a ski-town can be a challenge, particularly in the sparsely settled Interior of BC. It's a renter's market in the Kootenays, there being more ski-bum vagrants than available properties to let so you hear stories of people piled into the oddest quarters, paying drastically over the odds for rent. Aside from the usual ten-Aussies-crammed-into-two-bedrooms routine, I know one guy who spent a whole winter sleeping in a stairwell, another who'd snuggled down in the utility room beside the washing machine.

To secure somewhere affordable and vaguely habitable, it's advisable to get into town weeks or possibly even months ahead of the ski-hill opening. So when Maximilian and I decided, a mere week before the season kicked off, to spend the winter in Rossland problems could have been afoot.

What would our contingency plan be if we couldn't find anywhere to live, we worried? Stay in a grotty hostel dorm? Live down in Trail?

However, before any such drastic moves had to be employed, a friend of a friend tipped us off to a three-bedroom house advertised for rent. I rang the owner, a retired local widow who now spends the winters golfing in California, and gave her the two-lovely-girls-from-Ireland lowdown. She said the house was still available but that the monthly rent was on the steep side. I held my breath as she named her price. It was a steal. Evidently she had no idea the degree to which seasonal residents in a ski-town can be fleeced. So Maximilian and I moved into our new home along with a guy called Andy, an archetypically laid-back Vancouverite.

We've really "lucked out" with the house, as the North American phrase has it. Right at the top of upper Rossland, it's set into the hillside with two massive decks, unencumbered mountain views and ample space. My bedroom in particular is so large it's obscene. The living room has proved equally spacious enough for weekly yoga sessions, guided by a friend of ours who's training for her yoga teacher cert. She and her household are preparing vegan roast and a tofu-based dessert for Christmas Day. "That sounds very nice," I said politely when I heard of this festive repast. There's even a sheltered carport so I don't have to brush off my truck in the morning after heavy snowfalls. This winter being my swansong to Canada, it's nice to go out in style. Maximilian is here till the end of January and I'm going to eke out my dwindling funds for another month after that.

Equally as thrilling as the creature comforts of the house are its hidden treasures. This is after all a family home, built by our landlady's late husband, and the furnishings have accumulated with the generations. There are children's ski-trophies from the 60s and 70s, a personalised jacket from the 1983 BC Winter Games and grandchildren must have appeared on the scene soon after this if the toy cars and video collection (*Beauty and the Beast, The Little Mermaid, Jurassic Park*) are anything to go by.

We were looking through the presses today for board games – we're hosting a board game evening on Wednesday, it's going to be WILD – when Andy found a carry case full of tapes. And tapes of such unrivalled magnificence as will bring any social occasion back from the abyss! There's Kenny Rogers – *Ten Years of Gold*; Willie Nelson – *His Original Hits, Country Stories in Song* – A Compilation; not to mention the rather leftfield inclusion of *Hair* (The American Tribal Love-Rock Musical) – The Original Broadway Cast Recording.

I'm not vaunting these tapes in any sort of ironic-kitsch way, nor is this a backhanded way of slagging them off. I have a genuine affection for country music. Some of it at least. My limits were tested this summer in Alberta. Driving up and down to Fernie at the weekends with just the radio for company, I'd listen to hours on end of terrible, mawkish, God-bless-America stuff about freedom and dead owners of Cadillacs. I certainly don't seek to denigrate the memory of anyone who's died in combat and I equally don't want to jump on the anti-American bandwagon but being subject to such syrupy-sentimental patriotism over prolonged periods was enough to make me want to join an angry mob in Iran or other such hot-bed of fundamentalism and burn an effigy of George Bush.

But such moments aside I like a bit of honky-tonk now and then – don't we all? – and I've been getting great mileage out of the stash of tapes. My truck is of a vintage such that it has a tape deck instead of a CD player, which had hitherto only been used for connecting up Maximilian's iPod with one of those newfangled cable things. The discovery of the tapes, though, has meant a return of the tape-deck to its original use and I've formed an unhealthy attachment to the Kenny Rogers album in particular.

Andy was then rummaging around the shed recently when he came across two more carry-cases of tapes which, if our amateur anthropological datework is anything to go by, must have belonged to our landlady's now grown-up children during their late 80s/early 90s heyday. So it's U2 during their *Joshua Tree* to *Zooropa* phase, Guns N' Roses, Bruce Springsteen, James Taylor, Talking Heads. The regularity which with I've playing these new finds in the house and the truck alike leaves me a bit abashed. It's got to the point where I now quantify distance in terms of the tapes; i.e., it takes until the thunderous break in November Rain – "don't you think that you need somebody/don't you think that you need someone" – to get to the ski-hill. It takes all of Bryan Adams' *Reckless* to drive down to Trail and back.

I don't know where it all went wrong. Time was – long, long ago – when I was reasonably *au fait* with what was hip and new in the musical world. But since I first stepped onto a snowboard in 2002, I've been inhabiting a snow-flurried haze with the cultural developments of the Noughties permeating my consciousness only oh-so-faintly every now and then: resurgence of guitar music? Ibiza becoming passé? Lots of bands with "The" in the name? Mormons wearing eyeliner? Twins with bouffant hair? What's going on out there?

It's growing increasingly difficult to imagine that I'll ever successfully reintegrate into polite society upon leaving the wilds of BC.

Lisa

December 2009: Somebody Call A Doctor!

Hi again

Red Mountain (The Best Ski-hill in the World TM) opened last Saturday, a week ahead of schedule. It's difficult to describe the current conditions at Red without coming across as too triumphalist or gloating. In contrast to the snow-starved horror of this time last year, the early-season skiing and riding has been exceptional. And there's little in the world to rival fresh lines on a powder day. That weightless, almost transcendental feeling of flying through bottomless snow – oh. The pumping legs, the ecstatic cries, then arriving at the bottom, cheeks flushed, eyes aflame, hair matted damp under your helmet, panting with exertion – that's what I'm talking about. Whooping and high-fiving your friends then taking the chair-lift to do it over and over until you're too damp and cold for any more – Jesus, I can barely stand it.

As a doctor, Maximilian has dealt with her fair share of alcoholics and addicts. This evening she asked me a few rudimentary questions about my relationship with snowsports.

"Has it affected things with your family?"

"Let me see, I've spent two weeks in the past eighteen months at home…"

"Have other people commented about it? Have their comments made you angry?"

"Well, you know, just now and again?"

"Has it had a detrimental effect on your work-life?"

"Ha! I'm not going to even credit that with a response. You're talking to someone who duct-tapes over the holes in her snow pants."

"Is it the first thing you think about in the morning?"

"Fuck yeah. Looking out of the window and seeing how much it's snowed overnight. In fact, recently I've started sleeping with the blinds up for an unobstructed eye-opening view."

"Have you tried to give up and failed?"

Silence, and then, "Right, I see what you're getting at."

This is absolutely, definitely and positively the last ski-season I'm going to spend in Canada. I can stop anytime I want. Anytime I want.

Lisa

December 2009: Old Dudes Rip

Well now

You know the way the *National Geographic* sometimes runs articles about ethnic groupings/population pockets of exceptional longevity, eating fish oils or maintaining strong family ties or some other such key to long life? The next such feature should be about Rossland. At community-driven ski-hills like Red Mountain, every trail name tells a story. Newly gladed this year, for example, are Captain Jack's Trees, named after a white-bearded free-skiing legend who was killed in a road accident while biking this summer. Similarly there's Rino's Run, Rino being a 74 year old ski-patroller keeping the slopes of Rossland safe for over forty years. I then sat next to a guy on the chairlift the other day who's had a season pass for fifty-nine years, though this is far from exceptional around here. He told me about his friends and contemporaries. There's Louie, who's eighty-four and deaf in one ear but who's been skiing since the 1930s. Then there was Ernie, now sadly departed, who held his eighty-fifth birthday party in Rafters (the raucous ski-lodge bar which goes OFF) and whose worst day in his life was when they took his skis away from him after he turned ninety-six.

And make no mistake about it: these aren't doddery

geriatrics feebly snow-ploughing down the green runs. Oh no. Old dudes rip.

The south-facing side of Red is known as Paradise and the ski-lodge there is called, perhaps somewhat obviously, Paradise Lodge (or Paradise Lost as I keep inadvertently referring to it, adding a Miltonic ring to a day on the hill). Anyway, the other day we were reposing ourselves by the fire in the lodge when in came a weathered man, around sixty or so, wearing a faded fluoro jacket and with a slightly lop-sided gait. Retro 80s gear might be all the rage at the moment but a lot of it is still being worn in Rossland from first time around. As he pulled out the liners from his ski-boots and adjusted his orthodtics, he explained to us that this is his seventh season in Rossland but that normally he doesn't bother skiing Paradise. He prefers the more challenging ungroomed stuff off the North side. But as it's only the first week of the season he's easing himself back into things. And, in any case, he's been skiing differently since his hip replacement. None of this was self-aggrandisement, it was all said as simply and plainly as a glass of water.

"Unbelievable!" Maximilian kept saying, shaking her head in admiration, "unbelievable!" She was agog he was out on the hill at all, let alone conquering the off-piste, as hip replacements normally betoken the road to immobility.

Tim, his name was and we met him again a few days later back in the lodge. He offered to give us some pointers on our skiing and keenly we acquiesced. Down the groomers we went and he put Maximilian through a few drills for her technique. Then he turned to me.

"We should go do Short Squaw" he said.

Hmm. On my snowboard I love Short Squaw – or "Booty's Run" as that section of the hill has been renamed, "squaw" having fallen out of polite use – but I continue to be an appallingly bad off-piste skier and, well, I've had issues there before on skis. But hey, nothing ventured, nothing gained and can't let Tim down now can I? So we followed the ridge line along the top of the mountain before dropping in via the steeper and narrower of two chutes, of course, as per Tim's preferred route.

Tim – the sexagenarian with the hip replacement – ripped down the steep and deep with ease, and I following behind knock-kneed but resolute, puffing out my cheeks to psyche myself up for every acute-angled turn – watch that rock! – and eventually bam! smoking myself on a tree. It was one of those proper ski crashes where I ended up straddling the tree, legs oddly-angled and buried in the snow on each side. Ouch. Tim looked on pityingly as I disengaged myself from the branches, then we continued through the trees till we reached the cat-track. At which point I gingerly made my way to the base to tend to my bruised thighs and the indefatigable Tim headed back up the chairlift to do it all again. Like I said, old dudes rip.

Lisa

December 2009: Sweet Nothings

Hungry, anyone?

So there I was, sitting out on the Daylodge deck the other day enjoying my packed lunch. I waxed lyrical last winter about peanut butter but this season I'm moving up in the world by venturing out into a wider repertoire of nut butters. That day's treat was almond butter on homemade oat-and-honey loaf.

"Here, try a bite of this," I said proffering the sandwich in Maximilian's direction, "you don't even need jam on it because the bread is already sweet."

"Mmm, yeah, sweet bread," she said idly, then paused. "What are sweetbreads? It's some type of organ isn't it?"

"I think it's testicles," I said.

"I think you might be right," she replied, at which point we sniggered uncontrollably.

"Hang on though," I continued, "there's sweetmeat as well, isn't there? What's that then? Is it some kind of dessert?"

Back on the slopes for another bit, then home to investigate matters further, Maximilian shovelling the drive while I googled "sweetbreads" and "offal" and "cooking testicles". You don't even want to know some of the stuff I came across. My findings: sweetbreads are the thymus and pancreas, tenderly prepared. Sweetmeats on the other hand refer to marzipan, nougat and other such fondant delights. However – and this is really important for the next time you find yourself in a confectioners-cum-offal-restaurant – sweetmeats CAN also refer to testicles, breaded and fried. Don't say you haven't been warned.

On an entirely different note, you might have noticed that I haven't been injuring myself recently with the frequency which I did in my park-rat days. (Do you think there could be a connection?) But this morning I was going through some mellow bumps when I clipped a ski, ejected from it and flew several feet through the air before a face-first smackdown. This sounds more violent than it actually was, the snow so soft nothing was injured. Except my pride. But before clambering back uphill to retrieve my errant ski I noticed that its counterpart – still attached to my other foot – and the surrounding patch of snow was now flecked with blood. And very fresh blood, given the brilliant scarlet of the blots. I took off my glove and tentatively patted my face – nada. I ran my tongue around the inside of my mouth – again, everything still in place thank God – a few weeks ago a friend of a friend kneed himself in the face and knocked out two of his teeth in a particularly vicious crash. Nor was there the telltale metallic tang of

- 256 -

a nosebleed. I sat there for a minute, trying to work out what had just taken place.

Two possible explanations, both of which are somewhat improbable. First: someone had taken the exact same line and crashed in exactly the same spot only a minute or two beforehand. The blood was of so vivid a hue it couldn't have been any further back than that. The problem with this theory is that Red Mountain is sparsely skied at the best of times, especially this morning when visibility was low and the sky was a dismal gray against the freezing rain. There was no one up there. Second: the impact caused a minor nosebleed from the very front of my nose, so forward that all the blood splattered over the snow rather than trickling back down into my nasal cavity. Again, unlikely but unless anyone else has a better idea I'm stumped. Maybe it was a wounded Sasquatch limping his way back to his forest lair?

Baffled but unhurt I clicked back into my ski and went on my way. All very odd.

Lisa

January 2010: Gettin' 'Er Done

Happy New Decade!

Well now, New Year's Eve and its aftermath....It could be a headline from *The Onion*, the absolute predictability of it all: "Girl Castigates Self for Drinking To Excess, Vows Never To Do So Again". But, in brief, the Irish in Rossland (population: two) did not acquit themselves well while ringing out the old decade and in the new.

Strong drink was taken.

National stereotypes were reinforced.

Terrible, terrible atavistic slogans were chanted and in one instance written into a snowbank.

Reference was made to the continued prominence of a certain monarch on Canadian banknotes.

Local sensibilities were offended.

Amends will have to be made.

My penance for the New Year's Eve fiasco was forfeiting fresh turns on New Year's Day. In fairness, I was more tired and scutty-eyed than anything else but experience has shown that if I go shredding with anything less than full faculties, injury will ensue. I marvel whenever anyone sparks up a doobie out on the hill. Here amongst the grow-ops of the West Kootenays, the sweet smell of BC weed wafting down the lift line is so common to barely muster mention. I need all the reflexes and responsiveness I can get for snowsports.

So yeah, anyway, on New Year's Day I stayed home and shovelled the drive instead. Maximilian came out and took a photo of me doing so, the whole drive-shovelling thing still being somewhat of a novelty. Of course, for Canadians it's just part of the daily wintertime routine and they'd no more capture it in photos than Irish people would dash out with a camera when someone's hanging the washing on the line.

Looking at the photo afterwards I realised that my fashion muse these days is Old Man Marley, the gruff snow-shoveller from *Home Alone*. I recreated his look by teaming a fleece-lined hunting cap with my ski jacket, some fleece mittens completing my top half. On my bottom half I went for tracksuit bottoms inherited from my brother (vintage, darling), tucked into snow boots which were left in my truck by my housemate Ellie at the end of last winter. The boots are a size too big for me but, being the ingenious fashionista I am, I compensate by wearing thick merino wool knee socks. What I love most about this look is its versatility as with a few accessory changes it could be adapted for any social occasion (well, here in Rossland anyway.) It remains to be seen how I'm going to get on back in status-ridden middle-class Dublin.

See, for all my *Mise Éire* pronouncements of New Year's Eve, I'm a liminal creature now (as high-falutin' postcolonial theory would describe it) neither fully Irish nor fully Canadian and am going to have significant readjustment issues when I finally, finally leave the Kootenays for good. The other day at the base of Red I met two guys I know from last winter who'd just got back into town. We took the chairlift together and talked about current snow conditions, the sled they bought a while back, our various trucks – my '91 Isuzu Trooper to their '95 Ford F150 – and the usefulness of 4WD for rattling around Rossland in the ice and snow. "Oh yah, for sure eh," I found myself saying to express absolute agreement at one point. Let's break this sentence down into its constituent parts. "Oh yah," is a multi-purpose phrase which can function as either inquiry or affirmation depending on the intonation employed. Think Frances McDormand in *Fargo*. So you have "oh yah?" meaning "is that right now?" as well as "oh yah" for "you're right there boss." "For sure," again signals accord. And as for the ubiquitous "eh", loath as I am to reinforce national stereotypes, Canadians really do use it a lot. Whereas I'd once mutter "d'ya know what I mean" I now round off probably every second sentence with an "eh". Oh yah. I've become more than a little Canadian-ised over the past four years.

Let's see how it goes, eh.

Lisa

January 2010: Were you ever out in the Great Alone...

Ahoy!

The one regret I have of my time in Canada is not having made it up North. Properly North, that is. I like a bit of elemental struggle in my life. Coincidentally, I just finished rereading my absolute favourite book of all time and under all circumstances, *The Catcher in the Rye*, for about the millionth time. Holden's plan to hitch out west, live in a cabin and chop wood for the winter no longer seems like such a desperate and implausible strike. Do it, Holden, there are thousands of us scattered across BC of similar mind and I'm sure my friends would be happy to lend you their chainsaw for a day or two if needs be.

We were over in the trailer park for dinner last night with aforementioned friends. They bought a dilapidated trailer last year and have painstakingly roofed, dry-walled and renovated it into a cosy homestead. One of their cousins was there who's been living up in the Yukon for the past eighteen months. He told us what it's like to wake up in your cabin when it's 50 below, the wood-burner has gone out, there are icicles in your beard and you're too perishingly cold even to get up and light the fire again. Of what it's like up there on the brink of the Arctic Circle and to have twenty-one hours of darkness a day during the winter months. Of trappers and miners not talking to anyone for months on end and returning half-deranged into town in the spring.

So when reading reports of how Ireland has been propelled into a state of national emergency by the current "Arctic conditions" I have to think "really?" That said, I appreciate that it takes a while to acclimatise to the cold and it probably wouldn't be too pleasant if you didn't have the necessary gear. Winter tyres, snow chains, 4WD. Shovels, salt, grit. Thermals, toques, down booties, fleece pants.

Someone suggested last night that we should send an aid convoy from Canada to see Ireland through these crisis-ridden times. Every one could donate a bag of road salt, an extra snow shovel from their shed and an old toque. (We probably have more winter gear in our garage right now than in the whole of County Dublin.) We could then load up an airplane and deploy the Canadian Army to help salt and grit the roads. Of course, the Irish have their part to play as well. Maximilian has become an expert shoveller in her time in Canada so when she goes back at the end of January she'll be well positioned to become a national hero, hacking away at the ice. "You could be the Irish, what's-his-name, Stakhanov," I suggested, "you know, clearing the snow of ten men in a day or something."

Lisa

January 2010: How Do You Like Them Potatoes, or Rock'n'Roll Dreams Come True

What's that you're sayin'?

On Tuesday there was a bluegrass band playing in the Old Firehall, Rossland's token classy joint. Our friends Dani and Jenn invited us around to their house beforehand for wheat-free and dairy-free pizza topped with tofu and vegan cheese. These are the same friends who tucked into the vegan Christmas dinner. Maximilian and I thought it would be only right to bring some additional toppings along so we defrosted some of the Christmas ham from the freezer then stopped in the supermarket en route for a block of salty, fatty, melty mozzarella.

Now the thing about Rossland is that anything goes. If you want to get up and smoke a bowl first thing in the morning – fine. If you want to get up and head off on an epic backcountry trek – fine. If you want to get up, head off on an epic backcountry trek *then* smoke a bowl – well it doesn't get more Rossie than that. As long as what you're doing or ingesting isn't harming anyone else, so be it.

This live-and-let-live vibe extends to matters sartorial and, as I mentioned last year, thrift store couture is huge. Dani and Jenn are thrift store gurus and for the walk to the Firehall Dani bundled up in an oversized, deep-pocketed, multi-coloured tweed overcoat.

"Dani," I said admiringly as we were walking along, "if you wore that coat anywhere else in the world people would assume you'd just been released from a psych ward. But here it looks really cool."

Now the poster said the band would start at 8.00pm but naturally we assumed the event would be running on Kootenay time so we ambled on in just before nine. Actually they were half way through their set so we shuffled into some seats and listened appreciatively to the remaining songs – the Old Firehall is a more of a nod-your-head-and-finger-the-stem-of-your-wineglass place than a hoe-down dive-bar.

Fast forward to the end of the night and the guitar player came over and struck up a conversation with Dani and Jenn as we were making our way to the door. The band was on a tour across Western Canada and as this was their first time in Rossland we gave him the lowdown on West Kootenay life. I'm not sure how but somehow they got onto the topic of the thrift store, integral part of Rossland life that it is. Jenn mentioned that there were some nice dresses there at the moment but that they were on the pricey side: four dollars each.

"I mean, four dollars," she exclaimed, "I could get 30kg of potatoes for that!"

The guy from the band looked quizzical so they clamoured to explain.

"See there's a farmer just across the border –"

"Which is only six kilometres away. And he sells off sacks of potatoes –"

"The ones that are all misshapen so he can't sell them to the grocery stores –"

"And today we bought a 30kg sack –"

"For only five bucks!"

"Fresh from the farm."

I nodded vigorously. These are exciting times we're living through.

The other band members flocked over one by one and the virtues of potatoes – their versatility, their nutritional worth – were enthusiastically extolled by all. It was suggested that the band might perhaps consider bartering one of their CDs for some of these wondrous farm-fresh spuds. 10kg of potatoes was initially suggested as a fair exchange. Upon closer consideration, however, it was agreed by all parties involved that it would be excessive for the band to take so large a quantity of potatoes on the road. A compromise was reached: Dani and Jenn would part with 5kg of potatoes in return for a CD.

The guitarist handed over the disc. But how was he to get his potatoes in return? A deal is a deal, after all.

"Where do you live?" he asked.

Dani paused, thinking how best to explain how to navigate the winding, hilly streets of Rossland to find their house.

"Do you know where the Prestige Hotel is?" she asked

"Yeah, we're staying there," he said.

"Oh perfect!" Dani said, clapping her hands, "we live just round the corner. I'll drop the potatoes by first thing tomorrow morning. How's 9:00am in the hotel lobby? Is that too early?"

"No, no, that's fine," said the guitarist somewhat dazedly but now 5kg of potatoes better off. Probably not the outcome he'd anticipated upon approaching a group of girls in a bar. But hey, it's why every band goes on tour, isn't it: the gigs, the chicks, the potatoes.

Lisa

January 2010: Snowsports - cradle to grave

Let's hear it for the Kootenays!

Was it Sparta where babies were left out overnight on the cliffs so that only the hardiest would survive? There must be some sort of similar initiation here in Rossland before you're allowed to buy a house, or even start kindergarten.

They don't start skiing young in Rossland – they start *in utero*. Yesterday in Paradise Lodge I met a woman who was seven months pregnant and just about able to buckle her snow-pants up over her bump. Her companion was talking about what a pity it was that her fifteen-month old was a few months shy of being able to ski this year. Eighteen months, apparently, is the optimal age to start the groms on the hill. If they can walk they can ski.

Indeed, that morning I'd seen a five year old impatiently leaning on his poles and shouting "Come on Dad!" trying to hurry things along. God, parents can be such a drag sometimes. When Papa had finally finished fiddling with his goggles and poles, Junior then skate-skied along like a demon to get good air off a jump on the way to the bottom of the Upon reaching adulthood you then probably have to extricate yourself from a lair of grizzlies, make your way through the forest blindfolded then suture your own wounds with only a bottle of whiskey for pain relief before you can be considered a bona fide member of the community. The locals here are unilaterally hardcore if my recent chairlift encounters are anything to go by.

A few weeks ago I sat next to a man who works as an avalanche controller and forecaster. That's right, his job is to drive around BC bombing any cornices or slabs that are likely to slide. He told us about a group of his friends who went on a four-week ski-tour. Now ski-touring isn't the on-snow equivalent of wine-touring or anything. You don't sedately cruise from resort to resort enjoying the local specialties. Instead, it's where you strike off into the back country on skins or snowshoes, all your gear on your back, and enjoy fresh lines up and down mountain passes through avalanche terrain, dodging crevasses and the like if you're really striking out for the wild on a multi-day tour.

"What did they do for food?" I asked, "would you even be able to carry enough stuff for that long a trip?"

"Oh," my companion said, "they air-dropped four food parcels ahead of time. Two of the packages were lost though. The first one they couldn't find because the weather turned in so they possibly strayed slightly from their planned route. The other they reckon the ravens got into. They got to the site of the drop, the packages were all torn and empty and the birds were sitting around looking fat and well fed!"

Imagine – having travelled for days across the backcountry in the snow and cold to find your only food source destroyed? What on earth can you say in response? "Oh I know how they must have felt – this morning we nearly ran out of milk."

Then Tim (the sexagenarian with the hip replacement I mentioned a while back) told us about his escapade last winter in Chamonix whereby he had to be heli-evacuated after twenty-six hours stranded on the backside of a mountain. See, he skied down this particular face before realising there was no route out, he was just heading deeper and deeper into the Alps. However, whenever he tried to hike back up he just kept sliding back down. There was too much fresh snow and the pitch was too steep. He was stuck.

"I thought I was a goner when it started to get dark!" he told an astounded Maximilian and I. He survived the night by pacing back and forth on the same patch of snow in an effort to stay warm and alive. Luckily someone alerted ski-patrol to his disappearance and the helicopter found him the next day, by which point his body temperature had fallen to 32C and he had to be hospitalised. Within a few days, he was back out skiing.

Yesterday topped things off though. I got on the Motherlode lift with another two locals, one of whom was casually discussing his mountaineering feats and his most recent expedition to Everest. He said he was planning his next trip back to the region but that some of the 7000m peaks are "just too easy. It's about a fifty-five degree pitch so it's basically a long snowwalk." Totally. I mean, who among us *hasn't* felt the irritation of their Himalayan ascent lacking challenge?

We got to the top of the lift and he turned to me.

"Want to come ski Sarah's Chute with us?" he asked, referring to a notoriously steep and cliff-ridden section of the hill.

"Absolutely not," I said. When I hear "7000m peak" and "just too easy" in the same sentence, that's my cue to leave.

Lisa

February 2010: Winter Carnival

Oh yeah...

Sorry for being incommunicado there for a while but, like, get with the programme: Winter Carnival was going on! All sorts of enjoyments and entertainments take place in Rossland during Winter Carnival weekend: food stalls, a DJ booth and a mini-terrain park are set up. The steepest hill in town is iced down for a bobsled race, an ice-bar is sculpted out along the main street and a great time is had by all.

Run in tandem with the Winter Carnival is Blizzard Fest, a three-night music extravaganza, currently in its fourth year to the Winter Carnival's estimable one hundred and thirteen years. Proceedings kicked off on the Thursday with a funk band playing in the Flying Steamshovel, Rossland's premiere bar (in fact, Rossland's only real bar). My friend Gregor was wearing a flannel shirt I hadn't seen before.

"May I?" I asked, stroking the sleeve admiringly, "Is this –?"

"Mmm hmm", he said, "Real wool. Only three dollars from the thrift store."

"It's beautiful," I murmured.

I was a little…tired…the next morning but one cannot be a slug-a-bed during Winter Carnival weekend! Up to the ski-hill for some restorative fresh air, some easy groomers and to watch the King of the Mountain competition. The King of the Mountain is a three-lap race – or "multi-glisse triathlon" if you prefer – which takes place down the face of Red Mountain via a run called The Cliff. Yes, it's steep, the clue is in the name. Contenders to the throne have to zoom down the course on each of skis, snowboard and telemarks and whoever racks up the quickest time over all three laps, including gear-changes, yanking on and off the various boots and the lift-ride back up is crowned King. It's the ultimate Rossland accolade, the ski-bum equivalent of Olympic 100m gold.

The defending champion was Duncan, a half-British/half-Canadian, dreadlocked, volly ski-patroller, the archetypal Kootenay hippie. Now the odds were stacked against Duncan heading into the race this year. A few weeks ago he broke his hand in three places and then in a separate incident was caught up in an in-bounds avalanche. He lost a ski and a pole but luckily made it out alive with nothing broken. Well, nothing that hadn't been broken beforehand I mean. But gear-loss and fractures were no impediment to the King. He literally single-handedly (no, really – literally) powered to victory to retain his title for another year. All hail the King!

Back down in town that afternoon I put in a tortuous treadmill session at the gym (you'll see why I'm mentioning this later on), watched the Winter Carnival parade, checked out the outdoor pond hockey championship – obviously I'm referring to ice-hockey, this is Canada after all – and meandered by the ice-bar which by this stage had sold out of beer; everyone was off their rocker on mushrooms and whatnot.

But rather than tying one on I needed to get home to bed early(ish) in preparation for the next day. See, my friends and I were taking part in a five-person relay race from the top of Red Mountain to downtown Rossland composed of downhill skiing, mountain biking, cross-country skiing, snow-shoeing and running (my leg).

Given that I haven't mentioned running since the Dublin Marathon you wouldn't be blamed for thinking I'd vowed off the whole enterprise with a "never again" at the 26.2 mile marker. In fact, I continued running when I got back to Calgary, continued running while Maximilian and I were on the road trip and continued running after we got back to Rossland, the temperature dropped to minus 18 and my eyelashes and eyebrows would be frost-flecked white by the time I'd get back home. Since the ski-hill opened, however, my energies both physical and mental have been redirected towards snowsports and running has been put on the back-burner or is that mixing my metaphors? Some short'n'fast sessions on the treadmill have been the extent of things. As a result I've grown slightly more substantial through the hips than I might prefer but unfortunately the only way to get the streamlined leanness of running thirty miles a week is to, eh, run thirty miles a week. Oh well, I've only got four weeks left in Canada then the rest of my fucking life for running after that...

But anyway, back to the relay race! Let's have a run-down of the top-class racing pedigree of our team.

On skis, we had Peter "Buzz" Reed. This is Buzz's third winter in Rossland so he's not adverse to going fast and as an added bonus he's a master of the race tuck. The skiing leg of the relay was taking place down a run called Sally's Alley which is rolling at the top, flattens out into a cat-track then finishes in one final steep pitch. Buzz and I did a course inspection of it the afternoon before the race. Hmm. It was icy. Indeed, it was beyond icy – it had that horrible film of dusty snow which makes it nigh on impossible to dig your edges or to speed-check. Christ, I thought, I wouldn't fancy racing down this. Of course, I didn't say that to Buzz.

"Well!" I said instead brightly, "looks like it'll be a fast one tomorrow!"

Buzz did a few practice runs down the course and took his life into his own hands by straight-lining the final pitch. Maximilian happened to be watching from the Daylodge and said she'd never seen anyone go the whole way top-to-bottom without turning like that before. Buzz, for his part, said he'd never been so scared in his life.

On race morning Buzz turned up with a full-face helmet and temporarily traded his powder-friendly twin-tips for some dedicated just-waxed race skis. He meant business and gunned it down Sally's Alley – which thankfully wasn't quite as deadly as the day before – for the handover with our next team-member, the mountain-biker.

The mountain-biking leg was the most difficult leg to fill when we were recruiting for the team. Just as you can get winter tyres for your car, so too you can get studded bike tyres for grip in the ice and snow. Alas, no one we knew had any. So who could we convince to bike down the icy back-road on which the race was taking place without the proper set-up and with a pretty high risk of wiping out? Our friend Trav, that's who.

Travis took outdoor leadership in college, spends his summers either kayaking or working as a wrangler on a cattle ranch and is qualified in wilderness first aid. Unfortunately we don't get to see him much this winter because he's usually attending to some sort of maintenance issue in his trailer. The past few times I've rung him he's variously been dry-walling, lacquering a table and fixing a hole in the roof. But he was able to put aside his household duties for long enough to take part in the relay race, in lieu of studded tyres going for full-face helmet, body armour and balls of steel.

As soon as Buzz reached the changeover point, Travis rattled down the rutted and potholed course at full throttle, skidded to a stop, handed over to Shannon, our cross-country skier, and spat a few gloppy blood-tasting mouthfuls onto the snow.

Shannon! Now there's a girl who can paddle her own canoe. She's extremely hardy and never complains about any sort of discomfort, just gets on with things, earning the nickname "The Terminator" last winter. Cross-country skiing regularly gets vaunted as the most demanding cardiovascular sport there is, arms and legs a-pumping as you fly along and by the time Shannon reached the end of her leg she was in a bad way, according to Maximilian, official team physician and photographer. She went very, very quiet – no complaining here – then bent over and was close to vomiting.

Time for Dani, our snowshoer, to come into her own. Dani is five feet nothing and tiny in all dimensions but currently on her fourth snowboarding season, training to be a yoga teacher; and she spent her youth on 400m and 800m relay teams. Dani has her own snowshoes for backcountry jaunts but for optimal race performance she borrowed her housemate's lightweight pair. She snowshoed with all her might along the steep and icy trail then handed over to me, the runner, for the final leg.

I was off! Down and up and down again along a snowy bank before emerging at the bottom of Rossland's main street for a full-on sprint to the finish line. Let's take this sucker anaerobic! I gave it everything and then some more, got to the end then bent over, panting, vision blurry, hands on my quads, head between my knees.

Man...felt far worse at the finish line of the relay than I did after the marathon. Going from zero to max-effort with no warm-up when it was about minus six and in the mountains: yup, that's going to hurt. I've never felt lung burn like that before – I always thought when people talked about "burning lungs" it was just poetic licence or something. But owwww my chest was on fire and owww breathing deeply wasn't going to work right now.

The rest of the team came along, we high-fived, we cheered, we winced, we coughed and hacked like we had emphysema. Maximilian disappeared into the supermarket and returned with a four litre plastic container of water which we swigged, swashed around our mouths and spat back out.

We waited for the results to be announced and considering that we took it to the line and then beyond we were mildly disgusted that we didn't even place on the podium. We came fourth out of thirteen teams which sounds respectable enough but one "team" was a guy who did the whole thing solo, another was a group of ten-year old girls. Evidently our willingness to destroy ourselves was no match for consistent training and raw speed.

So we did what any dedicated group of athletes would

do under the circumstances: we went into the liquor store to stock on up some post-race refreshments. Reposing over beers and boozy coffees, we conducted some performance analysis – in short: fuck it, we couldn't have gone any harder, we're winners in our own minds and that's what counts – then siphoned hot chocolate and Malibu into thermoses to bring to the rail jam taking place back downtown.

Our friend Jessy, another trailer park boy, was taking part.

"I didn't know Jessy was into rails," I commented to Trav.

"No he totally wasn't," Trav said, "but then he put up this super sketchy looking rail in the trailer park and he's been hitting it non-stop for the past two days."

And then he went in the rail jam. Well why not? Fortune favours the brave.

Now I know that "random" is both misused and over-used as a descriptor. But try as I may, I'm struggling to find another word to describe the fact that Jessy had a pork chop taped to his helmet for the event.

"Jessy," I asked choosing my words carefully, "why do you have a pork chop on your head?"

"Eric asked if he could tape a piece of meat to my helmet and I said okay," Jessy said as if that explained it all. Right so. I shouldn't have asked. But who's Eric?

We watched Jessy and the other jibbers do their thing, people set up their deckchairs along the edge of the course, snowballs were thrown, then my feet went numb so I went home. I clambered into bed still wearing my running tights and thermals then a couple of hours later clambered back out to drag myself to the culminating event of Blizzard Fest at the Miner's Hall.

Rossland is mellow as ski-towns go, more about pot-lucks, cardigans and weed than the Euro-pop and disco balls of other resorts. There are no nightclubs in town – mention "clubbing" around here and people would probably think of baby seals – but there is the Miner's Hall. When Rossland was still in its gold-mining hey day it was some sort of union headquarters but it's since become a venue for things like the Rossland Film Festival, the monthly Joe Hill Music Night, visiting bands, big dance parties and that sort of thing. People get FUCKED UP at the Miner's Hall. Mushrooms, acid, MDMA: choose your own adventure. Last year my housemate Ellie was talking animatedly and at length to this guy who stared at her, paused for a second, said, "You're fucking hot but you need to stop talking," gave her a foil packet of magic mushrooms and walked away.

Not generally being one for means chemical myself, last winter I drank a bottle of Amaretto before going to the Miner's Hall one night (only one of the small bottles, admittedly, but still) in an effort to Get Drunk and Get On It. Unfortunately I instead ended up in a bleak hole of despondency and doom, couldn't handle all the wreckheads and promptly came back home. This year, however, I was still so buoyed by the excitement of the relay race – not to mention still beset by a rattling cough – that I danced about and waved my hands in the air like I just didn't care. Which I didn't, by that point.

The next morning we shuffled our way down to see the Olympic Torch passing through town en route to Vancouver for the Winter Olympics next month. For every fresh-faced family there was a group of ski-bums hiding their deathly pallor behind large sunglasses and oversized toques. Seeing the hallowed Olympic flame up close was, in a word, anticlimactic. Whatever. Can't say the weekend hadn't been fun overall.

Lisa

February 2010: Ask and ye shall receive

Greetings.

The skiing in BC is the best in the world and the skiing in Red Mountain is the best in BC. Ergo, the skiing at Red Mountain is the best of the best. Nothing like starting off with a few bold and completely subjective claims. Someone asked me today where else I'd like to ski and I was stumped: I wouldn't want to be anywhere else but here. Now and for the rest of my life. Come on Canadian Immigration. Canada's massive. Sure you wouldn't notice me at all if I stayed. I went into lengthy rhapsodies last year about the trees, the glades, the death-defying pitch etc. so I won't repeat myself on that point. However, enjoying this natural terrain at its best requires ample snowfall so thankfully there hasn't been a repeat of the no-snow doom of last year. The December and early January dumps have laid down a solid base and most or many of the cliff-bands/rocks/miscellaneous hazards have been covered up. That said, we could do with a top-up. There's only been one snowfall in the past two weeks so everything is entirely tracked out, the trees are mogulled, the south-facing glades are sun-baked, the northern-facing ones aren't quite as dire but it's still not the bottomless BC pow I've grown to know and love.

Now I'm sure that the snow has only slackened off temporarily and it's not that fresh corduroy doesn't have its charms but once you get a taste for the untracked there are only so many groomers you can ski before you go mad (about three or four is my limit). So rather than staying in-bounds and frothing at the mouth for the next snow, everyone is venturing into the slack country to earn their turns, the upside of the current conditions being a relatively stable snowpack. I was waiting for a friend at the top of one of the lifts the other day and I'd say twenty-five of the thirty people who whizzed by were heading off with touring gear.

I, alas, can't follow suit, lacking such gear as I do. So as everyone else ventures off on these backcountry adventures, I stay behind, sadly waving them on their way before doggedly making my way down an icy mogul-field instead. (And if everyone else jumped off a cliff, would I jump off a cliff as well? Probably. If the landing was soft enough.)

You see, boot-packing isn't practicable on longer hikes, particularly if you're breaking trail. You'd be sinking knee or thigh deep down into the snow on every step, skis precariously balanced over one shoulder. Though you'd probably develop massive deltoids on one side from toting your skis like this and as a result you'd look great wearing those asymmetrical one-shouldered tops, it's hardly compensation enough. By the time you'd get to the top of the hike you'd be so exhausted that your friends would be advised to carry a defibrillator to perk you up for the ski down. What you need are touring bindings and climbing skins. Touring bindings, as well as allowing you to ski downhill like normal bindings, have a hinged mode to allow you to "walk" uphill while skins are these fuzzy nylon strips you stretch over the base of your skis to give you traction on the snow.

More important still for ducking the ropes and venturing in the great beyond is avalanche gear: beacon, shovel, probe and the nous to use them if shit goes down. There's no ski-patrol in the backcountry to monitor and bomb any formations that look unstable, nor are they close to hand if anything goes wrong. You need to wear a beacon so that your buddies can locate you if you get caught in a slide or conversely if someone else gets buried you can switch over to "search" mode. Then a shovel and probe so that you can hopefully pinpoint and dig out the poor fucker before they suffocate to death in the rapidly solidifying slough (note: it's not the lack of oxygen that's the killer, it's the build up of CO_2). If they're not already dead from the impact trauma, that is.

In the light of the above I'm ashamed to admit that I've done one or two (or three or four) gear-free hikes with some avvy-savvy friends. Just very, very short hikes right by the resort boundary and in very stable conditions and with people who knew what they were doing, I hasten to add, not that that makes it even remotely alright. We were heading out the other day when this other group who were skinning up at the same time looked at us in disgust.

"Do you guys have beacons? All of you?"

The fact that it was only a ten-minute hike and Dani's mumbled response – "we're not going all the way up to the ridge, we're just dropping in here" – was no excuse and we knew it. We felt like fucking idiots and rightly so. Just because loads of people hike that pitch without gear and just because the avalanche risk is extremely low at the moment doesn't justify it at all. Going out of bounds without the right gear could be considered the on-snow equivalent of drunk driving. What if you trigger a slide that buries someone lower down and you're powerless to help?

So suitably chastened, I'm now firmly restricted to the resort area and trying to work out how I can afford touring gear and whether I place a higher value on financial solvency or fresh turns (really, though, I think we all know the answer to that). I've burnt through my savings account to be able to stay in BC this winter – I'm living in the moment, man – and really can't afford the set-up without banging it all on the credit card in anticipation of my next chunk of income. Alberta tax return here I come! Chary as I am to get into debt, I'm severely tempted to do so.

But wait! I haven't even got to the good part yet! A few days ago, fretting on my penury, I updated my Facebook status – yeah, yeah, I'm a social networker, deal with it – to "Lisa McGonigle is hoping a rich and mysterious benefactor will surprise her with skins, a touring set-up, transceiver, shovel and probe." Closely followed by, "Touring gear, touring gear, my kingdom for touring gear." Paula, the owner of a local cat-skiing company wrote back to say that although she couldn't furnish me with the hard goods, she'd arrange for me to go cat-skiing if I helped her clean her house in return. Would I what? I'd do practically ANYTHING for fresh turns. The day before I'd announced to Maximilian, "God, I'd sell my (as-yet nonexistent) first born for some more snow right now." "That's terrible," was her response.

As for cat-skiing – well when I told my brother about the arrangement he asked if cat-skiing was the M&S of snowsports. Nah buddy. It's the Fortnum and Mason of snowsports. It's the Harrods of snowsports. It's the gold-dipped, platinum-edged $400/day how-do-you-like-them-apples of snowsports. Accompanied by two guides, a snowcat rumbles along to drop you off at the type of terrain that you'd hike for hours to get into. You're guaranteed a fresh line, then at the end of the run the snowcat picks you up again and all you have do is repose and enjoy the home-baked cookies and gourmet sandwiches which are to hand ahead of the next equally sensational descent.

I was prepared to clean out Paula's septic tank, get up on a rickety ladder and shovel the snow off her roof, dance the Dance of the Seven Veils for any assembled houseguests: anything for that sort of return. Instead I arrived up to Paula's condo the morning after Maximilian's going-away party – where we sent her off to Zambia with one final orgiastic blast of November Rain – and simply had to give the bathroom a quick wipe-down, sweep the kitchen floor, whip the mop around a bit and pick up and fold any clothes scattered around the living room (Paula and her husband have three girls between the ages of four and nine.) It was like cleaning my own house except for someone else if that makes sense. In any case, it all seemed too good to be true.

But it wasn't! The following morning when I arrived at the cat-skiing lodge I was fully prepared to be told that I'd evidently misunderstood the terms of the deal and there was no way on earth I'd earned a day's cat-skiing in return for three hours' light housekeeping. But no, the guide cheerfully checked off my name on the list, we all bustled onto the bus, I strapped on one of the beacons all guests have to wear – "you don't really want this old thing back at the end of the day, do you? What? Right, right, I see. Well, can't blame me for trying" – we clambered into the snow-cat and off we went.

To bust out the vernacular, it was a super awesome day and we ripped freshies run after run. At one point, admittedly, we had to traverse across a creek after coming through some interestingly tight and crusty trees but having learned to ski at Red I'm familiar with the "oh fuck" factor and it isn't really much of a day on the hill if there isn't at least hairy moment.

I'm not sure why all this good karma has been bucketing down on me recently but whichever deity looks out for skint ski-bums up there sure has been pulling out all the stops.

Lisa

February 2010: Powder to the People

And finally…

Just as it was inevitable that I'd end up staying for the season – or at least a sizeable part thereof – once the idea was in my head, so too was it inevitable that I'd crack and buy touring gear in the end. It was simply a question of psyching myself up for the not unsubstantial financial outlay. Given that I'm on borrowed time in the Kootenays at this stage, touring gear might not appear the most sensible investment right now in my life but when have I ever tended the way of prudence when snowsports are involved?

I was galvanised into action when I went up the hill a few weeks ago for just another ho-hum day inbounds. I've become appallingly spoilt from skiing at Red. I expect it as my absolute due that there'll be fresh snow and no lift-lines and I'm entirely disgruntled with anything less. As I was getting on the chair for my first run, one of the lifties looked at me and went, "Lisa you look terrible! You must have made a night of it last night."

"Eh no, actually. I was in bed by ten. You're not looking so hot yourself though..." *You still have blood encrusted around your right nostril, you fucking cokehead.*

"At least I have an excuse!"

What can I say? This is just the way I look these days. SPF 15 notwithstanding, so much time spent outdoors over the past few years means that I'm now decidedly weather-beaten, ravaged by the elements.

Nice confidence booster to start the day though.

I skied around, disconsolate, on the tracked-out stuff, stopping half-way down the mogulled crud of Mini-Bowls (a very mellow tree-run) to gaze longingly at the figures trekking up the ridgeline opposite. Fuck it. That was it. I traversed out of the trees, took the nearest cat-track down to the base, went home, ordered a beacon, shovel and probe online from MEC and rang around the local ski-shops for deals on skins and touring bindings. One of the shops over in Nelson had some good deals going so before the afternoon was out I'd driven there and back, touring bindings had been mounted on my skis and climbing skins had been cut to size. Bada-bing!

Next step: work out how to use these things, simultaneously avoiding being smoked by an avalanche. My friends had taken an avalanche course with Jim, one of the ski-patrollers, the week before and had mentioned that he was potentially willing to accept childcare for his toddler in lieu of the course fee. So hot on the heels of the cleaning-for-cat-skiing deal, a babysitting-for-avalanche-training exchange was brokered and I launched into story-reading and nappy-changing with gusto.

It turned out the avvy course was starting that very afternoon though. Shit! I hadn't had a chance to try out my touring set-up yet, having only got it two days beforehand. This was going to be a daunting intro to the backcountry. Oh well, it's the Rossland way. Figure things out on the way down. Or, in this case, on the way up.

The first evening was classroom-based (more specifically, ski-hill-condo-conference-room, leather-armchairs-and-flatscreen-TV-based) and we learned about the various factors affecting the snowpack on any given terrain: the aspect, the pitch, any recent temperature rises or dips, wind-loading, whether it's been sun-affected or not. Complicated, multi-factorial stuff, the take-home message of which is that snow settles in discrete layers, some of which are stronger or weaker than others. So if you're planning to tramp around up there on skis or a snowboard it's important to understand the interaction between these different layers in gauging if anything is likely to slide.

Jim emphasised that, terrifying as they are, avalanches happen every day. Sometimes no one gets buried. Sometimes someone get partially buried. It's only when someone gets completely buried that you have a situation on your hands. Prevention, as ever, being better than cure, the best tactic is to try to avoid arriving at such a situation in the first place. So rather than regaling one horror story after another or issuing dire warnings to never venture into the backcountry again, the course instead focused on risk management and assessment when choosing trips and terrains, opening our eyes to the tools and resources, both first-hand and second-hand, which can be employed to that end.

The next two days were spent in the field, as it were, digging pits to test the snow stability and examine the different types of snow crystals and learning to identify potential terrain traps like gullies or convex rolls. Time was also devoted to avalanche rescue techniques, familiarising ourselves with our beacons and practicing how to locate and dig someone out with the least panic and greatest speed.

At the start of Day One of touring we took the chairlift up, stopped off in Paradise Lodge for coffee – nothing like doing things in style – then made our way to the resort boundary for the start of our uphill adventure. Everyone strapped on their beacons, the snowboarders buckled on their snowshoes and the skiers peeled apart their skins. Jim said that on one of the other courses he'd recently run there'd been someone who'd never used skins beforehand. Imagine!

"Well," I said, with a cough, "it's funny you should mention that…"

He and the others in the group were extremely patient as I got to grips with all the new equipment. Using skins for the first time reminded me of the first time I drove an automatic: I refused to believe that I didn't need to engage the clutch or pull up the handbrake when stopped on the uphill, that the transmission would take care of it all automatically (hence the name: automatic, I suppose). Similarly when we reached a steep section out touring, rather than keeping my skis flat and trusting the skin fibres to grip to the snow, I'd instinctively dig my edges into a wedge. That of course meant leaving less surface area for the skins to grip so, Bambi-legged, I'd slide back down the track or flop over into a free-heeled heap. More than once the others had to pull me back up to standing. Changing direction proved tricky as well. By the end of the two days of touring I was aching, not in my legs as might be expected, but across the fleshy pads in my hands. Apparently I'd been gripping my ski-poles extra hard to compensate for a certain unsteadiness on the skins themselves.

In any case, such…character-building moments aside, how

amazing is touring gear! Learning to ski was worth it alone for being able to cover ground so efficiently on skins. Don't get me wrong – it's still intensely physical, I'm still soaked with sweat and my heart is pumping in the 150s by the time I get to the top of whatever peak or ridgeline we're approaching but compared to boot-packing or even snowshoeing with a board on my back – wow.

You might wonder why I've committed to skis rather than snowboard for touring, particularly since this means foregoing powder turns on a board, epic and mind-blowing and other such hyperbolic adjectives as there are. See, I'm quite firm about this: skis are a poor second to a snowboard for slaying the pow. There's just something about the fluid all-body motion of being on a board for deep snow-slashing which is decidedly lacking when two skis and two poles are involved. The advice for powder skiing is to maintain a slightly narrower stance than normal so your skis approximate one surface rather than two. Or, eh, else you could just snowboard and have one surface to begin with.

But nonetheless, not only does touring on skis mean not having to haul my board up then ride down with snowshoes on my pack, clonking me in the back of the head on every turn, I'd also rather the manoeuvrability of skis for any dodgy moments which may arise. For example, at the end of a day touring the Plewman Basin on Tuesday, three of us got lost in discomfortingly tight trees on the way back to the highway. Well, no, saying we were lost is a bit sensationalist. We knew we'd reach the road eventually if we kept going. We just chose a less than optimal route. Bad as the bushwhacking was on skis, branches smacking in our faces as we tried to find a clearing, it would have been more frustrating still on a snowboard. True, I had to take my skis off at one point to crawl out of a gully on my hands and knees, shunting my gear up in front of me through the maddeningly soft snow, but otherwise I could at least sidestep or scoot myself along the flat. The boarders, on the other hand, kept having to strap and unstrap, not to mention stalling in tree-wells and having to haul themselves up by grabbing onto overhanging branches every few turns.

That was quite the day, really, that last section being the least of it, more of an annoyance than anything else. Earlier on, however, I'd had significant issues along the top section on our way up. Some of the switchbacks were so acute it was like trying to do the splits on skis to get around them. Mid-turn, I kept feeling like I didn't have a secure enough foothold and any second was going to slip out and ragdoll backwards down the entire mountain face through the avalanche zone. One of the guys with us had to stand behind me on every turn, propping up my ski-tails with his snowshoes to make sure I didn't slide back downhill, and talk me through every manoeuvre:

"Okay, place all your weight on your right ski. Good! Right, now kick your left ski out into the air behind you. Really hard! Like you're trying to kick me in the face! Okay, now move it around to beside your other foot. That's it, that's it, dig those poles in to steady yourself! Attagirl! You got it!"

A few times he had to resort to a hands-on-ass-full-force push to shunt me around into a stable position. By the time we reached the ridgeline I was drained, demoralised and in the slough of despond. I felt like an idiot: what the fuck was I doing out there touring when I'm so terrible on skis? There's pushing your comfort zone and then there's being mildly traumatised and feeling like a liability to the group.

I suppose I have to take a step back and realise what "so terrible on skis" equates to in Rossland. I class myself as a weak skier because having used my skins oh, seven or eight times I struggled to get my kick-turns in firmly enough along the top of the heart-racingly steep Plewman Basin. Or because the day before, on the peak of nearby Mt Roberts, instead of dropping into the fifty degree cliff-banded chute down which the Canadian Freeskiing Open is run, I took a less precipitous route. I'm such a lame-ass sometimes.

The norm here is almost impossibly hardcore: we had a potluck tonight at which one girl described her six-week trek across the Patagonia ice-cap, an experience which sounded absolutely amazing and absolutely miserable in equal parts, and another guy mentioned how his friend was struck by both pulmonary and cerebral oedema in Nepal. (Don't you just hate when that happens?) Mere marathon running doesn't even rank around this crowd. This week I had three big days touring in a row, culminating in the Plewman affair. The following day I went up the hill for some lazy lift-accessed turns, more out of habit than anything else, but was so wrecked I only half-heartedly did a few groomers before coming home and spending the rest of the day reading and eating chocolate in bed. I was disgusted with myself for being such a lightweight before realising oh yeah, we powered up four mountains in three days so it's fair enough to be a bit tired.

Oh whatever. I love touring and that's what counts. I love the challenge, the adventure. I love becoming entirely unaware of the passing of time, so engrossed am I in the task at hand. We could have been out there for twenty minutes or four hours for all I know and am always surprised how late it is when someone checks their watch at some point in the day. I love how your entire world is telescoped down to the three or four others in your group. If anything happens these are the people who are responsible for your life, and you theirs. I love getting back to the house at the end of the day absolutely spent, feeling like I've accomplished something. After the final day of the avvy course I was buzzing so much I couldn't sleep that night. Apart from when I'm stricken by The Fear, I even love the uphill slog. And of course I love the fresh lines. In short, touring is everything I love about snowsports magnified to the nth degree.

But in other news, my time, money and legal status in Canada are all finally up and then some, alas. I'm leaving Rossland this Saturday, overnighting in Calgary – yay – then flying back to Dublin the following day. We've been over all this before: I love the Kootenays with almost elemental force and want nothing more out of life than to one day take my place amongst the old dudes up at Red but, hey, you can't always get what you want. So! Onto the next life stage. Fuck it. I'll go back and finish that PhD after all. Just don't think that I don't feel like I've been punched in the stomach by it all.

See, there comes a time in every ski-bum's life…Has anyone else read or seen *Into the Wild*, my undeclared urtext over the past few years? Even Chris McCandless realised when it was time to head home for a bit. After shunning society and striking out for the Alaskan wilderness alone, the transcendental insight he achieves is "happiness only real when shared." Ski-seasons are, after all, as much about the people as they are the pow. The solidarity forged through injuries, penury and euphoric highs, not to mention mini-meltdowns in the back-country. Nope, there's no friend like a snow-friend.

But there's only a short window in one's life for such footloose ski-bumming and I've just about expended mine. And more immediately, all my visas.

Canada, it's been real. But you've made it clear we don't have a future together, that this was only ever intended to be a temporary thing. Casual, a bit of fun. I can't take any more sleepless nights worrying about where we're headed. These things need to be two-sided, you know. And you can be so cold and inhospitable sometimes. No! Not another word.

Suppose I'd better get on with things so.

Lisa

Acknowledgements

Thanks to everyone whose stories, glories and ignominies have made their way into this book, not least of all those unsuspecting locals who may be astonished to find themselves featuring herein, be that as a result of chairlift conversation or picking up hitchers to and from the hill.

Many thanks also to the organisers of the Fernie Writers' Conference who saw fit to grant me a scholarship to attend the 2009 event. The encouragement and support of the Creative Non-Fiction group led by Sid Marty at the Conference was the fulcrum in these pages being transformed from a disparate sheaf of emails to something resembling its present form. The indefatigable Susan Toy from Alberta Books Canada has been a constant source of guidance and advice and I couldn't have asked for more personable, professional and confidence-inspiring publishers than Ron Smith and Randal Macnair from Oolichan Books.

My friends and colleagues at Fernie Physiotherapy - Dan McDonald, Jaime Ellis, Lynn Ferguson, Sue van Evra, Heather Kerr and Anna Chow - variously fed, clothed, sheltered, diagnosed and treated me through some very lean times and I can only hope to repay their generosity and kindness some day. The Medical Training department of the Royal College of Physicians of Ireland, under the redoubtable helm of Grace Turner, and everyone who worked volly crew at Red Mountain 2008/09 also enlivened two very different work environments. Yeah SpR training schemes! Yeah B-netting!

No matter where I was - or indeed they were - in the world, Lena Murphy and Clare O'Hara were only ever a phonecall away and as a result have been on the receiving end of far too many rambling, involved and no doubt teeth-grindingly tedious stories about my latest emotional misadventure. Thank you both, and sorry for all the drama.

What parent doesn't love to receive the "I'm-dropping-out-of-Oxford-to-go-snowboarding" phonecall, or indeed the "I-won't-make-it-home-for-Christmas-again-this-year" one? Thank you Alison and Ben for taking it all in your stride.

Most especially, however, I have to thank everyone whose friendship and camaraderie I've shared both on and off the snow over the past five years. Alex and Jethro Cotton, Ali Murfitt, Ellie Maxfield, Gerry Thornton, Mike Cattie, Min Millen, Jenn Cumpsty, Renee Male, Racquel Green, Brendan Seredynski, Matt "Pado" Patterson, Emma Padgett, Colin Ball, Julian McCartney, Eve Markstein, Darren Ovinge, Kristen Thams, Erin Farrell, Tanya Arman, Marshall Smith, Lindsay and Steven Tallott, Yosi Assis, Johnny Price, Aongus McGreal, Hailey Rhyne, Travis Baldwin, Jessy Hill, Matt Aird, Kym West, Peter "Buzz" Reed, Shannon Noonan, Kyle Sedola, Andy Wright, Vanessa Benwood, Dani Cole, Jenn Noakes, Greg Hogg, Gregor Graham, Graeme Thompson, Bonnie Hook and everyone else with whom I've cranked snowboard bindings or clicked into skis: this book is for you and about you. Happiness only real when shared.

Lisa McGonigle
December 2010

Photograph by Joe Harrison

Lisa McGonigle grew up in North County Dublin, Ireland. She attended Trinity College Dublin and the University of Aberdeen, Scotland before coming to British Columbia in 2005. Having spent several years skiing, snowboarding and hiking in the Kootenays, she is currently studying for a PhD in Irish Studies at the University of Otago, New Zealand.